Climber's Guide to
Pinnacles
National
Monument

Climber's Guide to
Pinnacles
National
Monument

DAVID RUBINE

Chockstone Press
Evergreen, Colorado

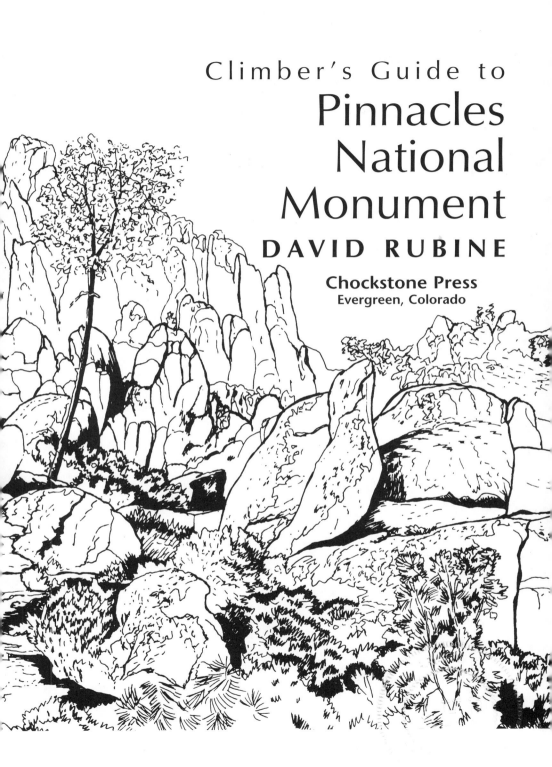

CLIMBER'S GUIDE TO PINNACLES NATIONAL MONUMENT

ISBN 0-934641-89-7

Published and distributed by:

Chockstone Press, Inc.
Post Office Box 3505
Evergreen, Colorado 80439

Front cover and title page drawings by Shelley Cost.

Back cover photo by Tim Corcoran: Tom Davis on *The Druid (5.12b)*, The Back Door, page 53 .

All uncredited photos are by author.

To my beautiful wife Ruselle,

who belays me not only on the rock,

but in life.

WARNING: CLIMBING IS A SPORT WHERE YOU MAY BE SERIOUSLY INJURED OR DIE.
READ THIS BEFORE YOU USE THIS BOOK.

This guidebook is a compilation of unverified information gathered from many different climbers. The author cannot assure the accuracy of any of the information in this book, including the topos and route descriptions, the difficulty ratings, and the protection ratings. These may be incorrect or misleading and it is impossible for any one author to climb all the routes to confirm the information about each route. Also, ratings of climbing difficulty and danger are always subjective and depend on the physical characteristics (for example, height), experience, technical ability, confidence and physical fitness of the climber who supplied the rating. Additionally, climbers who achieve first ascents sometimes underrate the difficulty or danger of the climbing route out of fear of being ridiculed if a climb is later down-rated by subsequent ascents. Therefore, be warned that you must exercise your own judgment on where a climbing route goes, its difficulty and your ability to safely protect yourself from the risks of rock climbing. Examples of some of these risks are: falling due to technical difficulty or due to natural hazards such as holds breaking, falling rock, climbing equipment dropped by other climbers, hazards of weather and lightning, your own equipment failure, and failure or absence of fixed protection.

You should not depend on any information gleaned from this book for your personal safety; your safety depends on your own good judgment, based on experience and a realistic assessment of your climbing ability. If you have any doubt as to your ability to safely climb a route described in this book, do not attempt it.

The following are some ways to make your use of this book safer:

1. **CONSULTATION:** You should consult with other climbers about the difficulty and danger of a particular climb prior to attempting it. Most local climbers are glad to give advice on routes in their area and we suggest that you contact locals to confirm ratings and safety of particular routes and to obtain first-hand information about a route chosen from this book.

2. **INSTRUCTION:** Most climbing areas have local climbing instructors and guides available. We recommend that you engage an instructor or guide to learn safety techniques and to become familiar with the routes and hazards of the areas described in this book. Even after you are proficient in climbing safely, occasional use of a guide is a safe way to raise your climbing standard and learn advanced techniques.

3. **FIXED PROTECTION:** Many of the routes in this book use bolts and pitons which are permanently placed in the rock. Because of variances in the manner of placement, weathering, metal fatigue, the quality of the metal used, and many other factors, these fixed protection pieces should always be considered suspect and should always be backed up by equipment that you place yourself. Never depend for your safety on a single piece of fixed protection because you never can tell whether it will hold weight, and in some cases, fixed protection may have been removed or is now absent.

Be aware of the following specific potential hazards which could arise in using this book:

1. **MISDESCRIPTIONS OF ROUTES:** If you climb a route and you have a doubt as to where the route may go, you should not go on unless you are sure that you can go that way safely. Route descriptions and topos in this book may be inaccurate or misleading.

2. **INCORRECT DIFFICULTY RATING:** A route may, in fact, be more difficult than the rating indicates. Do not be lulled into a false sense of security by the difficulty rating.

3. **INCORRECT PROTECTION RATING:** If you climb a route and you are unable to arrange adequate protection from the risk of falling through the use of fixed pitons or bolts and by placing your own protection devices, do not assume that there is adequate protection available higher just because the route protection rating indicates the route is not an "X" or an "R" rating. Every route is potentially an "X" (a fall may be deadly), due to the inherent hazards of climbing – including, for example, failure or absence of fixed protection, your own equipment's failure, or improper use of climbing equipment.

THERE ARE NO WARRANTIES, WHETHER EXPRESS OR IMPLIED, THAT THIS GUIDEBOOK IS ACCURATE OR THAT THE INFORMATION CONTAINED IN IT IS RELIABLE. THERE ARE NO WARRANTIES OF FITNESS FOR A PARTICULAR PURPOSE OR THAT THIS GUIDE IS MERCHANTABLE. YOUR USE OF THIS BOOK INDICATES YOUR ASSUMPTION OF THE RISK THAT IT MAY CONTAIN ERRORS AND IS AN ACKNOWLEDGMENT OF YOUR OWN SOLE RESPONSIBILITY FOR YOUR CLIMBING SAFETY.

PREFACE

The aim of the second edition of this guide book, as with the first, is to include the entire Pinnacle's climbing experience—to be a complete documentation of all the climbing activity that has ever been reported. After the flurry of first ascents in the late '80s and early '90s first ascent activity slowed drastically. The number of first ascents that have been reported since the last guide is but a fraction of those added to that addition. Growth slowed way down, probably due to the scarcity of good rock, coupled with the boldness required to put up a route on lead. (This style of first ascents has largely been honored as a park-wide standard.) This rate of growth is probably a good thing. The regulation of climbing by the park service in the '90s is inevitable. A very slow expansion of climbing development, along with climbers' commitment to a "treading lightly" use of the park's resources, will minimize regulations. All in all, climbers have demonstrated this commitment by promoting climber's work days, cooperating with the park service in trail and plant renovation and respecting cliff closures due to raptor nesting. Continued work like this can set the groundwork for a long-lasting and successful partnership between climbers and the park service.

I want to acknowledge and thank Brooks White for his magnanimous aid in data entry and setting up systems to compile information that will make further additions much easier.

Thanks to all the climbers who sent in not only first ascent data, but also took the time to compile and send useful and important editing changes, along with route description changes and suggestions. All of this contributed to what, I hope, is a first-rate guide.

I specifically want to thank Bruce Hildenbrand, Clint Cummings and Brad Young for their extra effort with corrections and updates.

Also, thanks to all the climbers who have contributed time, money and muscle replacing many of the inadequate bolts that abound in the park. Your efforts to minimize additional bolt holes by drilling out existing holes, along with making Pinnacles a safer climbing area, have not gone unnoticed. (See the section "Rebolting versus Retro-bolting" for an explanation on bolt replacement.)

Please continue to send current route information and corrections to the address below.

Climb safely,

David Rubine, September1995
P.O. Box 1057
Soquel, CA 95073 - 1057

CONTENTS

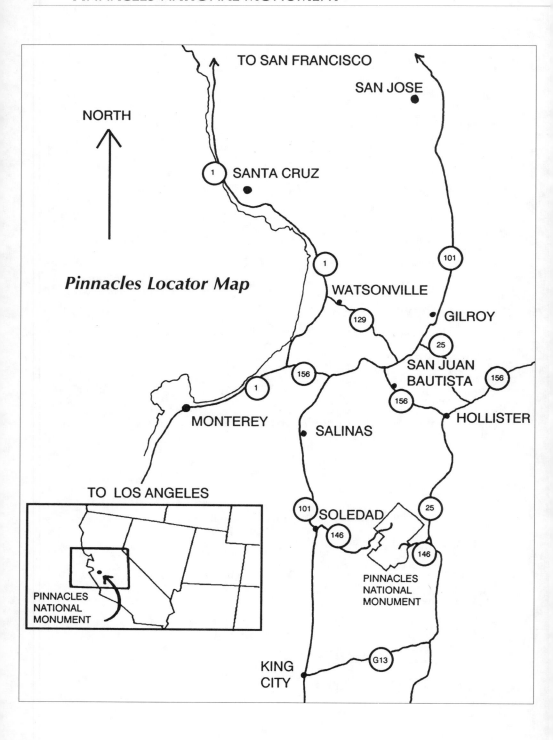

INTRODUCTION

Every climbing area has a unique flavor—a kind of mini-culture that characterizes the styles and attitudes of its climbers. These local personalities are created by the area's history, by who has climbed there, and by the type of climbing the area has to offer. However, personalities are not a static phenomena; they change and fluctuate as an area evolves, and with the evolution of climbing in general. In the years since the publication of Paul Gagner's 1983 Pinnacles guide, a handful of local climbers struggled behind a veil of opinion that Pinnacles was a climbing nightmare on Earth, and established numerous first ascents. Images of volcanic rock characterized by decaying, zero-grit surfaces kept many would-be first ascentionists from considering Pinnacles an area where they could apply their craft. It was this outdated opinion that provided a window of opportunity for local climbers to produce many high-quality routes, permanently altering the climbing experience at Pinnacles. What was created on that "bad rock" was an area of abundant, excellent cragging. Determination and exploration revealed areas of rock with vertical to overhanging routes of surprising quality.

Since the publication of Paul Gagner's guide, the number of routes at Pinnacles has nearly tripled. It seems that the growing popularity of climbing has affected even an "out of the way" place like Pinnacles. Rock climbing was originally something you had to do to get to the top of a mountain—or you practiced it to prepare for the mountain. It was a skill used to get to the top of something. Rock climbing now is a sport in itself. A single pinnacle or wall will have multiple lines ascending it, with each route comprising a complete, documented climb. Climbers, more often than not, tackle routes for the thrill of executing the moves, as opposed to bagging another summit.

In the early years of climbing at Pinnacles, the summit was the goal. Climbers used whatever methods needed to gain the top. Many ascents were achieved by merely tossing a rope over the top of a rock, fixing one end and prusiking the other end. Numerous early ascents were achieved by short bolt ladders, or a single aid bolt to get past a "hard" section. Many of these aid sections later were freed, and a lot of these sections went free at ratings of 5.8 or less. Climbers seemed to be on a summit-hunting spree. By the early '70s, a great majority of the summits had been hunted down. By the mid-70s, a transition began. Prompted, possibly, by the breakthroughs in Yosemite, climbers re-examined the many cliffs and spires for new possibilities. The goal of the summit began to be replaced by the creation of free lines of increasing difficulty. By the mid- to late '80s, the existence of multiple free routes on any given formation was firmly established. As an example, the East Face of the Monolith now has, on its 100-foot length, 17 mostly independent climbs. Up until 1974, only six climbs were recorded on the entire formation.

SERVICES

Presently, there is limited camping inside the park. Campsites are located on the west side. The future of these services, however, is uncertain. The park service presently is in the process of creating a master plan for the park that may include eliminating camping altogether within its boundaries. There is a privately owned campground just outside the entrance to the east side. The campground has a small store, showers and a swimming pool (coveted on those sweltering summer outings).

CLIMBING SEASON

Pinnacles is an excellent fall, winter and spring climbing area. It often remains dry in winter when everywhere else is wet. This makes year-round climbing available; however, the summer months can be sweltering.

GEOLOGY

Written by Charissa Olson Reid

To trace the beginnings of Pinnacles geology, one needs to have more than a little imagination! The area is the remnant of an ancient volcano, which was formed approximately 23 million years ago, when the plates that make up the earth's crust were pushing the Coast Range of California into existence and jockeying for position along the ocean floor. The lighter, more buoyant continental plate (North American Plate) scraped the surface of the oceanic plate that was diving beneath it, forming huge rubble piles that became the Coast Range. As the Farallon Plate subducted, it was melted into magma, which eventually made its way to the surface, creating volcanic activity in the newly formed mountains. One of these was the Pinnacles Volcano.

The Pinnacles Volcano's eruptions varied. The flowing hot lava streams of its youth gave way to a thick, pasty lava flow (toothpaste-like) that squeezed through previously formed fissures and joints. These flows were followed by alternating explosive bursts of rock and hot lava blobs, and quiet periods, when the only display was the venting of hot steam and blowing ash. The variety of activity defined the Pinnacle Volcano as a stratovolcano.

With the volcanic ingredients already formed, Pinnacles was ready for the second great force that shaped it — the movement of faults in the earth's crust. The San Andreas Fault was created when the Pacific Plate collided with the North American plate and broke off a chunk of the continent. (This piece of modern-day California continues to move in a northwesterly direction, along with the ocean floor that covers the Pacific Plate.) This newly created fault cut the Pinnacles Volcano roughly in half. The area we now know as the Pinnacles traveled north and west, leaving its other half 195 miles to the south near Lancaster.

The Chalone Creek Fault and Pinnacles Fault also played a role in the movement of the monument. Running roughly parallel to each other, the movement of these faults caused the area to sink several hundred feet, while areas adjacent to Pinnacles rose. This movement protected Pinnacles temporarily from erosion as it traveled northward.

Erosion later became a major factor in the evolution of Pinnacles, cutting deep canyons along the vertical joints in the rocks, and wearing away the less-resistant layers of volcanic ash that surrounded the magma ooze, forming the spires of the High Peaks. The forces of water and wind also caused large boulders to slide down the steep canyon walls, roofing what are now the caves. The talus caves in Bear Gulch and Chalone Creek are not "true" caves – rather, they are composed of the narrow canyon floor beneath the boulder piles.

Modern-day Pinnacles is a geologist's playground, with the silica-rich rhyolite forming pinkish tuff, layered lava flow bands and perlite pockets of green volcanic glass. The infamous protruding handholds of such areas as The Monolith tell the story of ancient mud flows and volcanic explosions. These forces formed the breccia boulder fields of the Bear Gulch area and the pinnacles themselves. The rock here holds not only recreational opportunities, but stories in stone of ancient Earth.

Andrews, Phillip. *Geology of Pinnacles National Monument.* University of California Press, 1936.

Chronic, Halka. *Pages of Stone: Geology of Western National Parks and Monuments, Volume 2: Sierra Nevada, Cascades, and Pacific Coast.* The Mountaineers, 1986.

Hill, Mary. *California Landscape: Origin and Evolution.* University of California Press, 1984.

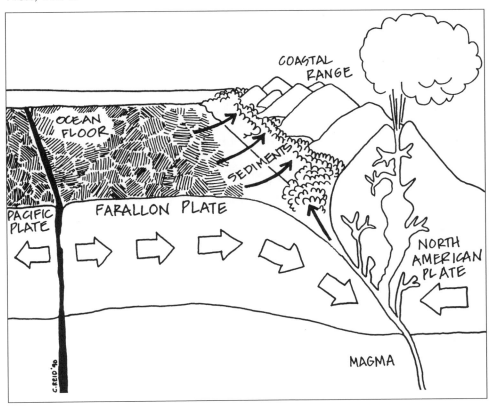

NATURAL HISTORY OR
"IT'S THEIR WORLD. WELCOME TO IT!"
Written by Ruselle Rubine

If you stop...just for a moment....long enough to hear the quiet sounds, see the subtle colors, smell the fresh dryness, touch the earth and sense its gentle aliveness, then you can experience the magic of Pinnacles. Like most of the earth, this area has undergone some extreme changes. Once the site of molten lava flow, thrusting faults and shifting continental plates, Pinnacles National Monument, as it is currently known, has cooled, settled and eroded into the rolling hills, gigantic rock formations and exotic, craggy peaks we see today. This harsh landscape seems so still, so dry and even lifeless at times; yet its gentle breezes nudge, urging us to awaken our senses. The native life—or natural history—of Pinnacles is more complex than it may appear. Stepping into this world of rock, dry brush, trees and grasses, you'll find creeks, caves and canyons, cool meadows and steep, barren mountains, a varying landscape where the wildlife—both flora and fauna —are diverse, interdependent and very well adapted to their environment.

There basically are four biotic communities found in Pinnacles National Monument — Chaparral, Foothill Woodland, Riparian, and Xeric (rock and scree). Each community is characterized, affected and often limited by environmental factors such as topography, soil, moisture and fire.

While plants tend to be more specific to a particular biotic community, the animals have more options in their distribution and can be found in various communities. They will be included in the description of the community in which they're most commonly found. For those interested in further exploration or more complete species information (identification, distribution, behavior, etc.) numerous resources are available in the Visitor Center.

The Chaparral community is the dense, scrubby brush on the hillsides, and covers about 82% of the monument. The plants living here are well-adapted for water conservation so they can survive long periods of heat and drought in coarse, gravelly soil. Chamise (or greasewood) is the most common chaparral plant, and like most, it is specifically adapted to and dependent on a "fire ecology." The clusters of short, needle-like leaves contain highly volatile compounds that allow it to burn even when green. Its narrow, brittle branches begin to die after 15 years, making ideal kindling. The plant becomes more flammable with age, since 30% of it may be dead within 30 to 50 years and when it burns it nearly explodes, clearing away surrounding brush to make room for new seedlings and to ensure new growth from the burl, or base, of the old plant. Ceanothus (otherwise known as buckbrush or wild lilac) and manzanita also have hardy burls, and their seeds germinate better after being toasted in the intense heat of fire. Manzanita has a smooth red bark like an extra skin, and its leaves turn edge-wise to the sun to limit long drying exposure in the summer. The leaves of the hardy holly leaf cherry have a shiny, waxy surface that reflects sunlight thus increasing its drought resistance. The berries of the manzanita (meaning "little apple" in Spanish) and toyon (Christmas berry or California holly) were used extensively by the Indians and early Spanish settlers, and continue to provide a reliable winter food source for small birds and mammals. The gray pine (formerly known as the digger pine) is the only pine native to Pinnacles. The presence of this large tree in the chaparral indicates a long period without fire (which is currently the case at Pinnacles). This deeply rooted tree is characterized by the spindly growth of dull gray-green needles and huge cones. The abundant seeds are enjoyed by squirrels, big-eared kangaroo rats and brown towhees.

As anyone knows who has attempted off-the-trail bushwhacking (not recommended!), chaparral can be quite brutal and relentless. The south-facing slopes are even hotter and dryer than the denser, greener north faces. But this dense, brushy habitat is ideal for sparrows, scrub jays, towhees and the commonly heard wrentit with its distinctive call. Predators and prey—rodents, rattlesnakes, kingsnakes, hawks and bobcats—are an integral part of this ecosystem. Plants and animals, fire, rain, shade and sun all maintain the ecological balance of this hardy environment.

The sparser, rolling, grassy hills dotted with blue oak trees and gray pines comprise the Foothill Woodland community. It provides food, shade and shelter for many animals, though it comprises only about 13% of Pinnacles' acreage. The volcanic layer beneath this fine, rich and shallow soil and, again, a lack of water, permit only the survival of the few trees with roots that reach deep enough to find a permanent water source (sometimes down 150 feet), and the grasses and annuals which sprout, grow and seed before the dry season arrives. With the spring rains come beautiful bright wildflowers to paint the landscape. Hawks and kites soar above, and the woodpecker's familiar tap-tap-tap echoes through the stillness. The mysterious feral pigs (long ago introduced as domestic, and now hairy and wild, with tusks) can be found in the valleys, along with the gentle Black-tailed Deer, rabbits and ground squirrels. California quail, other birds and rodents eat the plentiful seeds, acorns and grasses in this "bread basket" of the monument. In turn, they're eaten by the predators found here: red-tailed (and other) hawks, gray fox, bobcat, and an occasional mountain lion.

There are two members of this community potentially harmful to visitors — rattlesnakes and poison oak (also common in riparian areas; see illustration). Both can be illusory or mistaken for other species. If you think you see a rattlesnake, walk away slowly. They normally only bite if provoked. Poison oak, on the other hand, can strike without you even knowing...until later. Avoid all of its many forms! Animals may browse on it, but it's usually toxic to humans, and immunity can change with time.

Containing some of the more fragile plants, which are dependent on constant moisture, is the Riparian community. This includes the spring and streambed zones that comprise only about 3% of Pinnacles' total acreage. Although stream beds and creeks appear dry, water runs year-round beneath the surface, and feeds the lush green life above. Food is abundant in the valleys of Chalone Creek, Bear Gulch and West Chalone Creek. Even in the driest summer months (so far), there stands enough water for many birds, mammals, reptiles and amphibians to thrive. Owls, raccoons and coyotes feast in the stream areas, though mostly at night. The huge, deciduous valley oaks, evergreen coast live oaks, and white-barked California sycamore provide shade, shelter and food for the abundant bird life. In return, the birds fill the trees with song (and acorns). Cottonwoods, willows, blackberries, ferns, cattails, stinging nettles and duckweed depend on the constant water source, as do salamanders, lizards and snakes. In wet winter and spring months, the creeks can become full and river-like. Most of the animals in the monument may visit a riparian area at some time, but look to the verdant plants to find the hidden wet wonderlands of Pinnacles.

Probably of greatest interest and importance to readers of this guide is the Xeric or Rock community. Though the smallest in acreage, this rugged, dynamic environment—characterized by aridity and extreme, fluctuating temperatures—is the "main attraction" of the monument. Very little soil gathers on the exposed cliff faces of the rock formations. A few grasses and flowers can be found where a hollow in the rock has accumulated some soil, but the plants common to this community—lichens, mosses, spike mosses, and a few from the appropriately named Stonecrop Family—are very tough, drought-resistant and adaptable. That flakey stuff climbers want to scrub off the rock is lichen, fungi and algae in a symbiotic relationship. Lichens lend the rocks their faint colorful hues of red, orange, yellow, rust, green, brown and black. Over 90 species of this ancient plant gradually are breaking the Pinnacles rock down into sand. They're slow-growing pioneers though, taking 20 to 100 years to cover one square inch.

The xeric community's animal population is not quite so abundant, though the silent, soaring turkey vulture, the squawking raven, the bat guano-laden cracks and the lizards doing pushups on 5.12 faces all are fairly conspicuous. Not so obvious or numerous are the raptors, or birds of prey, inhabiting the high, rocky ledges. The soaring "fully protected" prairie falcon and the "endangered" peregrine falcon, both speedy and precise hunters, nest in the shallow caves and ledges of the crags, as does the golden eagle, a protected "species of special concern." Breeding peregrines once were near extinction due to detrimental "human alteration of natural ecosystems" — specifically the accumulation of DDT in their food chain. Some estimates say that if the current trends of pesticide use and human persecution (including the destruction of habitats) continue, "as many as 100 of the more than 300 species of raptors world-wide are in serious jeopardy of extinction by the year 2000." Public education, observation, research and conservation management all will help to support the survival of these magnificent birds. Even the California condor (currently extinct in the wild) which used to nest in the Pinnacles spires, may return thanks to these efforts. Pinnacles is one of the proposed sights for future release of the condor in an attempt to re-establish these birds in their natural habitats.

Although Pinnacles is a very harsh, rugged environment, it also can be very fragile. It is one of the few remaining magical places where plants and animals can survive and flourish in relative peace. This is an old community (by our standards) worthy of respect for the way its members adapt and work together. Interdependency means survival here; every element plays an important part. Remember: You are only a visitor.

BIBLIOGRAPHY
Keith, Sandra. Text for book on Pinnacles, 1990.

Johnson and Cordone. *Pinnacles Guide*, La Siesta Press, 1986.

Webb, Ralph C. *A Guide to the Plants of the Pinnacles*, 1971.

Moses Spring Self-Guiding Trail pamphlet, Southwest Parks and Monument Association, 1990.

Avery, Michael L. and van Riper III, Charles. *A Checklist of the Birds of Pinnacles National Monument,* 1987.

Fellers, Gary M. and Arnold, Brian W. *A Checklist of Amphibians, Reptiles and Mammals of Pinnacles National Monument,* 1987

Santa Cruz Predatory Bird Research Group pamphlet, Santa Cruz, CA.

Previous guide books.

RAPTOR PRESERVATION

To minimize disturbance of raptors, the park service seasonally closes certain areas or formations. These birds (like most wild animals) are sensitive, and disturbance from climbers may affect the survival of their species. At area headings and some routes in this book, a hawk symbol will denote possible closure. Also, heed closure policy notices posted on the climbers' bulletin boards at trail heads, and avoid these areas. Usually closures take effect in mid-January and continue until mid-July.

POISON OAK *(Toxicodendron diversiloba)*

Similar in both appearance and habitat, California blackberry and poison oak are sometimes mistaken for each other. Although both have tri-lobed leaf arrangements, poison oak leaves and stems are shiny and smooth, where blackberry leaves and stems are covered with thorny hairs. During the winter months when both plant species are dormant, poison oak stems can still cause intense allergic reactions. The Ohlone Indians developed an immunity to poison oak by eating small amounts each spring to insure continued resistance to the plant. This is not a recommended treatment, however, because varied responses by individuals make the practice unpredictable and sometimes hazardous.

Drawing and text by Lisa Vincente

CLIMBING AT PINNACLES – AN ETHICAL CONCERN

With the intense growth of climbing activity and the creation of a few rap-routes at Pinnacles came the predictable concerns and problems appropriate to such change. Climbers began to grapple among themselves to resolve ethical questions such as rap-bolting versus "ground up" climbing. Unlike many areas, local climbers created a forum for discussion where the topic was addressed. Meetings were held to express opinions and concerns. Although the dialogue was at times heated, it led to an understanding and cooperation in regard to the bolting issue. The result was the recognition of Pinnacles as an historic "ground up" area. All but a few routes at Pinnacles have been put up on lead, and the great majority of local climbers strongly request all climbers to respect this historical precedent. Please climb at the monument honoring the "ground up" standard that has so firmly been adhered to and, as importantly, be committed to the park's environmental preservation. If the overriding ethic is one of preservation of the natural resources, climbers will always find a common ground to sort out differences in styles and ethics. It is the observation of this author that Pinnacles has remained pristine in most of its areas because, by and large, people who climb here love the park for more than just a climbing area and have found that a "ground up" ethic is very compatible with slow development and "treading lightly" on the resources.

Pinnacles is fragile. The rock is crumbly, the ground is loose and easily overturned, and the vegetation is delicate. The impact climbers have had on this glorious place, at certain climbing sites, has been severe. This impact has resulted in the regulation and closures of some of the more popular sites. The Tourist Trap and The Back Door are now being limited as to the numbers of climbers using the area at any one time. The Ditty Boulder and Dead Point have been closed to climber use indefinitely. All these regulations have occurred due to intense erosion. It is vital that climbers, individually and as a group, address this reality and operate in the Monument as protectors of its wildlife and beauty. Climbers need to be at the leading edge of respecting and preserving this treasure.

FRIENDS OF PINNACLES

Friends of Pinnacles is a climbers' organization dedicated to preserving the natural resources at Pinnacles National Monument and climbers' access to those resources. Friends of Pinnacles will work cooperatively with the National Park Service, non-affiliated climbers, other interest groups, and the public to:

- reduce impact and rehabilitate high-use areas at the Pinnacles
- provide for effective and appropriate management of climbing activities
- provide for construction and maintenance of trails and facilities used by climbers
- develop and distribute educational materials
- generally promote the "LNT" (Leave No Trace) and conservation ethic of outdoor recreation

Friends of Pinnacles is a non-partisan group which any climber may join without requisite membership fee. A requested donation of $5.00 is gratefully accepted to cover expenses such as mailings, etc.

To join Friends of Pinnacles send your name and address to:

Friends of Pinnacles
208 Woods St.
Santa Cruz, CA 95062

You will receive a periodic newsletter and invitations to public Friends of Pinnacles meetings and events.

Access: It's everybody's concern

THE ACCESS FUND, a national, non-profit climbers' organization, is working to keep you climbing. The Access Fund helps preserve access and protect the environment by providing funds for land acquisitions and climber support facilities, financing scientific studies, publishing educational materials promoting low-impact climbing, and providing start-up money, legal counsel and other resources to local climbers' coalitions.

Climbers can help preserve access by being responsible users of climbing areas. Here are some practical ways to support climbing:

- **COMMIT YOURSELF TO "LEAVING NO TRACE."** Pick up litter around campgrounds and the crags. Let your actions inspire others.

- **DISPOSE OF HUMAN WASTE PROPERLY.** Use toilets whenever possible. If none are available, choose a spot at least 50 meters from any water source. Dig a hole 6 inches (15 cm) deep, and bury your waste in it. *Always pack out toilet paper* in a "Ziploc"-type bag.

- **UTILIZE EXISTING TRAILS.** Avoid cutting switchbacks and trampling vegetation.

- **USE DISCRETION WHEN PLACING BOLTS AND OTHER "FIXED" PROTECTION.** Camouflage all anchors with rock-colored paint. Use chains for rappel stations, or leave rock-colored webbing.

- **RESPECT RESTRICTIONS THAT PROTECT NATURAL RESOURCES AND CULTURAL ARTIFACTS .** Appropriate restrictions can include prohibition of climbing around Indian rock art, pioneer inscriptions, and on certain formations during raptor nesting season. Power drills are illegal in wilderness areas. *Never chisel or sculpt holds in rock on public lands, unless it is expressly allowed* – no other practice so seriously threatens our sport.

- **PARK IN DESIGNATED AREAS,** not in undeveloped, vegetated areas. Carpool to the crags!

- **MAINTAIN A LOW PROFILE.** Other people have the same right to undisturbed enjoyment of natural areas as do you.

- **RESPECT PRIVATE PROPERTY.** Don't trespass in order to climb.

- **JOIN OR FORM A GROUP TO DEAL WITH ACCESS ISSUES IN YOUR AREA.** Consider clean-ups, trail building or maintenance, or other "goodwill" projects.

- **JOIN THE ACCESS FUND.** To become a member, *simply make a donation (tax-deductible) of any amount.* Only by working together can we preserve the diverse American climbing experience.

The Access Fund. Preserving America's diverse climbing resources.
The Access Fund • P.O. Box 17010 • Boulder, CO 80308

ROCK CLIMBING AND ITS FUTURE AT PINNACLES
Written by Andy Artz—Climbing Ranger
Tim Reid—Former Climbing Ranger
Endorsed by Steve DeBenedetti—Resource Management Specialist

Compromise (kom'pre-miz') n. The fine art of....

1. a. A settlement of differences in which each side makes concessions. b. Something resulting from such a settlement.

As a climber and a park ranger, I find myself experiencing the unique perspective of belonging to the membership of two groups on opposing sides of the same issue. While straddling the fence dividing the camps of climbing community and land management agency can be unsettling at times, it also affords a uniquely objective view of a hotly debated issue...regulation of rock climbing on public lands. Thus, when David asked me to write a word on the subject from the agency perspective, I did not hesitate to tie into the sharp end.

Climbing, due to an exponential increase in popularity, has outgrown its former sleepy obscurity and now occupies a high-profile position in mainstream recreation. What once was a low-volume resource use is now significant – to the point of raising rock climbing to the top of many agency resource management priority lists. Climbers want to climb, and land managers must meet their responsibility to the resource. Webster's definition of compromise certainly pertains to the crux of the issue: How do park managers ensure that resources are protected for future generations while also providing for their appropriate use?

Recognition by the administering agency that rock climbing is a legitimate use of resource is, like it or not, a compromise. Conversely, rock climbers conforming to resource protection mandates is a reciprocal compromise. Somewhere in between there exists a minimally restrictive and workable reality. While at first glance it may appear that climbers are bearing the lion's share of compromise, this perception must be juxtaposed against the fact that rock climbing has been largely unregulated for most of its history.

Rock climbing is at a critical juncture in its evolution. Whether or not the sport reaches the future in a minimally restricted form is largely contingent upon the actions of the participants. For Pinnacles rock climbing to continue to be enjoyed in a minimally restrictive environment, the monument needs cooperation with, and perpetuation of, the following concepts:

- Observe all closures and regulations. Make sure that you and your peers are conversant with this information and climbing management concerns. Check the climbers' bulletin board at the trailhead on both sides of the park for current information.

- Prevent erosion by using the designated access trails and by not taking shortcuts.

- Avoid climbing on routes over park service maintained trails except on weekdays. A trail "sentry" should be posted to warn other hikers of the climbing activity and the potential of rockfall.

- Observe the voluntary "no climbing/hiking" closures in order   to protect falcons and eagles as they nest. Note the raptor symbol at the heading of routes and areas.
- Abide by the occasional area restrictions, such as The Back Door and The Tourist Trap, which minimize climber use to prevent further erosion of the site. Read the restriction signs posted at each site.
- All roto hammers are illegal in the monument.
- No new routes may be established above the trails.
- Adopt, practice and perpetuate a minimum impact frame of mind concerning climbing. Think before you place a bolt. Consider visual impact, camouflage hangers and anchors accordingly (see section on bolting), consider not using chalk or only using a chalk ball, only scrub individual holds, not large areas. If you're going to leave a sling, leave one that is colored so it blends with the rock. Backpackers have been practicing a minimal impact concept for years – it would behoove the climbing community to follow suit.
- Consider how your climbing activity might affect another visitor's experience. Be considerate.
- Think carefully about what a new route will add to Pinnacles climbing and the resource. Objectively separate personal gratification from the route...Now, is it still significant? If not, then consider a different route.
- Remember that the resource is finite and your impact can be permanent.
- Give something back to the resources: pick up trash and educate uninformed individuals.

Rock climbing in the 1990s will be regulated. This is unavoidable. Climbers can directly influence the degree of regulation through their actions...all in all, a small compromise to make in return for the well being of a magnificent activity.

Get involved! As this second edition goes to press, the park is developing a climbing management plan that will determine how the National Park Service deals with climbing at Pinnacles for decades to come. As climbers have worked with the National Park Service to repair erosion damage, clean up climbing areas, and otherwise help preserve the Pinnacles, so climbers are currently working with the National Park Service to develop a climbing management plan. Get involved in preserving the places where you climb.

PINNACLES—A UNIQUE HISTORY
Written by Tom Davis

The story that brings us to Pinnacles as we know it today is as colorful and bizarre as the landscape that makes the monument unique. It is a story of ancient explorers and banditos, of summit baggers and fun-hogs, of famous climbers in an infamous climbing area, and of infamous individuals attempting to become famous; it is a tale of purists in an impure age and of the adventures that inspired all these people to leave their mark on the pages of time. But most of all, it is a story of surprising depth for such an obscure climbing area.

The history of climbing at Pinnacles dates back almost as far as that of all the major climbing areas in the United States and involves many of the players more commonly associated with places like Yosemite. The human history of Pinnacles has become as colorful and convoluted as the tilted columns and fault-twisted terrain that greets the present-day visitor.

General George Vancouver is credited with the first recorded (non-indigenous) sighting of the rock formations that are the main attraction of the monument. In 1774, while his ships were being repaired in Monterey, he made an inland mapping journey and mentioned seeing some " remarkable formations of creme-colored stone."

History then catapults us forward to the times of the wild west, when a particularly successful bandito named Tiburcio Vasquez made his home in the great cave beneath the Monolith. His exploits included running off with a senora from San Juan Bautista and successfully pillaging the countryside for 20 years. A legend persists to this day that his booty lies hidden somewhere within the monument. In 1875, his career finally was ended on the gallows in San Jose.

In 1906, the Pinnacles became a government forest preserve, and in 1908, Teddy Roosevelt declared it a National Monument.

The area's climbing history begins in the early '30s, when a group of Sierra Club climbers made the first technical ascent in the Monument. Condor Crags was climbed in 1933 by David Brower, George Rockwood and Hervy Voge. The following year, the same crew, with the addition of David's brother Ralph, made the first ascent of North Finger and Tuff Dome. These three routes were done in the traditional style, with the exception that bolts were used to protect free climbing. This was, possibly, the first time in North America that bolts were used solely for the purpose of creating a free climb.

In 1935, David and Ralph Brower, Bill Van Vorris and George Rockwood made the first ascent of what would prove to be the most popular crag in the entire park. The **Left Hand Traverse** climbed the oak tree near the northeast corner of The Monolith and gained the ledge by traversing a small branch and stemming across to terra firma. Look at the branch today and imagine how big it must have been 56 years ago! That was 18 years before another, more "conventional," route was put up on The Monolith.

The year 1947 was an auspicious one for rock climbing in California. John Salathé and Anton Nelson accomplished the first ascent of a big wall on the continent of North America when they sweated out **Lost Arrow Chimney** and **Lost Arrow Spire** in an epic five-day push. Earlier that year, Salathé made a ground-breaking ascent on **The Hand** at Pinnacles. He lead a two-pitch route, up a near-vertical, crackless wall, using only pitons for protection. Modern climbers will be thankful for the few bolts that have been added since the first ascent. In spite of fortified protection, The Hand stands as an exciting 5.6 lead for a solid 5.9 leader!

The fifties were characterized by a classic mountaineering approach to climbing. Most of the summits in Pinnacles were obtained during this period, and very few formations hosted more than one route. In 1955, Dave Hammack published the first official guidebook to the area.

The sixties brought a new onslaught of talent and boldness to Pinnacles. Attitudes began to shift from pure summit orientation to a focus on new routes. Rope toss/prusik ascents and tree climbing gave way to the more familiar techniques of free and aid climbing. Steve Roper and Jim Bridwell were the driving force behind the blazing of dozens of new and difficult routes during this period.

Perhaps the greatest undertaking of the early '60s was the first ascent of The Balconies, one of the biggest walls in the Monument. Because of Roper's passion for climbing, he was guilty of inducting anyone who appeared remotely capable into the sport. One victim was Frank Sacherer, who became famous for his bold free climbs in Yosemite. The pair, along with Howard Bradley, pushed the first route up the 500-foot East Face of the Balconies. Perhaps the aesthetics of bolting one's way up a crumbling wall planted the seeds for Sacherer's vehement commitment to pure free climbing, which typified his career in Yosemite.

Pinnacles was unique in its need for the use of bolts—the use of bolts to protect free climbs was still in its infancy. Thus, the use of aid to place bolts was common. An intimidated leader often would drill a short bolt ladder to surmount a steep section, only to have the second free climb it on his way past. It wasn't until the late '60s that people like Frank Sacherer and Bob Kamps had developed a code of ethics governing the establishment of free climbs. It was their feeling that a free climb must be created as if one is climbing without a rope. This meant that a fall relegated one to the base of the route for another attempt, and that all protection was to be placed from free stances or not at all. Their example sparked a new generation of free climbing accomplishment.

New route activity reached a feverish pace in the mid-60s—a pitch that would not be seen again for over 20 years. Virtually all the classic, moderate routes were established during this era. What would become the most popular route at the Pinnacles was put up by Steve Roper and Andrew Emery. In yet another instance of corrupting his fellow youth, Roper led a suspicious and fearful Emery up **Portent** on Discovery Wall. On its notoriously exposed headwall, Emery sheepishly inquired what it was that Roper was anchored to. Steve calmly informed him that he was tied to a two-foot tree, and not to worry. Upon topping out, Emery was shocked to find Roper tied to a measly two-foot tall chaparral bush!

Bear Gulch was the scene of fiendish activity both on and off the rocks. In many ways, this was the "golden age" of Pinnacles climbing. The parking lot at the trailhead was a campground that served more to keep the adventure going through the night than as a place of recuperation after a hard day at the crags. Traveling south from the Bay Area, the adventurists would collect discarded tires for weekend bonfires. "Teton Tea" was brewed in multi-gallon batches, and served to both stimulate and inebriate the scene. Reportedly, a record was set when 13 tires were put on the fire at one time. As if this wasn't enough, Roper's father worked for a large chemical firm, which allowed Steve to occasionally procure huge chunks of magnesium. At critical moments, he would slip these onto the fire, with ferocious results. Eventually, a form of late-night Olympics would erupt, involving such events as long-jumping through fire and lightless ascents of The Monolith.

1965 was a big year. More first ascents were done than in any five years prior. Jim Bridwell particularly was prolific. He produced a series of climbs that were as difficult as any in the country at that time. **Premeditated** and **Trial**, at A4, were very serious undertakings, especially when one considers the crumbly nature of the rock and the groundfall/ledge-out potential that was possible on **Trial**. Bridwell also made the first free ascent of numerous 5.9s and the first 5.10 in the monument, **No Holds Barred**. He remains the unchallenged master of aid climbing at Pinnacles. It wasn't until 1971, when Barry Bates free climbed **Mechanic's Delight** (which many people feel is 5.11), that a harder route was accomplished. In 1966, Steve Roper published a very comprehensive guide to the climbs of the Pinnacles, and an era of unrestrained adventure began to draw to an end.

The seventies were a time of transition. The last of the prominent big walls were climbed, including **Machete Direct** by Glen Denny and Gary Coliver in 1974, and **Resurrection Wall** by Rupert Kammerlander and Anton Karuza in 1978. Direct aid was used less and less, and first free ascents became the dominant theme. Many of the old bolt ladders were pushed free, and first ascents began to reach toward new levels of boldness in free climbing.

Rupert Kammerlander exemplified a boldness that has been seldom matched. His routes have come to be known for the commitment and focus they require. Often run-out, you can easily picture Rupert moving up, more intent on the climbing than on protecting himself. His route **50 Meter Must** (5.7 R+) is a prime example of moderate and excellent climbing that will cause most leaders to consider their skill and commitment before venturing past the third bolt. His style of first ascents was an example of minimum impact climbing coupled with a pure "ground up" ethic.

Shake and Bake was the first—and is still one of the most impressive—of the modern free routes. In a stroke of true vision, Tom Higgins and Chris Vandiver launched themselves up the sheer wall of The Balconies with the intent of creating the first free climb on the wall. As if this wasn't enough, their goal was to place all the bolts without resorting to aid of any sort. After three days of strained and nerve-wracking effort, the pair gained the safety of the ledge at the top of the wall. Their audacity, combined with their use of ⅜-inch bolts, set a superlative example. Be forewarned: Until you are ready to handle 30-foot runouts on sustained 5.9 climbing, steer clear of this one. But when you are ready, you will experience one of the true gems to be found at Pinnacles.

As in the spirit of **Shake and Bake**, for over twenty years Jack Holmgren has always placed bolts in stance, often taking hours to drill a single bolt to avoid weighting a piece of aid. Jack has been known to climb up to a protection point to pound a few times on the drill only to downclimb to a natural resting spot or the ground, shake out and go back up to drill some more, doing this over and over until the hole is deep enough for a bolt. It might be accurate to say that Jack has led, by example, the way for Pinnacles to stand as a last bastion of "ground up" first ascents, which mostly has been respected by the climbing community. To this day, Jack Holmgren's **Nexus** (5.11c) is the most difficult route done by free-stance tactics.

Barry Bates had become firmly established as a top-notch free climber by the mid-70s. With routes in Yosemite such as **Vanishing Point** and the first free ascent of **New Dimensions** to his credit, people began to see that Barry's unassuming manner neatly disguised his climbing prowess. One weekend in 1978, with the help of Glen Garland, Barry made a serious effort to free climb the incredibly steep bolt ladder on the first pitch of **Machete Direct**. After a day's work, the pair became convinced that the pitch could be done. The duo met with success the following weekend. They conservatively rated it 5.11+, but the truth reads more like solid 5.12. It was ten years before a harder route was done at Pinnacles.

The end of the seventies was a time of diversification. People like Jim Beyer continued to push bold lines on improbably steep faces, but hooks were occasionally used to assist in placing bolts on vertical and overhanging terrain. An unknown party even went as far as to install three bolts, on rappel, on an impressive toprope problem on The Monolith. Their motives also were a mystery, as it is a 70-foot climb that could not be led with such sparse protection.

The dawn of the eighties saw a changing of the guard. Most of the prominent aid routes had been free climbed or put aside due to their obscenely loose nature. Paul Gagner, John Barbella, the McConachie brothers and Chris Bellizzi came to dominate the first ascent scene. Hooking was employed universally by this group as a means for lead-bolting on spectacularly steep lines. A new wave had begun that flowed toward the development of a pure cragging area. The higher grades began to fill out, particularly in the 5.10 range.

In 1981, Chris Bellizzi finished bolting The Monolith toprope problem, led it, and dubbed it **Post Orgasmic Depression (P.O.D.)**. At 5.10d/5.11a, **P.O.D.** sported ⅜-inch bolts and was prominently located. It became an instant classic, but was destined to undermine the "ground up" ethic that had flourished at the Pinnacles. **P.O.D.** also demonstrated the awesome potential for steep and difficult climbing that was yet to be tapped.

A few years later, James McConachie, John Barbella and Paul Gagner led a route that is even steeper and more intimidating than **P.O.D.** With one ¼-inch exception, they hand-drilled ⅜-inch bolts as they pushed their line over three consecutive overhangs and onto a long headwall. **Heat Seeking Moisture Missile** (5.10d) exemplified the limitless nature of "ground up" climbing on Pinnacles rock.

In 1987, the modern age discovered Pinnacles. Fresh from a summer in Europe, an enthusiastic climber named Mike Carville began to consider the possibilities existing on the steeper walls. Using **P.O.D.** as a justification, Carville began to employ European tactics on his first ascents. He had a great eye for a line, and in a very short time, Carville cleaned, toproped and rappel-bolted numerous routes in the Bear Gulch area. Due to the day-use nature of climbing at Pinnacles, it was several months before the "regulars" caught wind of his actions.

Carville was not the only one to see the unclimbed gems that still existed in the monument. At about the same time, a group of Santa Cruz climbers had begun to try their hand at lead bolting. Kelly Rich, David Rubine, Michael Harrington and Tom Davis were busy sniffing out new possibilities as well. Unfortunately, our boundless enthusiasm was accompanied by minimal experience with placing ⅜-inch bolts. The first route we attempted developed into a four-year comedy of errors, due in part to the botching of the first bolt placement and the two years spent trying to mount a hanger on a stud with stripped threads (duct tape works, but does not inspire the leader with confidence). Three-eighths-inch hand drilling gear was hard to come by, so we attempted to design our own. In the process of arriving at a workable design, we assembled about 20 pounds of useless and broken bolting gear. During this time, we managed to learn one important thing: there seemed to be no inherent limits to the hook-and-drill technique of lead bolting.

As our collection of trashed gear grew, so did the number of routes. Our activity, and that of Carville and the others, did not go unnoticed, and the likes of Gagner, Bellizzi, and the McConachie brothers renewed their efforts with increased vigor. It soon became known that Carville was bolting on rappel, and most people assumed that all the new lines were being done that way. Thus, an ethical conflict was already in the works when two other climbers dropped a bomb on the scene.

These individuals bolted a number of routes in a remote canyon on the West Side, and employed extremely high-impact techniques. Rap-bolting with a power drill, they scrubbed huge stripes on moss-covered faces. Upon closer inspection, it became obvious that many of the routes had never been climbed, as the rock was so loose that it broke away with little or no pressure. In more than one instance, would-be second ascentionists discovered a beautiful line with chalk on every hold, only to find that the holds could not support even a few ounces, let alone body weight. Along with the creation of fictitious routes aside, these climbers also carved a bermed trail up the Citadel Canyon. They cut down brush, dug out switchbacks and lined the trail with rocks and cigarette butts. These offenses, combined with all the new route activity, were seen as an out-growth of modern climbing. Because of these actions, the Park Service considered very restrictive parkwide regulations.

Many of the more seasoned veterans were concerned about the ethics of the newcomers, and with the threat of new, restrictive regulations including the possibility of a climbing ban, a meeting was called. Every faction was represented. Virtually every person who had done a first ascent at the Pinnacles in the previous ten years was there. Free-stance bolters, hookers and rap-bolters all sat down to discuss the development and preservation of Pinnacles. It soon became obvious that there were only two people rappel-bolting in the monument, and that the only person doing it with honesty was Mike Carville. The discourse was heated at first, but he quickly agreed to cease rap-bolting provided none of his completed routes be removed. A consensus was reached: Pinnacles would remain a "ground up" area. Also, climbers agreed to draft a letter in support of seasonal closures of certain formations to support raptor reproduction. Armando Menocal, chairman of the Access Committee, then presented the climbers' united agreements to the Park Service, and the final outcome was in favor of the climbers. Carville even went on to establish one route on lead (**Pistol Whipped**) before leaving the area and moving to Tahoe.

Back on the crags, the new route activity hardly missed a beat. Gagner, Bellizzi and the McConachies began to push even harder as they saw the enthusiasm with which the newcomers sought out new routes. Every weekend, the ring of hammers on drills could be heard. Between 1987 and 1989, Bear Gulch was transformed into the sportclimbing arena that it now is.

Future Shock was the first lead-bolted 5.12. It took over six months to establish, but since that breakthrough, a virtual landslide of 5.12s went up by hook-and-drill techniques. Mike Carville figured out a key sequence on **Forty Days of Rain** (after Kelly Rich and Tom Davis fixed the bad bolt). This pearl of wisdom allowed us to put a quick end to four years of agony. The next route to go was **Trial**. Using Friends, hooks and a piton, we added three bolts and pulled off the first free ascent in a mere three days. Over the next year, some ten 5.12s were established from the ground up.

With ethical conflicts seemingly resolved, there was a real feeling of camaraderie at the crags. All the activists now knew each other and the fun expanded exponentially. I can remember several occasions when Gagner and Bellizzi would laugh and poke fun at us as we sweated out the second ascent of one of their desperates, such as **Here Comes The Judge**. Fun and adventure were abundant. Once, while drilling from a hook some 30 feet in the air, David Rubine suddenly found himself dangling by one hand, holding onto the drill bit, when his hook placement crumbled. For fear of breaking yet another drill, his companions yelled at him to let go! The resulting lead fall was quite spectacular. Minutes later, Rubine established himself on yet another hook placement and finished drilling the bolt.

When the dust settled, it became obvious that Pinnacles had entered the modern age of climbing. With the numerous routes that were put up, 5.12 became firmly established and the number of 5.11s tripled. What appeared to be a modern sport-climbing area had been created primarily by a spirit that respected the styles that were the origins of climbing in the monument.

Along with the climbing history, the succession of Pinnacles guides should be noted. The first official guide came out in 1955 by Dave Hammack through the Sierra Club. Yet even before that, Dave Brower wrote an earlier report on Pinnacles for the Sierra Club Bulletin. Though these publications were small they represented the desire for someone to bring to the community the joy they found here. Following these guides, Steve Roper produced a guidebook in 1966. This marvelous edition marked the emergence of Pinnacles as a recognized climbing area an set a precedent for quality. Following Roper's book came Chuck Richard's in 1974. Chuck Richard's passion for climbing and life are clear in his zany and complete guide. Paul Gagner's guide in 1983 once again marked a turning point at the Monument. Paul's efforts to bring Pinnacles to life as a legitimate free climbing arena were precursory to these editions.

The story is far from finished. The spirit of adventure that lured Yosemite veterans to spend their weekends playing at Pinnacles still thrives, and new discoveries have hardly been diminished by the addition of more routes. If perchance you wish to add your name to the list of adventurers who establish routes in this monument, take a moment and consider the manner in which those who have gone before you have left their mark. Consider that the spirit of adventure dwells in the fear of the unknown and therein lies the reward. Pursuit of this spirit is the pigment that brightens the experience of those climbing in this bizarre and colorful landscape.

THE CLIMBING SCENE

Climbing at Pinnacles is truly an adventure. The rock ranges from mudlike to incredibly sound, producing routes of the highest calibre. The rock is volcanic, with many protruding knobs and pebbles that allow ascents of many vertical to over-hanging faces. You can find very sporty 5.4 to 5.8 climbing that requires absolute concentration because of the questionable permanence of the holds. You also can find "clip-and-go" 5.12s on perfectly sound rock—and everything in between. In general, the climbing is very steep, requiring a lot of endurance. Even on 5.7 or eas-ier climbing, above average stamina is a must. The rating of a climb says very little about the verticality of the route.

Most routes are short—around 80 feet or under—and need only one rope (although there are a number of multi-pitch formations). Routes mostly are bolt-protected, with crack climbs being a scarce commodity. Older routes (those established before 1980) should be approached with caution: bolts might be bad and the route runout. If you want to be humbled, venture onto some of the oldies for a thrill.

As with all "soft rock" climbing areas it is often best to stay clear of the harder, steeper routes for a day or so after a good rain. Especially on some routes 5.11 and harder, cruxes are often dependent on a few small holds which can become weak-er when wet.

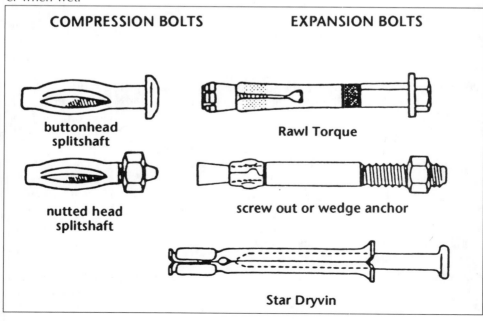

COMPRESSION BOLTS

EXPANSION BOLTS

buttonhead splitshaft

Rawl Torque

nutted head splitshaft

screw out or wedge anchor

Star Dryvin

SAFETY

Climbing at Pinnacles is uniquely dangerous. I say this not to dampen the potential enthusiasm in climbing here—only to point out the safest frame of mind with which one should approach these climbs. I have been on the scene of three accidents in the last three years. These accidents had two things in common—the reason they occurred, and broken bones of varying degrees of seriousness. All these leaders took serious falls due to the failure of protection. Nuts and camming units pulled out of the comparatively soft rock. On any climb where self-placed protection is required, expert skills are mandatory, regardless of the rating. You cannot place too much protection. Set aside the ego, place lots of gear, and understand that the rock is soft. If a climb has a required runout, climb with fanatical caution. You always can tell a longtime Pinnacles climber by the curious way they tap the holds. The sound of that tap can tell everything about the permanence of the hold.

As you venture onto the less-traveled climbs, the degree of caution should increase. The rock is likely to be less trustworthy, and the data less accurate. It is impractical (probably impossible) for any guidebook author to do every route in an area to verify data. Although this author has at least visually inspected over 90% of the routes in the monument, data may be wrong. Once you leave the familiarity of Bear

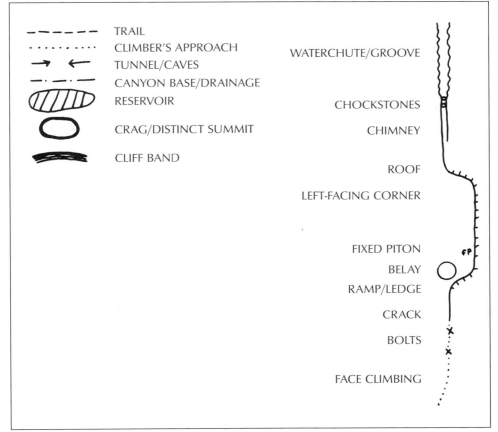

Gulch or the popular West Side valley, the stakes increase. Be prepared for no bolts, bad anchors and misleading information. Consider yourself warned. Have an adventure, get lost in the wondrous backcountry, but be prepared. The crediting section at the end of the book will contain some pertinent bolt and anchor data on the routes.

Bolt placements on a number of routes can unknowingly put you in danger of groundfall. Be aware of this potential when pulling the rope up to clip into the second bolt.

Also, don't take bolts for granted. They aren't necessarily "bomb-proof" protection. Always examine the state of any bolt. Ways of identifying and replacing bad bolts will be discussed in the section on bolting.

Remember, the rock is loose. Debris constantly is falling from the gravelly cliff tops. Always yell "Rock" if you dislodge something, and be aware of people above you when on the ground.

The most important tip on safety that I can offer is to train yourself properly. There is nothing more horrifying than finding yourself in the middle of a lead on something you have no business climbing. Pinnacles, in particular, is a nasty place to get into that predicament. Tell the truth: Am I ready to lead this climb? Am I ready to lead altogether? Am I ready to be climbing on my own? Classes are available from many mountain stores. Fortunate is the novice who finds a skilled and patient mentor.

EQUIPMENT

A standard rack of camming units (Friends and TCUs), nuts and quickdraws can be used. Long runners can be used to tie-off occasional knobs for protection. There are a number of routes where Tri-cams can be used in pockets. It is wise to carry a few on your rack, especially when climbing more obscure routes.

On many routes, bolts with lap (smash) links have been installed for rappelling. The links have been placed to prevent the need to leave a sling. Avoid leaving a sling on the anchor (to minimize visual impact) unless it's needed to back up the system.

BOLTING

Written by Clint Cummins and David Rubine

A large number of routes at Pinnacles rely on bolt protection, due to the scarcity of protectable cracks in the volcanic rock (breccia). An understanding of the types of bolts used and their strength is important, especially on the older and less-traveled routes. Bolt strength is a function of the compression strength of the rock, the size of the bolt and the type of bolt (plus its age).

Rock compression strength varies greatly at Pinnacles, from the light/white-colored "dirt" to the granite-hard rhyolite knobs (with every density in between). Bolts often are placed in the darker, moderately sound breccia, where water erosion has leached minerals to harden the surface. With the breccia, darker is better, although hidden flakes and hollow spots also are a factor. Tapping the rock and listening for a hollow sound is useful in determining where to place a bolt. All breccia is soft relative to granite, so when a bolt bends slightly under load, the rock can begin to crumble at the surface of the hole. This distorts and flares the hole, and can lever the bolt in a downward direction against its roots. Thus the "pullout strength" of the bolt is critical. In harder rock, "shear strength" is more important.

Large-diameter bolts are stiffer, so they bend less and reduce the problem of hole disintegration. They also tend to be longer, which means that more of the rock has to give way before they fail. The bolt itself rarely will fail in soft rock, unless it is severely rusted or abused.

There are three types of bolts—compression, expansion and glue-in. Compression bolts (split-shaft Rawl Drives) should not be used at Pinnacles. They are wedged in place by the compression of the split-shaft. They widen and damage the surface of the hole as they are pounded into the softer rock. Even in hard rock, the split-shafts eventually can lose their hold, become loose and spin in the hole. Quarter-inch Rawl Drives are absolutely unacceptable at Pinnacles, although quite a few have been used here. And, while ⅜-inch Rawl Drives may be adequate, they should be avoided in favor of the superior alternatives.

Expansion bolts, of at least ⅜-inches in diameter, are much better. The best kind are the "torque bolts" (Rawl Bolt, Petzl, and Metolius S.S.), which have a hex head that is torqued against a threaded cylindrical wedge in a long sleeve. A close second is the Star "screw-out," or wedge anchor, which uses a hex nut to pull the shaft tight against a small ring on a reverse-tapered section deep in the hole. The old Star Dryvin also is an expansion bolt, using a nail driven into a split sheath. Although a very popular bolt on routes put up before 1980, this protection bolt is barely adequate. Its weaknesses are that it is not very stiff, and its expansion is achieved solely by the force of the driven nail, not by the torque of threads against an active expansion mechanism. Because of this, the nail has a tendency to slip out over time. This type of bolt always should be watched for signs of this weakness. It easily can be pulled and replaced with a better bolt, which can be placed in the same hole.

Glue-in bolts have superior strength and durability in soft rock. These bolts are popular on soft limestone in Europe, and they eventually may be used at Pinnacles for the most popular belay/rappel anchors or as replacements for old protection bolts. They have a strong load-bearing surface along the entire depth of the hole, but the glue's long setting time (10 to 60 minutes) and the large diameter hole makes them impractical for protection on first ascents.

Most bolts are readily identified by looking at the head. You also can get an idea of the bolt type by knowing the date of the first ascent party or the names of those involved. Any ¼-inch buttonhead or hex nut can be assumed to be a Rawl Drive split-shaft. They are common on older routes, but have not been used much in the '80s. (Refer to the credit section of the guide for a more detailed accounting of bolts used on specific routes.) Extreme compression problems and a very short length have precluded the use of 5⁄16-inch button heads in Pinnacles. Larger button heads are extremely rare. The ⅜-inch Rawl Drive split-shaft (large hex nuts) have been frequently used in the '70s and '80s. They are difficult to distinguish from the

⅜-inch Star "screw-out" or wedge anchor more commonly used in the late '80s and early '90s. Torque bolts still are fairly rare. Star Dryvins usually have a five-pointed star stamped on the head of the nail. They come in both ¼-and ⅜-inch diameter, and are common on routes established prior to 1980.

If you are attempting an older route, such as one of the more obscure or remote spires, you should expect poor bolts and possibly poor hangers with holes requiring small-diameter carabiners. Carry a crescent wrench and a few hangers and nuts, plus tie-off loops (or wired stoppers). Or, better yet, take the time to replace the bad bolt by levering out the old bolt and enlarging the existing hole. One unusual, but clean, alternative for setting up a rappel anchor is to have your partner tie the rope to the base of one side of the spire (often to a tree) on the opposite side of the rappel route. A basic check list for putting up new routes and for bolting in general is as follows:

- Three-eighths-inch torque bolts or wedge anchors are mandatory, with a minimum length of three inches.
- Tap the rock to check for hollowness.
- Use silicone rubber between the hanger and the rock to prevent weathering. Polyester resin is best for this purpose; it is harder but more durable. Epoxy is too hard and should be avoided.
- Diminish visual impact by avoiding the use of colored hangers, and by painting bright hangers black (paint before installing).
- A set of large, split-chain (smash) links attached to the hanger (also pre-painted black) is suggested for rappel anchors, to avoid bright and/or rotting slings.
- Unused or abandoned bolt holes may be patched by filling the hole with a mixture of silicone and rock and gravel.
- Battery or gas powered drills are illegal in Pinnacles National Monument.
- The standard for putting up a first ascent at Pinnacles is that bolting for the lead be done from the ground up.

REBOLTING VS. RETRO-BOLTING

Rebolting means removing and replacing old, unsafe bolts, leaving the bolt in its original location. It may also mean adding a belay bolt to anchors when necessary. If you plan to contribute to the safety of climbing at Pinnacles by replacing an existing protection bolt make sure you know what you are doing. In general this is an accepted and appreciated practice. Here are a few rules regarding rebolting:

- Never add fixed protection points to an existing route without the first ascentionist's permission.
- Do not move a protection point from its original location without the first ascentionist's permission.
- If the first ascentionist is no longer available to ask, then the route remains unaltered.
- Do not place additional bolts next to existing old bolts.

- Always, when possible, pull the old bolt and drill out the existing bolt hole. If this is not possible, and this is a very, very rare exception, Star Dryvin bolts are easily pulled with a crow bar. Chop the old bolt, patch the hole with silicone and gravel and drill a new hole as close to the old one as possible. Make sure the new hole is not so near as to crumble into the old one.
- If you are unsure of how or where to rebolt something, contact Friend of Pinnacles to get feedback on your concern. Members of the organization, many who are leading first ascentionists in the Pinnacles climbing community, will gladly give you their opinion.

Retro-bolting means adding additional protection bolts to an existing route. In general, the climbing community does not approve of this. Protection bolts added to existing routes, without the first ascentionist's agreement, will undoubtedly be removed. If you are not up to leading a fixed protection route (as opposed to a crack where protection can be placed more often), as the first ascentionist climbed it, then find a climb that suits your level of skill and boldness.

The author of this guide is not advocating bolting. If climbers are going to lead at the Monument, bolts are needed to protect them and adequate knowledge of the technology of bolting is mandatory before placing one. Drilling a bolt creates a permanent defacement of the rock and is a huge responsibility for the climbing community. This responsibility always should be considered before placing a bolt. A bolt never is placed solely for the use of the first ascentionists. It is a permanent protection piece for all those who do the route. Other lives will depend on a properly placed bolt; it is not just a reminder to others that someone was there first.

Before placing the bolt, consider the need for it. Is the route worth doing? Is the bolt solely being placed to mark territory? Will anyone do the route after you? Could it just as easily be toproped? Grappling with questions like these creates the basis for personal ethics in regard to bolting, and personal ethics are desperately needed in this age of "machine gun" bolting. Remember, once the drill is tapped, the rock is changed forever. Consider this important question: What is the environmental impact of my climbing at Pinnacles, and does it demonstrate a commitment to minimum impact use of the Monument?

RATINGS

Ratings truly are subjective. They are a consensus-derived opinion of the difficulty of a route. Depending on the number of people who have done the route, that consensus may be the opinion of one or many. Ratings do not take into account individual abilities, strengths or body types. Ratings merely point at the possible difficulty of the single hardest move of any given route. On occasion, a rating will be derived not by the single hardest move but by the sum of all the moves making up the route. For instance, The Verdict may not have a 5.11b move anywhere on it, but the length and overhanging nature of the route add up to the rating in the opinion of many who've done it.

Along with the number rating may be an R or X rating. An R rating indicates that at some point on the route, a fall of 20 feet or more is possible, protection may be dubious, and there is a great possibility for injury from a fall. There may be other routes with points on them where falls of 20 feet or more could occur, but the fall may be clean and the protection excellent, or the section is significantly easier than the rest of the climb.

An X rating means that at some point on a climb, there is a chance of an extremely long fall or groundfall, and the likelihood of a serious injury or fatality is great. A route may have a runout section where, if a fall occurred, results could be disastrous, but it would not be given an X rating if the runout is, let's say, 5.5 on a 5.11 climb. The rating is used to indicate a true "death climb," not to point out every runout section in the monument. Just because a climb has no R or X rating does not mean it is inherently well protected. Conditions change and guidebook authors are only as accurate as the information gathered.

STAR SYSTEM

Certain routes will be given a star rating to further shed light on the potential of a route. One star ★ means the route is above average. The rock usually is fairly decent, and the climbing good. Two stars ★★ means the route is highly recommended. The rock usually is good and the climbing is excellent. Three stars ★★★ means the route is a Pinnacles classic. The route is an all-time favorite of most climbers, the line captures the spirit of "true" Pinnacles climbing, the rock is usually great, and the climbing is the best that the monument has to offer.

Of course this system started with my personal opinion and evolved with the opinions of a handful of climbers. The stars are meant to be an aid in determining a day's agenda. If you have opinions about route quality, please send that info to the address listed in the front of the book.

HOW TO USE THIS BOOK

The Pinnacles landscape can be approached by road from the east or west, and that is how the guide is organized. In addition to the East Side and West Side sections of the book, the High Peaks separating those respective sides is described in its own section. Maps and written description are supplemented with the occasional cliff photo and topo.

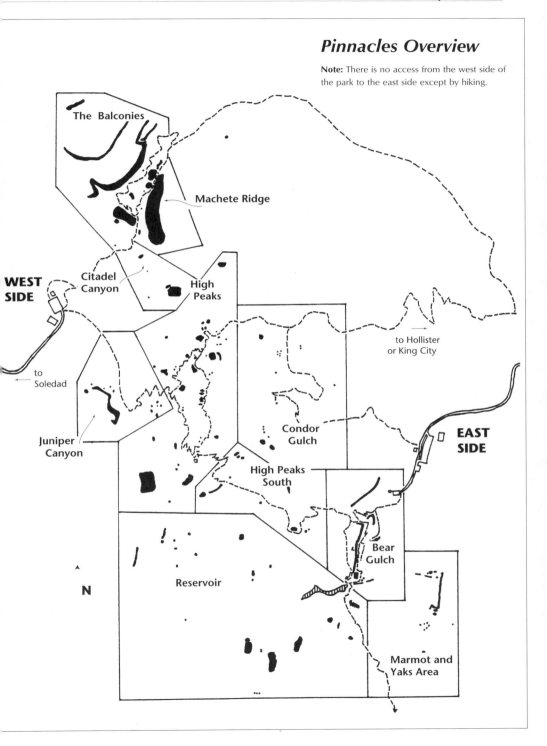

Pinnacles Overview

Note: There is no access from the west side of the park to the east side except by hiking.

The Balconies

Machete Ridge

WEST SIDE

Citadel Canyon

High Peaks

to Hollister or King City

to Soledad

Juniper Canyon

Condor Gulch

EAST SIDE

High Peaks South

Bear Gulch

N

Reservoir

Marmot and Yaks Area

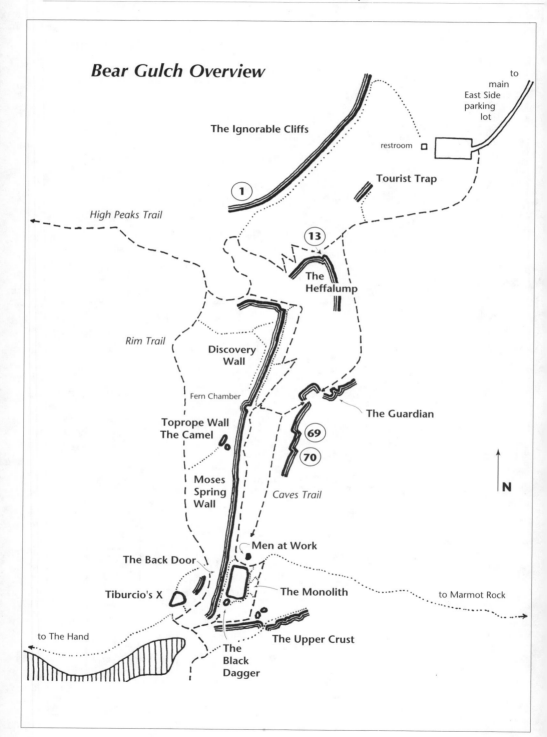

Bear Gulch Overview

The Ignorable Cliffs

to main East Side parking lot

restroom

Tourist Trap

(1)

High Peaks Trail

(13)

The Heffalump

Rim Trail

Discovery Wall

Fern Chamber

The Guardian

Toprope Wall
The Camel

(69)

(70)

Moses Spring Wall

Caves Trail

N

Men at Work

The Back Door

Tiburcio's X

The Monolith

to Marmot Rock

to The Hand

The Black Dagger

The Upper Crust

EAST SIDE

Bear Gulch Area

Bear Gulch extends from the upper East Side parking lot to the reservoir and includes all faces and formations both in the gulch and on either side of it. Access to all routes in Bear Gulch, and all East Side climbing, originates at the East Side Visitor's Center. Approach descriptions will be given as if you are walking up the canyon.

Bear Gulch has the highest concentration of routes, the best rock and the easiest access of any climbing area in the monument. It also provides high-quality climbing at all levels. For these reasons, it has become the most popular area at Pinnacles. In the last eight years, many new routes have gone up, nearly doubling the number of climbs in the gulch. Quite a few routes come highly recommended. **Wet Kiss** (5.9) is a steep, well-protected face climb on superb rock. In the vicinity of the **Wet Kiss** are **Portent** (5.6) and **Ordeal** (5.8), two moderate and wonderfully exciting climbs. For the climber looking for a challenge, you can hop on **Forty Days of Rain** (5.12c), a dynamic route sporting reachy face moves to a ten-foot roof/handcrack. In general, most any route on The Monolith, Back Door or Upper Crust will be of quality. The classic **Post Orgasmic Depression** (5.10d) will pump you up on its gradually overhanging wall. The historic **Regular Route** on The Monolith (5.8) will make you pause as its angle takes you by surprise. **Cataract Corner** (5.12a/b) will impose some agonizingly intricate sequences as you battle up the steepening arête. Playing on **Rocket in My Pocket** (5.10d) can be rewarding: fun sequences getting you to the jug of your dreams. **Heat Seeking Moisture Missile** (5.10d), on Moses Spring Wall, will provide an authentic portrayal of "true Pinnacles climbing" for the ambitious and dedicated crag master.

The Ignorable Cliffs

Usually an ignored and shunned area, The Ignorable Cliffs are the long, high band of cliffs directly above the upper Bear Gulch parking lot. The cliffs actually have three moderately hard and excellent free climbs. On The Pub Wall, **Anchor Scream** (5.11a) and **This Bolt's for You** (5.11d) are two tasty clip-ups. **Bat Cave** (5.11), a recently freed aid line at the other end of the cliff from The Pub, also makes this area worth a visit. The other routes on this cliff band mostly are discussed for historical reasons. They are aid climbs on mostly loose rock, requiring unknown aid placements and utilizing archaic bolts that could possibly take one into the A4+ realm. Venture on these lines with fanatical caution.

The main area is marked by two large, east-facing overhangs (which serve as boundaries of The Pub Wall) seen directly above the upper Bear Gulch parking lot. Triangle Skirt is the overhang on the right and Delusion Overhang is on the left.

The best approach to The Ignorable Cliffs is to take the Moses Springs Trail to the High Peaks Trail junction. Follow the High Peaks Trail up past the second switch-

back to a point where it comes closest to the long Ignorable Cliff band on the right.
Take the trail skirting along the base of the cliff. Approximately 100 yards after leaving the main trail, you'll be directly below Bat Cave. To get to The Pub Wall and the
rest, continue along the trail, staying directly below the cliff, for approximately 400
yards, until you reach the obvious overhangs of **Delusion Overhang** and **Triangle
Skirt.** To descend from the area, either walk along the top of the cliff to the
right/north end and down an obvious gully/break, or rappel from the anchors at
the top of **Anchor Scream** or **This Bolt's for You.**

1   **BAT CAVE 5.11 ★**   Originally an aid line, this route now is an improbable-looking free
     climb. As such, it stands as an example of the tenacity and commitment Pinnacles
     climbers have had in freeing some of the old, intimidating aid routes. Once on top,
     walk south to the High Peaks Trail. Fifty feet to the right of the start of **Bat Cave** is a 15-
     foot left-arching corner (5.10+), which makes an excellent toprope.

1a   **BAT CAVE – DIRECT FINISH 5.11b TR**   Go directly over the apex of the roof, follow-
     ing a left-diagonalling thin crack.

The Pub Area

2   **CONTRABAND CRACK 5.8 A2**   This aid line is located 150 feet left of **Delusion
     Overhang.** It is an offwidth crack that begins about 25 feet off the ground. Aid has
     been used to get to and enter the wide crack above.

3   **DELUSION OVERHANG 5.7 A3**   This is the largest roof immediately left of **Anchor Scream**. It is split in the middle by a thin crack. Follow this crack through the overhangs and to the right.

4   **DELUSION OVERHANG RIGHT 5.10**   Follow a left-facing corner up to the extreme right side of **Delusion Overhang**. As the corner becomes an overhanging offwidth/chimney, continue out the right side of the roof to the top.

The Pub Wall

5   **ANCHOR SCREAM 5.11a** ★★   A superb climb on surprisingly good rock, topped off with a committing mantel.

6   **THIS BOLT'S FOR YOU aka The Price 5.11d** ★★   The thin boulder start is a good warm-up for the roof above.

7   **TRIANGLE SKIRT 5.5 A2**   This the roof/corner just right of **Anchor Scream**.

The Ignorable Cliffs

1 **BAT CAVE 5.11** ★
1a **BAT CAVE–DIRECT FINISH 5.11b TR**

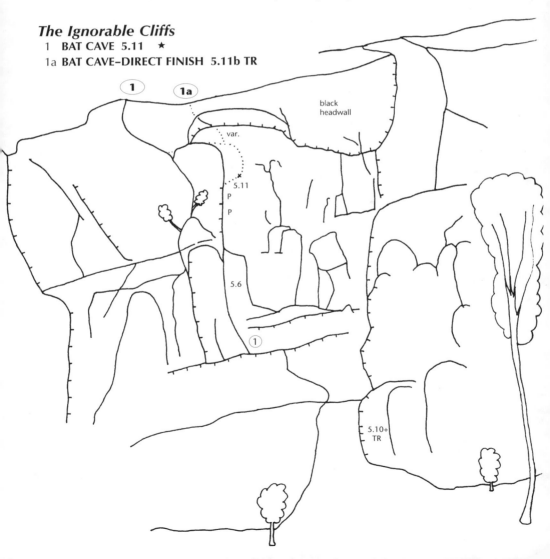

The Pub Wall

The Ignorable Cliffs
3   DELUSION OVERHANG 5.7 A3
4   DELUSION OVERHANG RIGHT 5.10

The Pub Wall
5   ANCHOR SCREAM 5.11a ★★
6   THIS BOLT'S FOR YOU 5.11d ★
7   TRIANGLE SKIRT 5.5 A2

The Tourist Trap

This area is to your right just before the Moses Spring and High Peaks Trail junction. It is a small cliff band directly below Bat Cave on The Ignorable Cliffs. The obvious left-facing corner with a five-foot roof at the top is **Rat Race**. An easy scramble across the boulder-filled gully takes you directly to its base. Descend from the top by either rappelling off the bolts above **Thrill Hammer** and **Pastie** or by following the trail at the base of The Ignorable Cliffs back out to High Peaks Trail. The climbs on this wall are like a "preview of coming attractions" for visitors, as they come to terms with the possibility that there are ways to enjoy the monument other than hiking the trails. Please observe the site restriction posted at the trail head to The Tourist Trap.

7a   **ANGSTROM'S AWAY 5.10a**   This route is 50 feet left of **Rat Race** and follows the arête past three bolts to a chain belay.

8   **RAT RACE 5.7 ★★**   How can a five-foot roof be only 5.7? It's worth finding out on this route. A belay on top is set up by tying off a block. Protection to four inches is needed for the roof.

9   **HAPPILY MARRIED BACHELOR 5.9**   This shaky-looking, double-crack system lies on the right wall of the **Rat Race** corner. Start up **Rat Race** and traverse right into the crack system.

10 **THRILL HAMMER 5.8+ ★★** This fun route can be done in one or two pitches. For those wanting to avoid the initial difficulties, a third-class ledge enables one to climb a shorter and easier pitch. A direct finish over the summit block can be protected by carefully placing small camming units in the horizontal crack at its base.

11 **PASTIE 5.7**

12 **NIPPLE JAM 5.8 ★**

Also in the area:

12a **WILD BERRY CRACK 5.10a** Located north across the creek and upstream from Steve's Folly. Start in an overhanging, left-slanting fistcrack. Lieback the crack and finish on the face. A fixed piton, #3 TCU and an assortment of larger camming units are the protection.

The Tourist Trap

7a **ANGSTOM'S AWAY 5.10a**

8 **RAT RACE 5.7 ★★**

10 **THRILL HAMMER 5.8+ ★★**

11 **PASTIE 5.7**

12 **NIPPLE JAM 5.8 ★**

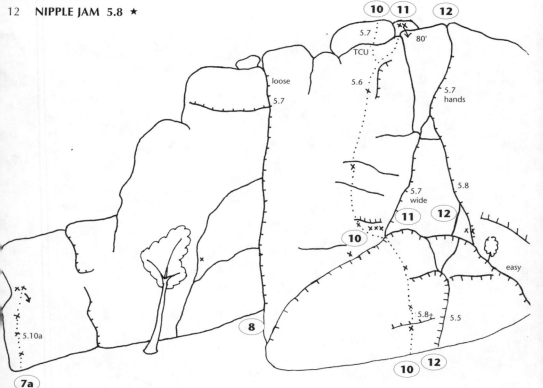

Photo: Tim Corcoran.

Jeff Goris on **Ordeal** *5.8.*

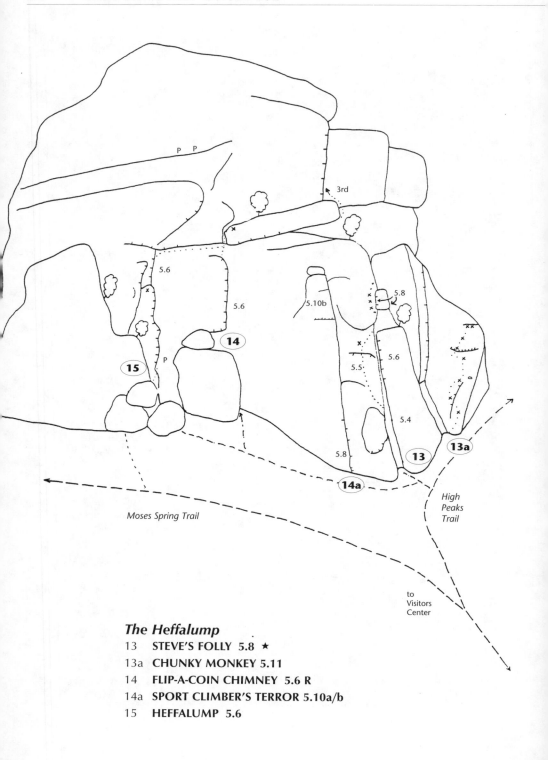

The Heffalump

13   **STEVE'S FOLLY 5.8 ★**
13a **CHUNKY MONKEY 5.11**
14   **FLIP-A-COIN CHIMNEY 5.6 R**
14a **SPORT CLIMBER'S TERROR 5.10a/b**
15   **HEFFALUMP 5.6**

The Heffalump

This is the large formation located in the angle formed by the intersection of Moses Spring Trail and the High Peaks Trail. It has three seldom-done routes, although **Steve's Folly** has some very pleasurable, mixed climbing on decent rock.

13 **STEVE'S FOLLY 5.8** ★ This route starts from High Peaks Trail at the point where it first turns sharply to the right (about 50 feet past the intersection). Ascend the steep, enclosed waterchute just left of the trail to a ledge on the left. From the right side of the ledge climb a short, bolted face to another ledge with a tree. Belay from here to eliminate rope drag. Above, a wedged boulder forms a right-facing and a left-facing corner. Either climb the steep right-facing corner (the original route and the crux) past three bolts, or the left-facing corner (protected by Friends) to another ledge, joining **Heffalump** and **Flip-a-Coin Chimney**. Intricate but easy scrambling up to the right takes one to the Discovery Wall Trail.

13a **CHUNKY MONKEY 5.11**

14 **FLIP-A-COIN CHIMNEY 5.6 R** This east-facing route starts about 160 feet past the trail junction, just off Moses Spring Trail. It is the obvious and enticing right-facing flake/chimney in the middle of the wall. Make your way over boulders to the start of the flake. From the top of the flake, tunnel under the block above to meet the same ledge as the belay on the second pitch of **Steve's Folly**. The finish is the same as **Steve's Folly**. This climb is very difficult to protect.

14a **SPORT CLIMBER'S TERROR 5.10b** This is a left-leaning crack, left of **Steve's Folly**. TCUs to #3 Friend are needed for protection.

15 **HEFFALUMP 5.6** **Heffalump** starts in a chimney/flake about 30 feet to the left of **Flip-a-Coin Chimney**. Scramble down through the boulder-filled gully to the bottom of the chimney/flake. Climb the chimney to a bolt. Face climb up and right to the long narrow ledge known as Pterodactyl Terrace, and traverse right until you are directly above **Flip-a-Coin Chimney**. Tunnel under the block above to the shared belay ledge.

The Guardian

The Guardian is the pillar on the left (southeast), just before entering the man-made tunnel approximately 100 yards past The Heffalump. The area has several excellent routes, two on the pillar and two on either side. **December Shadows** and **No Holds Barred** are two of the hardest of the few crack climbs at Pinnacles. **No Holds Barred** (5.10a and 5.10c) in particular warrants attention; it engages one in classic liebacking and fingerlocks up a vertical 50-foot corner. **Daddy Long Legs** (5.11d) and **Tarantula** (5.12a/b) are two incredibly beautiful lines of vertical, sequential face climbing.

To approach **December Shadows** and **Daddy Long Legs**, follow the obvious trail a short ways to the left side of the pillar. Surmount a short but sketchy lieback (5.6) to a ledge with a belay bolt used for both routes. **No Holds Barred** and **Tarantula** are approached via the obvious, easy fifth-class gully just before the tunnel. Watch out for poison oak on the right side of the gully.

16 **DECEMBER SHADOWS 5.12a** ★ Battle up a flaring slot with a fingercrack in the back, leading to an oak up and right.

17 **DADDY LONG LEGS 5.11d R** ★★ Wild face moves up the left-slanting seam. Bring a long runner to tie-off a knob after the last bolt.

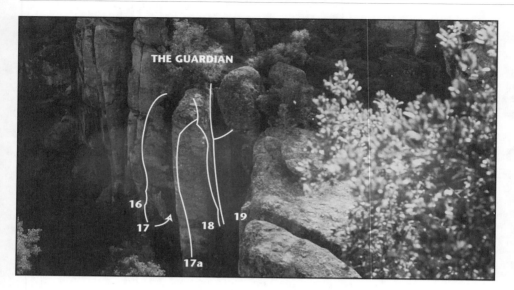

17a **TIME STANDS STILL 5.11b R ★** Follow a line of bolts up the left side of the prow facing the trail. The first clip is hard to reach, requiring a stick clip to make it safe. A final runout to the last bolt on **Tarantula** makes this great lead unnecessarily dangerous.

18 **TARANTULA 5.12a/b ★★★** A fierce sequence of moves.

19 **NO HOLDS BARRED 5.10a ★★** If one cuts out right before the final corner. Protection to four inches.

19a **NO HOLDS BARRED – DIRECT FINISH 5.10c ★★**

20 **OVERHANG CHIMNEY 5.7** Almost never done, this climb is the obvious bomb bay squeeze chimney at the southwest end of the tunnel. Possibly protected by Friends and a slung knob or two, this route mostly is a solo.

Couch Potato Wall

Couch Potato Wall is the north face above The Guardian, behind the large pine tree.

20a **THIS SPUD'S FOR YOU 5.10a** This is the left-hand route. Two bolts.

20b **NOTHIN' BEATS A SPUD 5.10b** This is the right-hand route. Three bolts.

Discovery Wall

Discovery Wall undoubtedly is the most popular climbing spot in the Monument. Graced with a huge assortment of climbs, it has a route at every level on consistently good rock. One easily could spend a whole day here.

Discovery Wall has a fair number of cracks on it. As with all cracks at Pinnacles, one needs to be an expert at placing nuts and camming units. Remember that the rock is volcanic and relatively soft. Although good nuts can be placed, they also can pull right through the rock. Well-placed camming units are the best bet. There is no such thing as too much protection here. More than one over-developed ego

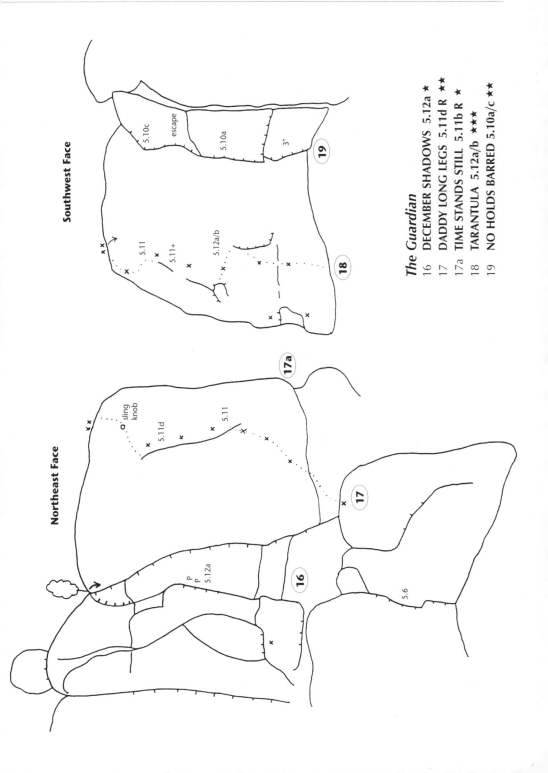

Southwest Face

5.10c

escape

5.10a

3"

19

5.11

5.11+

5.12a/b

18

Northeast Face

sling
knob

5.11d

5.11

17a

7

P
P
5.12a

16

17

5.6

The Guardian

16 DECEMBER SHADOWS 5.12a ★
17 DADDY LONG LEGS 5.11d R ★★
17a TIME STANDS STILL 5.11b R ★
18 TARANTULA 5.12a/b ★★★
19 NO HOLDS BARRED 5.10a/c ★★

has received an abrupt deflation on this cliff. If in doubt of your capabilities, use a toprope.

Running the entire length of the east face of Discovery Wall is a designated Climbers Access Trail that is distinct from the main Discovery Wall Trail. It is marked at either end by a sign with a locking carabiner on it. This trail can be caught at either end of the wall and also from below Portent. The access trail was created to prevent erosion between the two trails. Don't cut between them.

There also is a marked descent trail on top, leading northwest to The Rim Trail. This can be followed north to The High Peaks Trail and back to the north face of Discovery Wall. The trail starts at the big boulder/summit block on top of the wall.

Discovery Wall: East Face (Left)

21 **PILLBOX CRACK 5.5**   There is poison oak around the base of this climb.

22 **NAILBOX CRACK 5.8 ★**   (Recommended to bolt belay.) A fun crack requiring unexpected concentration.

23 **COFFIN NAIL 5.11a R**   A bold finish to **Nailbox Crack**. The rock gets shaky up higher. Protection to four inches.

24 **MUSTACHE 5.5 A3**   An unnerving crack shoots up the wall forming the right side of the **Nailbox** corner. Initially, this aid romp was achieved by slamming an unknown quantity of iron into the crack. A clean solo ascent has been made.

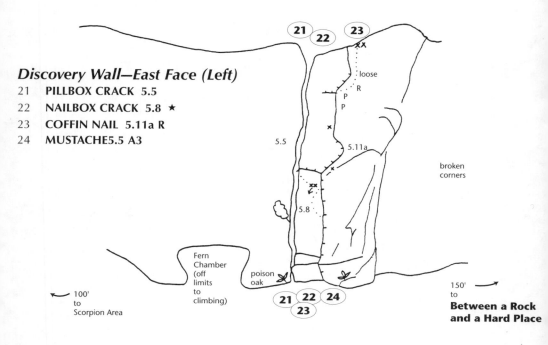

Discovery Wall—East Face (Left)
21 **PILLBOX CRACK 5.5**
22 **NAILBOX CRACK 5.8 ★**
23 **COFFIN NAIL 5.11a R**
24 **MUSTACHE5.5 A3**

photo: Kevin Kilpatrick

24a **RACING STRIPES 5.10a** ★ An interesting succession of crack, chimney and face moves. One can climb **Racing Stripes** to set up a toprope on **Melvin**. **Racing Stripes** goes up the chimney/crack coming out of the alcove just left of **Between a Rock and a Hard Place**. Several bolts, supplemented with some nuts and camming units, makes this a unique Pinnacles climb. Once out of the chimney move right past a final bolt to anchors at the top of **Melvin**.

24b **MELVIN 5.11a** ★★ Once the final headwall is reached, the climbing is dynamic and steep—well worth getting past the loose rock at the start. Climb past the initial bolt on **Racing Stripes** and exit up and right to an overhanging headwall bordering the crack system. Climb past four bolts to the shared belay.

Discovery Wall: East Face (Center)

25 **BETWEEN A ROCK AND A HARD PLACE 5.11a** ★ A quality face route with some length to it. A little loose at the start.

25a **LABOR OF LOVE 5.11** Although the rock is excellent, this climb is a little contrived. Consider stick clipping the first bolt for the lead. Probably a better toprope.

26 **PORTENT 5.6** ★★★ A wonderful face route on quality rock. Recommended as two pitches. Nuts and camming units can be used on the first pitch.

26a **FAT LIPS 5.11b** ★★ After first bolt, one- to two-inch camming units needed for horizontal crack after first bolt.

27 **THE BIG PUCKER 5.10d** ★★ An awkward crack to reachy face moves. Can easily be toproped after doing **The Wet Kiss**.

28 **THE WET KISS 5.9** ★★★ The runout to the second bolt can be protected by a sound stopper. An untimely fall getting to the second bolt can be bad news with a slack belay. **The Wet Kiss** rivals **Portent** in popularity.

29 **PLAGUE 5.10a R** ★ The bottom moves can be protected with large pieces.

30 **TRAUMA 5.9+** ★ **Trauma** has been the scene of some horrendous falls. It requires masterful protection skill to be led safely. It is a quality crack climb.

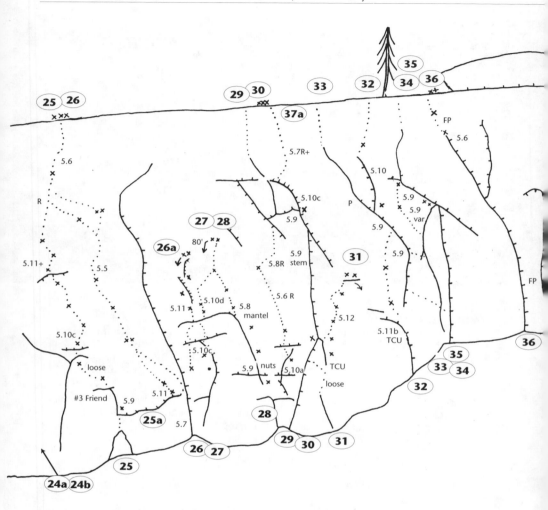

Discovery Wall
24a **RACING STRIPES 5.10a** ★
24b **MELVIN 5.11a** ★★

East Face (Center)
25 **BETWEEN A ROCK AND A HARD PLACE 5.11a** ★
25a **LABOR OF LOVE 5.11**
26 **PORTENT 5.6** ★★★
26a **FAT LIPS 5.11b** ★★
27 **THE BIG PUCKER 5.10d** ★★
28 **THE WET KISS 5.9** ★★★

29 **PLAGUE 5.10a R** ★
30 **TRAUMA 5.9+** ★
31 **ZIPPETY-DOO-DAH 5.12d** ★
32 **THE GLADIATOR 5.11b** ★
33 **DEAD BIRD CRACK 5.9**
34 **BYE-BYE FLY-BY 5.9 R**
35 **FLY-BY 5.9** ★
36 **SWALLOW CRACK 5.6** ★★★

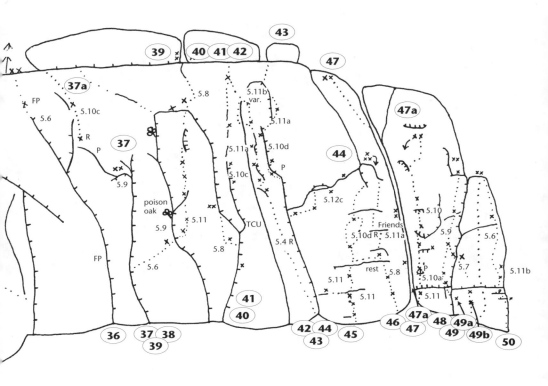

36   SWALLOW CRACK 5.6 ★★★

East Face (Right)

37   JORGIE'S CRACK 5.10a ★★
37a JORGIE'S CRACK CONTINUATION
      5.10c R ★
38   FEBRUARY FOOLS 5.9
39   PWEETER 5.11a ★★
40   ORDEAL 5.8 ★★★
41   BUFFALO SOLDIER 5.11a ★★★
42   BROKEN ARROW 5.10d ★
42a BROKEN ARROW direct var. 5.11b
43   HERE COMES THE JUDGE 5.11a R ★
44   TRIAL 5.12b/c ★★

45   THE VERDICT 5.11b ★★
46   PISTOL WHIPPED 5.10d R ★
47   THE CLEFT 5.6 ★
47a LITHIUM 5.11a/b

North Face

48   STUPENDOUS MAN 5.10a ★★
49   ENTRANCE 5.7 ★
49a POWER POINT 5.11d/12a
49b MAMMARY JUNK 5.10d TR
50   MAMMARY PUMP 5.11b ★★

30a **TRAUMATIZE — DIRECT FINISH 5.10c** ★ Climb the initial corner of **Trauma**. As the corner arches left continue straight out the right side of the roof past a bolt. Once the roof is surmounted either step left to re-join **Trauma** or move up and right and climb (5.7) unprotected to the top. A #3.5 Friend and a TCU can be used just over the roof.

31 **ZIPPETY-DOO-DAH 5.12d** ★ A little loose to get to the beginning of the "real" climbing. A severely overhanging route requiring great stamina. Its name was inspired by a long "zipper" fall on **Trauma**, which occurred while the first ascent was in progress and inspired all the protection cautions.

32 **THE GLADIATOR 5.11b** ★ An improbable-looking route demanding boldness. The start can be adequately protected by camming units and the rock is a lot better than it looks. Beware of some loose flakes getting past the second bolt. Wide protection is needed in the short section shared with **Dead Bird Crack**.

33 **DEAD BIRD CRACK 5.9** An awkward crack that takes one into guano realms. Protection to 3½ inches.

34 **BYE-BYE FLY-BY 5.9 R**

35 **FLY-BY 5.9** ★ Another Pinnacles crack climb requiring a very skilled leader to ensure safety.

36 **SWALLOW CRACK 5.6** ★★★ A fine and moderate crack climb.

Discovery Wall—East Face (Right)

37 **JORGIE'S CRACK 5.10a** ★★

37a **JORGIE'S CRACK CONTINUATION 5.10c R** ★

38 **FEBRUARY FOOLS 5.9** The legendary poison oak bush that inspired the climb's name occupies this crack up high.

39 **PWEETER 5.11a** ★★ Once the arête is mounted, the rock becomes amazingly good. The traverse from **Jorgie's Crack** can be protected with camming units.

40 **ORDEAL 5.8** ★★★ A Pinnacles classic!

The author on **Trial** *5.12*

41　**BUFFALO SOLDIER 5.11a ★★★**　This spectacular line escaped notice until just recently. Once above the **Ordeal** roof, the climb will astound you with its complexity of moves and rock quality.

42　**BROKEN ARROW 5.10d ★**

42a　**BROKEN ARROW — DIRECT VARIATION 5.11b**　Straight up between the last two bolts. This variation is a little contrived, as the arête to the left is just an arm's span away.

43　**HERE COMES THE JUDGE 5.11a R ★**　A very bold lead on slightly loose rock. An assortment of camming units can supplement the sparse bolts.

44　**TRIAL 5.12b/c ★★**　This once-dreaded aid climb first was envisioned as a free climb by Tom Davis. Once you leave the initial corner, the rock improves greatly.

45　**THE VERDICT 5.11b ★★**

45a　**THE VERDICT – DIRECT START 5.11c ★★**　A way to extend the sprint.

46　**PISTOL WHIPPED 5.10d R ★**

47　**THE CLEFT 5.6 ★**　A surprisingly nice climb for a chimney.

47a　**LITHIUM 5.11a/b**　Belay anchor is somewhat hidden, 40 feet above last bolt and slightly to the right under the overhang. This route is harder for shorter people.

Discovery Wall—North Face

48　**STUPENDOUS MAN 5.10a ★★**　An airy route following the arête over **Entrance.** Starts with a wild mantel. The moves to the first bolt over the roof can be protected with camming units.

49　**ENTRANCE 5.7 ★**　Wide crack climbing past two bolts.

49a　**POWER POINT 5.11d/12a**　Joins **Stupendous Man** at the fourth bolt.

49b　**MAMMARY JUNK 5.10d TR**　Toprope the face right of **Power Point.**

50　**MAMMARY PUMP 5.11b ★★**　This reachy climb moves out over successive tiers of roofs and has a loose start.

51　**LOST HORIZONS 5.8 ★**　This seldom-done climb actually is a fine route. Loose start.

52　**COSMOS 5.11b ★★**　A spectacular route that puts the leader in very photogenic positions. The first bolt quickly becomes worthless and extreme caution is needed in getting to the second bolt (even though it's fairly easy). The clip to the second bolt can be backed up by TCUs in the corner. Loose start.

53　**FORTY DAYS OF RAIN 5.12c ★★★**　A true roof crack, this route goes out a succession of ceilings that combine to make a ten-foot roof problem. Moves are very sequential and strenuous. A #3.5 Friend is needed in the roof before the "lip clip."

54　**THE GUTTER 5.10b**　This route is dirty, awkward and hard to protect up higher.

55　**THE ROOF 5.10a**　The fixed pins and bolts on this old climb should be used with caution, especially if used as toprope anchors. Back them up! Bring an assortment of TCUs and Friends.

56　**THE SLOT 5.9 ★**　This actually is a fine handcrack.

57　**WELCOME TO THE MACHINE 5.7**　A flaring chimney and a little hard to protect.

57a　**SPACEMAN SPIFF 5.9**　This climb ascends the leftmost buttress of the series of buttresses below Discovery Wall. It is about 100 yards left of The Heffalump. The base of the climb is about 20 feet above a large gray pine. Climb 60 feet up the left side of the buttress past six bolts. The start is bouldery, but well-protected by two closely spaced bolts. Six pre-existing bolts provide the belay someways back from the top. To minimize impact, the climb should be approached by rappelling from the belay.

57b　**DISMEMBERMENT GORGE 5.4 X**　Forty feet right of **Spaceman Spiff** is a very deep chimney. Climb the 20-foot waterchute, five feet left of the chimney and follow the chimney to the top. This climb is possibly protectable by tying off a bush and using protection in the back of the chimney.

Discovery Wall–North Face

47a LITHIUM 5.11a/b
48 STUPENDOUS MAN 5.10a ★★
49 ENTRANCE 5.7 ★
49a POWER POINT 5.11d/5.12a
49b MAMMARY JUNK 5.11
50 MAMMARY PUMP 5.11b ★★
51 LOST HORIZONS 5.8 ★

52 COSMOS 5.11b ★★
53 FORTY DAYS OF RAIN 5.12c ★★★
54 THE GUTTER 5.10b
55 THE ROOF 5.10a
56 THE SLOT 5.9 ★
57 WELCOME TO THE MACHINE 5.7

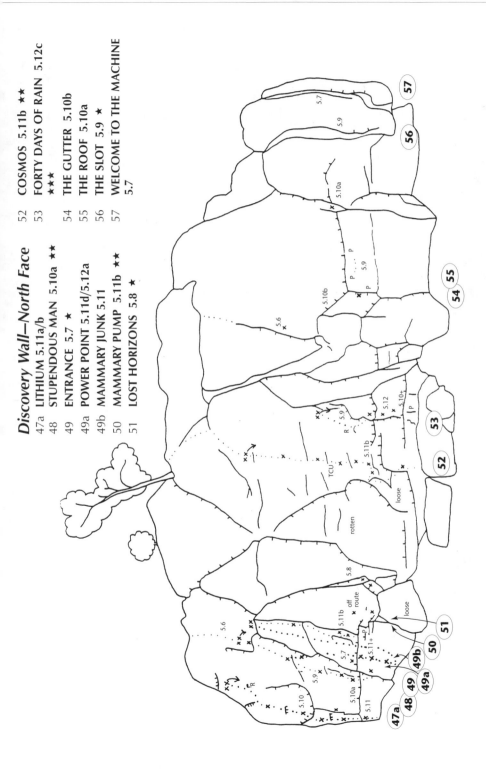

Moses Spring Wall

Moses Spring Wall actually is a continuation of Discovery Wall. It starts at the Fern Chamber and goes until it meets The Monolith. Although there are some high quality routes on this wall, most of them are directly over the trail. Check with the Park Service for the current protocol regarding climbing over the trail. Whatever the rules might be, extreme care must be taken to not dislodge any loose rock onto hikers, particularly on the **Surf's Up**, **Zig-zags**, **Anarchy**, **Scorpion**, **Crash Buds**, **Agrarian** and **Happy Birthday George**.

The quickest descent from the wall can be made by the switchback scramble just north of Tiburcio's X; it takes one directly down to the west face of The Monolith. A detailed description also is given in the approaches to The Back Door. Skirt north along the base of the west face of The Monolith to get to the Moses Spring Trail.

Moses Spring Wall—Left

58 **HAPPY BIRTHDAY GEORGE 5.9 X**   This loose climb is over the trail and has heinous runouts.

59 **AGRARIAN 5.8 R+**   This climb is really loose (widowmaker material); the first pitch is hard to protect past the fixed pin. There is 5.10a direct start that makes for a bold boulder problem. This line goes directly over the trail.

60 **EXILES 5.10a R ★**   This fairly sporty route is an exercise in nerve maintenance on mostly decent rock.

61 **HEAT SEEKING MOISTURE MISSILE 5.10d ★★★**   This is the best route on the wall. Wild sequences over three increasingly difficult bulges.

62 **CRASH BUDS 5.10a ★**   Awkward moves up the groove over the trail.

Moses Spring Wall—Left

58 HAPPY BIRTHDAY GEORGE 5.9 X
59 AGRARIAN 5.8 R+
60 EXILES 5.10a ★
61 HEAT SEEKING MOISTURE MISSILE 5.10d ★★★
62 CRASH BUDS 5.10a ★
63 BUZZARD BAIT 5.9 R+ ★

The Camel and Toprope Wall

115 TOPROPE WALL 5.4 to 5.9 TR
116 THE CAMEL – ALI BABA 5.10b ★★

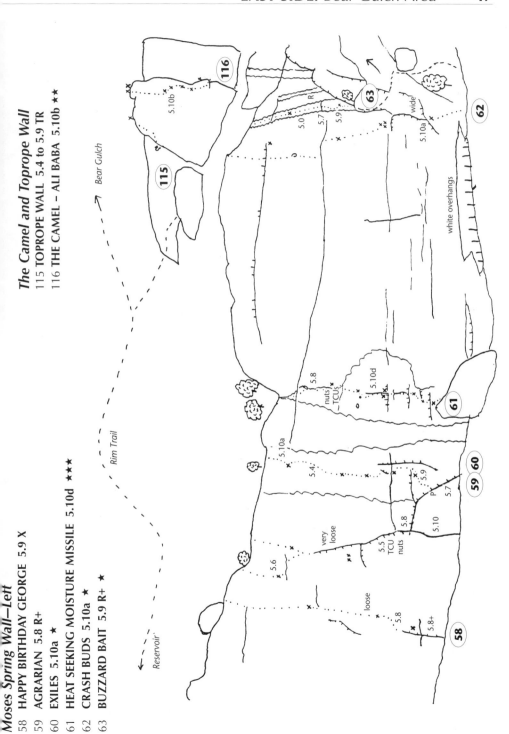

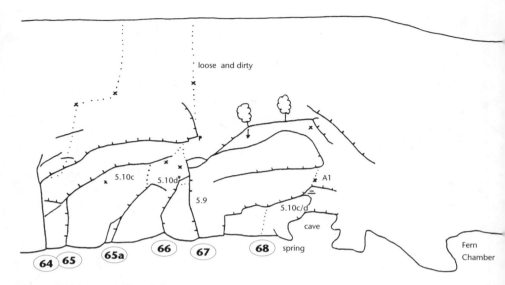

Moses Spring Wall—Right
64 **SCORPION 5.8**
65 **AN-ARCHY 5.10c** ★
65a **ZIG-ZAG MAN 5.10a**
66 **ZIG-ZAG LEFT 5.10d/5.11a** ★★
67 **ZIG-ZAG 5.9** ★
68 **Surf's Up 5.10 A2**

63 **BUZZARD BAIT 5.9 R+** ★   Approached by climbing the first pitch of **Crash Buds** or third class scrambling. This route has good rock but long runouts.

63a **VOYEUR 5.9** ★   Fifty feet right of **Buzzard Bait**, climb a right-facing corner to a slab and headwall past three bolts and a fixed piton. Medium-size Friends can supplement the fixed protection.

Moses Spring Wall—Right

64 **SCORPION 5.8**   Over the trail. Loose and mossy up top.

65 **AN-ARCHY 5.10c** ★   This corner has deceptively hard undercling/lieback moves. It can be led to the bolt just above the **Zig-Zags** by using that bolt and the top bolt on the **Zig-Zags** to lower off. It does go all the way to the top but the rock deteriorates and the route becomes a vertical lawn. Over the trail.

65a **ZIG-ZAG MAN 5.10a**

66 **ZIG-ZAG LEFT 5.10d/5.11a** ★★   This route is difficult to protect and usually is toproped. Over the trail.

67 **ZIG-ZAG 5.9** ★   Over the trail.

68 **SURF'S UP 5.10 A2**   Some half-hearted attempts at freeing this route have been made. It is almost never done as an aid climb because, unfortunately, it overhangs the trail.

Also in the area:

The next two routes on the east wall of Bear Gulch can easily be seen from the obvious canyon viewpoint approximately 50 yards past Moses Spring and just before the huge, white overhangs in the middle of the Moses Spring Wall. Honeycomb is the prominent straight-in handcrack slightly back down the canyon on the opposite side. **Torque Twister** is in the next recess to the left as the right of two parallel cracks.

69 **TORQUE TWISTER 5.10a** One can negotiate a direct approach to the climb starting at the trail junction of the **Moses Spring Trail** and the **Caves Trail**. Beware of poison oak. Pro to six inches.

70 **HONEYCOMB 5.9** This climb is approached by walking all the way to the **Monolith**, cutting back along the rim to the top of **Honeycomb** and rappelling to the base of the crack. You also can get to **Honeycomb** by scrambling to the base of **Torque Twister** and skirting around the pillar between the two climbs until another deep gully/chimney is reached. Climb this (5.4) and traverse back left to the climb. One bolt on top.

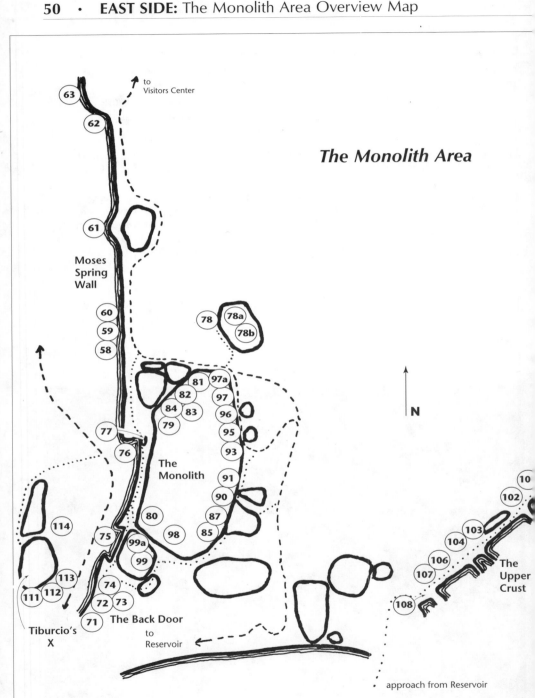

The Monolith Area

THE MONOLITH AREA

The Back Door

The Back Door has a series of great routes. The rock is sound and the climbing is varied enough to provide a challenge for everyone. This area is the last stretch of the long cliff band that includes Discovery Wall and Moses Spring Wall. It starts at the point where the Monolith almost meets the cliff.

There are four approaches to The Back Door. The first: skirt along the base of the east face of The Monolith, past **Subterranean Tango**, and around and down to the shady "pit" directly below **Bridwell Bolts**, The Black Dagger and Pearl Sheath. Third class up boulders to the left of The Black Dagger to reach The Back Door. Second: at the point where the Moses Spring Trail meets The Monolith North Face, cut right onto a trail that runs along the entire length of The Back Door (between it and The Monolith). This also is the approach to all west-face Monolith routes. Third: one can switch back down from the Rim Trail just north of Tiburcio's X at a point where the view of The Monolith is best. The fourth approach: rappel from the anchors on **Auto Cream**. There is a thriving poison oak grove between **Vigilante** and **Fringe Dweller.**

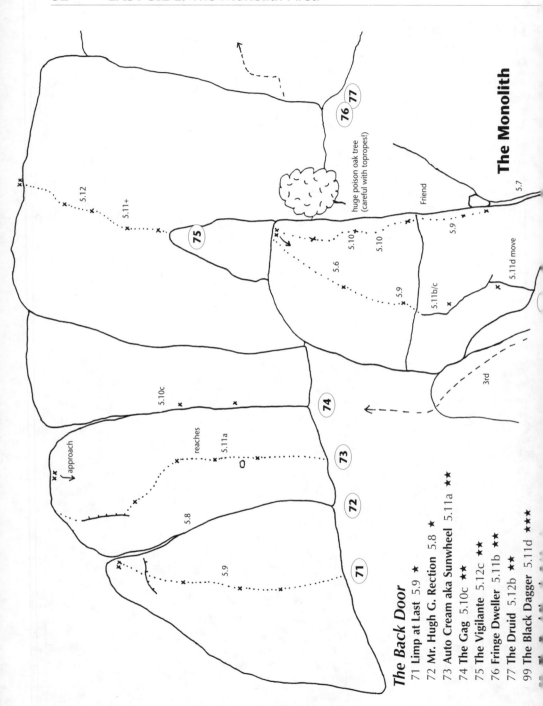

The Monolith

huge poison oak tree
(careful with topropes!)

Friend

5.12

5.11+

5.10c

reaches

5.11a

approach

5.8

5.9

5.10

5.10

5.6

5.9

5.11b/c

5.9

5.7

5.11d move

3rd

The Back Door

71 **Limp at Last** 5.9 ★
72 **Mr. Hugh G. Rection** 5.8 ★
73 **Auto Cream aka Sunwheel** 5.11a ★ ★
74 **The Gag** 5.10c ★ ★
75 **The Vigilante** 5.12c ★ ★
76 **Fringe Dweller** 5.11b ★ ★
77 **The Druid** 5.12b ★ ★
99 **The Black Dagger** 5.11d ★ ★ ★

The Back Door

71 **LIMP AT LAST 5.9** ★   A short, but fun face route.

72 **MR. HUGH G. RECTION 5.8** ★   An enjoyable crack.

73 **AUTO CREAM aka Sunwheel 5.11a** ★★   As good as it looks!

74 **THE GAG 5.10c** ★★ Deceptively difficult.

75 **THE VIGILANTE 5.12c** ★★   5.11 sequences to a hard crux move.

76 **FRINGE DWELLER 5.11b** ★★   A deceptively hard route on unbelievably good rock. This route and **The Druid** are in the narrow corridor directly across from **Ranger Bolts** and the west face of The Monolith.

77 **THE DRUID 5.12b** ★★   Very overhanging with a blind move around the arête.

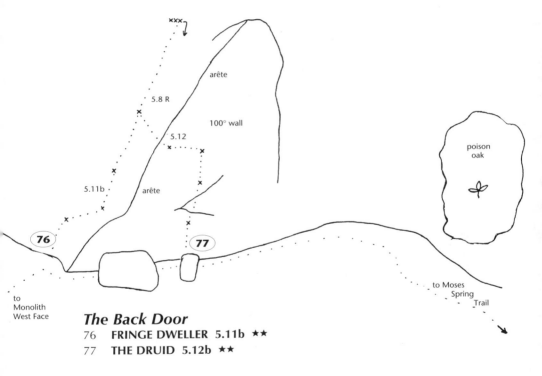

The Back Door
76 **FRINGE DWELLER 5.11b** ★★
77 **THE DRUID 5.12b** ★★

Men at Work Boulder

78 **MEN AT WORK 5.11a/b** ★   This rock is located on the opposite side of the trail from the northeast corner of The Monolith. **Men at Work** follows a left-facing, left-slanting corner past four bolts on the west face of a large boulder. Be aware of the poison oak around the base of the route.

78a **THE JERK 5.11a R** ★   From the first bolt on **Men at Work**, continue past two more bolts, then run it out to the top.

78b **WET WILLIE 5.10a** ★★   Climb past four bolts 15 feet right of **The Jerk**. Watch for poison oak.

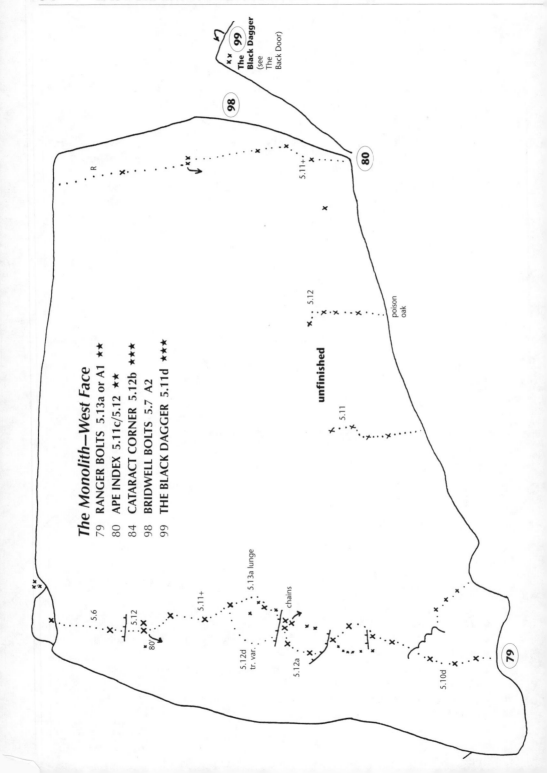

The Monolith—West Face

79 RANGER BOLTS 5.13a or A1 ★★
80 APE INDEX 5.11c/5.12 ★★
84 CATARACT CORNER 5.12b ★★★
98 BRIDWELL BOLTS 5.7 A2
99 THE BLACK DAGGER 5.11d ★★★

The Monolith

The **Monolith** has some of the best rock in the monument, making it the most popular single formation. It also has the highest concentration of routes of any formation on the east side of the park, ranging from 5.6 to 5.13a—and almost every route on it is recommended. People quite often climb a moderate route on the **Monolith** and toprope the harder routes on the east face, making **Lunch Rock** (the boulder leaning against the east face) the center of a lot of fun and socializing.

The Monolith originally was summited on February 17, 1935, by Dave and Ralph Brower, Bill Van Vorrhis and George Rockwood. The first ascensionists climbed the oak tree leaning over the right side of the east face and leaped across the abyss to join the **Regular Route** at its first belay. Climbing the tree is 5.7.

The Monolith—West Face

79   **RANGER BOLTS 5.13a or A1** ★★   The route initially was led free to the hanging belay halfway up (5.12a). The entire route eventually was toproped and then led to the top of the **Monolith** as one continuous pitch (5.13a). This route stands as a monument to the many climbers who have attempted to free it. The route originally traversed in from boulders on the right. There is now a direct start (5.10d), straightening the climb.

80   **APE INDEX 5.11c/5.12** ★★   A wicked right-leaning arête climb; this route is distinctly a reach problem. If you're under 5'8", the start is 5.12.

The Monolith—North Face

81   **LOWER NORTH FACE 5.11b or 5.6 A1** ★   This route originally was a bolt ladder.

82   **ROCKET IN MY POCKET 5.10d** ★★★   A thoroughly enjoyable climb.

83   **FUTURE SHOCK 5.12b** ★★★   The crux of this climb is very intricate, demanding focus and balance.

84   **CATARACT CORNER 5.12b** ★★★   A classic arête climb.

The Monolith—East Face

85   **FOREPLAY 5.11b** ★★★   Can you get a no-hands rest in the big scoop? This spectacular climb originally was led without the first bolt.

86   **SEVERAL SMALL SPECIES 5.11b TR** ★

87   **POST ORGASMIC DEPRESSION (P.O.D.) 5.11a** ★★★   This route is a Pinnacles classic!

88   **INDIRECT TRAVERSE 5.8+ R** ★★   This very sporty, traversing route makes a bold lead for both ends of the rope.

89   **HAWAIIAN NOISES 5.10d** ★★   Although the route initially was led directly to the second bolt on **Indirect Traverse**, it can be led using the first bolt on **Indirect Traverse**.

90   **SUBTERRANEAN TANGO 5.11a** ★★

91   **THE MONOLITH EAST FACE – DIRECT ROUTE 5.6 R+** ★★   Take care getting to the second bolt; it's a long ways up. Originally, this route was led boldly, by using the first bolt and somehow protecting the rest of the pitch with pitons.

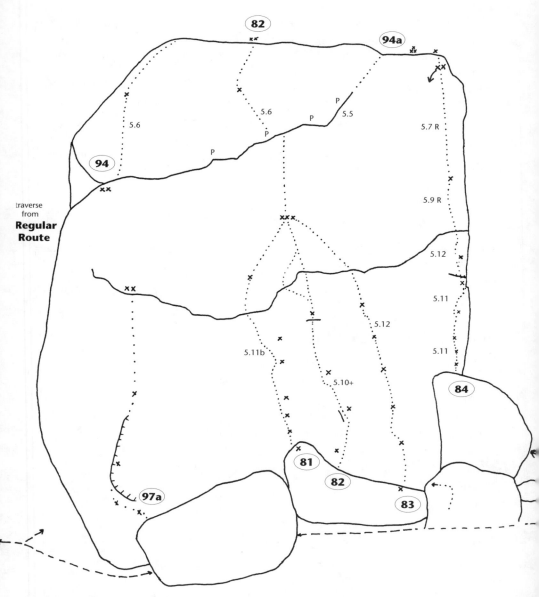

81 **LOWER NORTH FACE 5.11b or 5.6 A1** ★

82 **ROCKET IN MY POCKET 5.10d** ★★★

83 **FUTURE SHOCK 5.12b** ★★★

81 **LOWER NORTH FACE 5.11b or 5.6 A1** ★

84 **CATARACT CORNER 5.12b** ★★★

The Monolith—East Face

94 **NORTHEAST CORNER 5.7** ★

94a **PITON TRAVERSE 5.5** ★

97a **LARD BUTT 5.13c**

91a **WAY BELOW THE DIRECT 5.11/5.12 R+**   This dangerous route starts at **Subterranean Tango** and traverses under the block at the base of **The Direct** and continues out the right side, then up, to a two-bolt belay just over the bulge. One has to consciously avoid using the block while negotiating pointless runouts that put one in ground-fall potential at about every clip. The route has been led past the last three bolts. Although still run-out, it makes for a much better climb.

91b **BABY BLUES aka Post-Partum Depression 5.11c TR ★**   Climb just left of **Richnak's Revenge** using the anchors of **Way Below The Direct**.

92 **RICHNAK'S REVENGE 5.11a ★★**

92a **LODESTONE VARIATION 5.11 TR**

93 **THE MONOLITH EAST FACE – REGULAR ROUTE 5.8 ★★★**   This route can be done in one pitch, but the rope drag makes it 5.12. This spirited climb makes for a marvelous introduction to Pinnacles climbing. Another Pinnacles classic.

93a **HARD VARIATION 5.10c R**

93b **GOD IS GRAVITY 5.10d TR ★**   Toprope the face ten feet left of **Feed The Beast**.

94 **NORTHEAST CORNER 5.7 ★**   From the first belay on the **Regular Route,** continue right along the ledge to the arête. Ascend just right of it.

94a **PITON TRAVERSE 5.5 ★**   Continue along the crack past the northeast corner, diagonalling up and right on the upper north face.

95 **FEED THE BEAST 5.11c ★★★**   This fine route is an overhanging knob sprint that ensures a good pump. If toproping this route or **Hot Lava Lucy,** be aware that the overhanging nature of these routes makes for great swings.

96 **CANTALOUPE DEATH 5.10c ★**   This route starts by stepping off the boulder over the trail.

96a **CANTALOUPE DEATH – DIRECT START 5.12a**

97 **HOT LAVA LUCY 5.13a ★★**   This was the Pinnacles first 5.13. The first two bolts usually are pre-set from the boulder at the base and the rope is left clipped in the first bolt, so the initial moves actually are toproped. A spotter is advised.

97a **LARD BUTT 5.13c**

The Monolith—South Face

98 **BRIDWELL BOLTS 5.7 A2**   This quarter-inch bolt ladder is on loose rock. Hooks are needed to bypass hangerless or non-existent bolts, and on the last move. The belay is either via the bolts above **Post Orgasmic Depression** or by the summit block rappel station. Both are to the side and create a potentially hazardous pendulum for the second after unclipping the last bolt. Starting at the southwest corner, follow a wandering line of bolts into an obvious corner system to the top. Originally, a few pins were used intermittently.

99 **THE BLACK DAGGER 5.11d ★★★**   This excellent route goes up a left-arching this crack to face above. Climb past four bolts to a two-bolt belay. The climb is located on the huge boulder leaning against the south face of The Monolith, directly below **Bridwell Bolts**. It starts out of the "pit" mentioned in the first approach to The Back Door. (See topo for the Back Door area.) On the first ascent, the small oak was not used to place or clip the first bolt.

99a **THE PEARL SHEATH 5.10c ★★**   This wild climb offers some exposed cragging. 1.5 to 2.5 Friends can be placed just before the third bolt. (See topo for The Back Door area.)

The Monolith—East Face

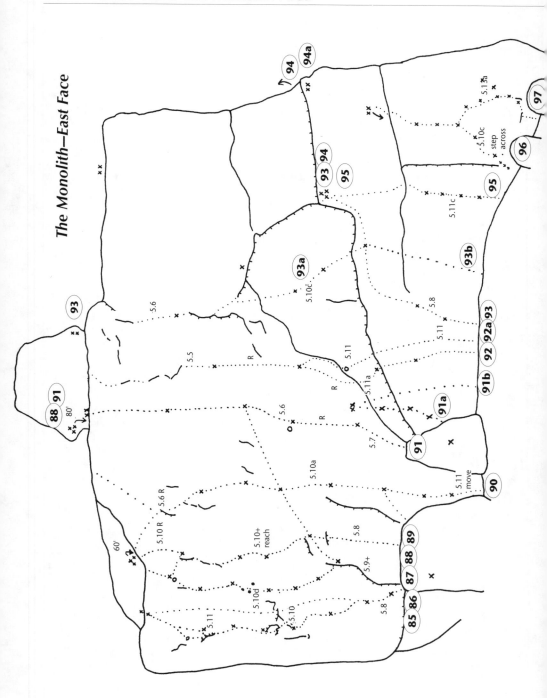

The Monolith—East Face

85 FOREPLAY 5.11b ★★★

86 SEVERAL SMALL SPECIES 5.11b TR ★

87 POST ORGASMIC DEPRESSION 5.11a ★★★

88 INDIRECT TRAVERSE 5.8+ R ★★

89 HAWAIIAN NOISES 5.10d ★★

90 SUBTERRANEAN TANGO 5.11a ★★

91 THE MONOLITH EAST FACE – DIRECT ROUTE 5.6 R+ ★★

91a WAY BELOW THE DIRECT 5.11/5.12 R+

91b BABY BLUES aka Post-Partum Depression 5.11c TR ★

92 RICHNAK'S REVENGE 5.11a ★★

92a LODESTONE VARIATION 5.11 TR

93 REGULAR ROUTE 5.8 ★★★

93a HARD VARIATION 5.10c R

93b GOD IS GRAVITY 5.10d TR ★

94 NORTHEAST CORNER 5.7 ★

94a PITON TRAVERSE 5.5 ★

95 FEED THE BEAST 5.11c ★★★

96 CANTALOUPE DEATH 5.10c ★

96a CANTALOUPE DEATH – DIRECT START 5.12a

97 HOT LAVA LUCY 5.13a ★★

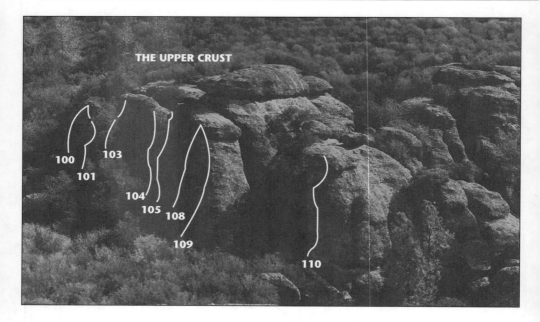

The Upper Crust

The Upper Crust is a superb area if you are looking for moderate climbing on great rock in the shade.

To get to The Upper Crust, follow a designated trail from the reservoir back northeast to the formation. The original approach, which started near The Monolith, is closed due to intense erosion caused by climbers.

100   **CASTLES MADE OF SAND 5.10b** ★

101   **SOUND CHASER 5.10a** ★★

102   **SOUND CHASER INDIRECT 5.9**   This variation bypasses the initial crux by a traverse in from the right.

103   **RELAYER 5.10c** ★★★   It's steeper than it looks.

104   **ORGANGRINDER 5.8+** ★

105   **ME AND MY MONKEY 5.9+** ★

106   **BABOON CRACK 5.10a R** ★   After climbing to the second bolt on **Me and My Monkey**, downclimb and start **Baboon Crack** to the right. Diagonal past the second pre-clipped bolt. An awkward move can be protected with Friends. Run it out to the last bolt on **Me and My Monkey**.

107   **WHEN IN DOUBT RUN IT OUT 5.7 X**   A rumored bolt and lost arrow placement have been reported as protection on this route. The author, after intense scrutiny, has located neither. This route is a solo or a toprope.

108   **JAPANESE WATER TORTURE 5.7 R** ★

109   **NODAL LINE 5.6 R** ★

110   **HARD AS A ROCK 5.12b** ★★   It's a lot steeper than it looks.

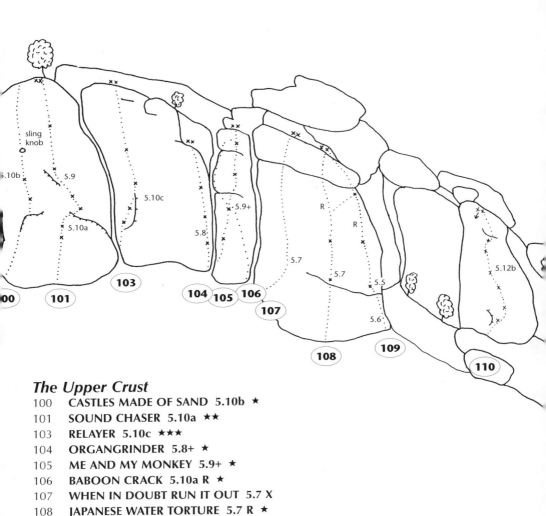

The Upper Crust

Tiburcio's X

Tiburcio's X is the 150-foot rock directly above The Back Door. It is distinguished by an X formed by two cracks that slice the side facing the reservoir. The rock is a little crumbly, and the belayer should sit far enough back to avoid any chance of getting pelted. One can either rappel the southeast face (two ropes) or downclimb/rappel the **Backside** route.

111   **CROSS YOUR HEART 5.10a/b**   Fairly sporty at the top. A little loose.

112   **COYOTE UGLY aka Bienvenidos a Pinnacles 5.9** ★   This full-pitch route has some very exciting moves on the way to the top of Tiburcio's X. Number 2 to #3 Friends needed in crack.

112a   **COYOTE UGLY – DIRECT FINISH 5.10c TR**   It had to be done, but is very loose.

113   **SIDESADDLE 5.7** ★   This short, alternate start has fun moves on decent rock. You can finish at the belay of **Cross Your Heart** or continue up **Coyote Ugly**.

114   **BACKSIDE 4th class** ★   This route ascends the northwest shoulder and is approached by hiking up and around via the Rim Trail. One bolt.

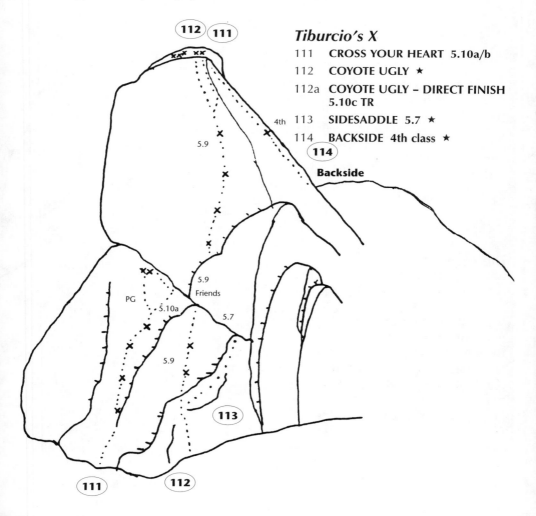

Tiburcio's X

111   **CROSS YOUR HEART 5.10a/b**

112   **COYOTE UGLY** ★

112a   **COYOTE UGLY – DIRECT FINISH 5.10c TR**

113   **SIDESADDLE 5.7** ★

114   **BACKSIDE 4th class** ★

Backside

The Camel and Toprope Wall

These routes show on the topo on page 47. A "camel" can be discerned by scrutinizing the rock from the area just after the tunnel on the Moses Spring Trail (try squinting).

115 **TOPROPE WALL 5.4-5.9 TR** There's a series of bolts on top, enabling one to set up topropes on a number of routes on the northwest face. There is a nice range of routes: 5.4 up the obvious center chute, 5.8 up the face ten feet left (past the hole) and 5.9 up the left side. Of course, there are numerous variations in between.

116 **THE CAMEL – ALI BABA 5.10b** ★★ **Ali Baba** ascends past five bolts up the steep north face of The Camel. It is approached by dropping off the Toprope Wall's backside (just as you get to it) and walking down the gully between the two formations. **Ali Baba** starts on the right side of the northeast face of The Camel. Step from the gully past a bolt to attain the main face. A little crumbly at the start. Two bolts on top. The Camel was originally summited by the easy descent route.

Ruselle Rubine on **Ali Baba,** *The Camel*

photo: Tim Corcoran

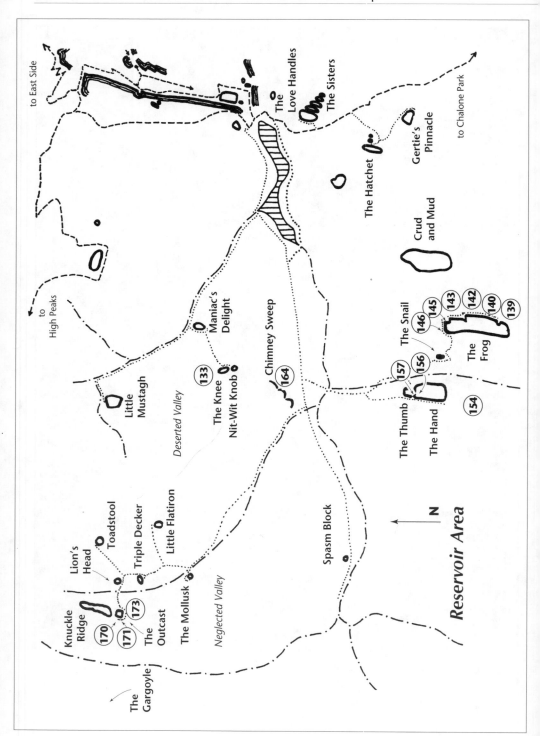

to East Side

to High Peaks

to Chalone Park

The Love Handles

The Sisters

Gertie's Pinnacle

The Hatchet

Crud and Mud

Maniac's Delight

Chimney Sweep

(164)

(133)

The Knee
Nit-Wit Knob

Little Mustagh

Deserted Valley

The Snail

(146)
(145)
(143)
(142)
(140)
(139)

The Frog

(157)
(156)

(154)

The Thumb
The Hand

Toadstool

Triple Decker

Little Flatiron

Lion's Head

Knuckle Ridge

(170)
(171)
(173)

The Outcast

The Mollusk

Neglected Valley

Spasm Block

The Gargoyle

N

Reservoir Area

THE RESERVOIR AREA

As you hike up to the upper end of Bear Gulch you eventually will come to a body of water. Bear Creek Reservoir is held by a man-made dam just southwest of the caves. It presents a beautiful contrast to the arid landscape characteristic of the rest of the monument. The reservoir marks the beginning of a large, spread-out area with a number of individual crags. The rock is more varied and less is known about the quality and difficulty of a number of the routes here. This area also marks the beginning of backcountry climbing at Pinnacles. If you are looking for quiet and a respite from the crowds, then consider venturing out past the reservoir.

117   **THE LOVE HANDLES 5.10d** ★   The Love Handles is the voluptuous, multi-tiered formation located 100 yards slightly northeast of the reservoir and just north of The Sisters. To get to the rock, cross the dam and head up and left just as the trail curves back right/south around the reservoir, following a natural break in the chaparral. Follow an indistinct trail to the base of the rock. A belay bolt has been placed on the slab at the base. The route ascends the north face past six bolts, starting at a short right-curving crack with the first bolt at its base. From the last bolt, head left up the shoulder. The crack can be protected with medium-sized Friends. There are two belay bolts on top. Walk off the back side. This climb is a wild succession of very steep bulges.

The Sisters

The Sisters are the obvious leaning slabs just east of the reservoir. The First Sister is the closest to the reservoir, with the others in a line behind it.

The First Sister has one of the most popular faces in the Monument. A wonderful 5.4 route goes up the center, providing a perfect introduction for beginning climbers.

To get to the First Sister, follow an obvious, worn trail up and left just as the North Chalone Peak Trail rises above the reservoir. The easiest way to get to the Third, Fourth and Fifth Sisters is to skirt up and left along the base of the First Sister, continuing up the hillside until it is easy to walk over to the Fifth Sister. From there, one easily can drop down to Three and Four. Or, circumvent the Sisters by going right from the base of the First Sister. This is also the approach to the Second Sister and Silhouette Arête.

118   **FIRST SISTER – LEFT ROUTE** 5.5 ★★   A thoroughly enjoyable and lengthy route.

119   **FIRST SISTER – CENTER ROUTE 5.4** ★★★   This popular line can be started from the left route with a traverse right into the high chute. Or, you can climb directly to the chute from the block at the base (no protection). A double-rope rappel is needed for the front face.

120   **FIRST SISTER – BACK SIDE 5.7**   This route is attained by climbing the Second Sister, leaning over to the First and manteling on to the backside ledge. There is one bolt protecting the mantel.

121   **SECOND SISTER 4th class**   The summit of the Second Sister can be reached by chimneying between it and the First or by fourth-class scrambling further to the right on the south face.

First Sister, West Face

118 **FIRST SISTER –
LEFT ROUTE** 5.5 ★★

119 **FIRST SISTER –
CENTER ROUTE** 5.4 ★★★

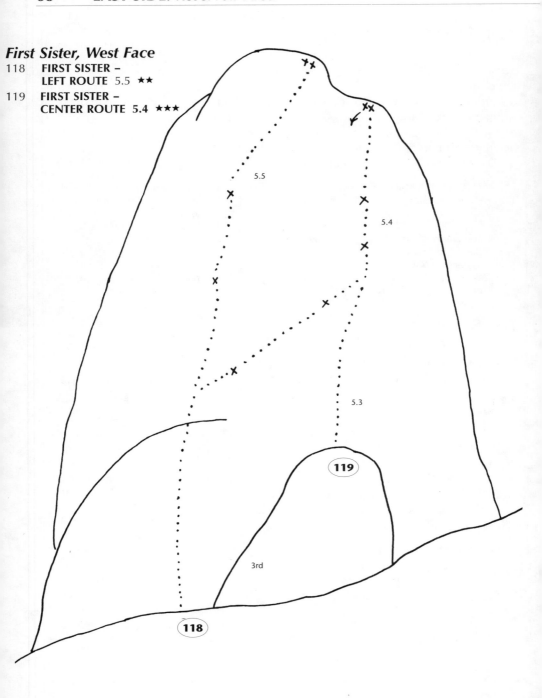

The Sisters seen from the Back Door

122   **THIRD SISTER 5.10a** ★   This short route climbs into the notch of the Third Sister, starting in the gully between it and the Fourth Sister. Climb past two bolts into the notch, until a third bolt is reached. Climb up and left to a two-bolt belay.

123   **THIRD SISTER – LITTLE SISTER SPIRE 5.6 R**   This little off-shoot sticks up from the south side of the Third Sister. Continue down the gully between the Third and Fourth Sister to another notch on the right separating the main Sister from Little Sister Spire. Climb out of the notch past one bolt at the bottom and run it out to the top. The belay and rappel anchor is an ancient bolt and a slung block.

124   **FOURTH SISTER – WEST FACE 5.5 X**   Good rock, but no bolts. Ascend the face directly opposite the regular route on the Third Sister. Can be toproped from two bolts on top.

125   **FOURTH SISTER – NORTH SHOULDER 5.1 X**   There is one hangerless bolt at the bottom of this route. It is basically a solo. This route makes its way up the shoulder to the left of the 5.5 route.

126   **FOURTH SISTER – SILHOUETTE ARETE 5.8 R**   Follow a "prominent" ramp on the south face, up and right, past a fixed pin to a small alcove. A long reach to a knob on the left and a 5.8 mantel (protected by friends in a crack at your feet) leads to a two-bolt belay about ten feet higher. On the next pitch, climb 30 feet to a large knob that has a bolt. Work up and left to the southwest arête and follow it to the top. A knob can be slung on the final runout.

126a   **GHOST OF TIBURCIO'S 5.6**   Climb past four bolts, from the notch between the Third and Fourth Sister, directly to the top. Two bolts on top.

126b   **GOING THE WONG WAY 5.7**   Just right of **Silhouette** area on Fourth Sister, scramble up a narrow gully to a small scrub oak. Three bolts lead up a short face to third class climbing. Ascend a pedestal to a short horizontal crack leading to easy face and the summit.

127 **FIFTH SISTER 5.6 X** One bolt on top. This climb essentially is a dangerous boulder problem. From the northeast shoulder, climb a pedestal and make a move onto the summit block.

128 **THE HATCHET 5.10a or A2 ★** **The Hatchet** is the striking blade of rock south of the reservoir, opposite the **Sisters**. Ascend the right side of the east face past a line of ancient bolts, climbing past the "nail puller" slot to attain the summit ridge. Work up along the exposed ridge to a bolt belay. Be careful of loose rock at the start.

The Hatchet has been the stage for a number of historic and entertaining efforts to reach its taunting summit. In 1946, Jim Wilson reached the summit first in one of the most creative approaches to climbing ever attempted. He flew a kite over the top, landed it on the other side and pulled a line over to prusik. Later that same year, Anton Nelson, Robin Hansen and Dick Houston somehow were able to achieve a conventional prusik. The front prow finally was bolted sometime later by Don Evers, Bill Dunmire and Floyd Burnette, who ceased their efforts at the "nail puller" slot. Eventually, Jim Moore fired in another bolt over the slot and managed the summit.

By 1966, the route had been freed (5.9), excluding the use of the first bolt to get started. Since then, the route has been completely freed, making for a challenging climb and a breathtaking summit.

129 **GERTIE'S PINNACLE 4th class** Gertie's is the next pinnacle uphill (southeast) and left of The Hatchet. The original lines go up the chimney/cracks on opposite sides of the rock. You can either rappel from bolts or downclimb.

130 **GERTIE'S PINNACLE – RAMBLE AND GAMBLE 5.7 R** Lost arrows and angles to one inch are needed for the belay. This route is another exercise in creative protection, as you must figure out the best way to get up this little known line.

Climb the north face of Gertie's Pinnacle (the side facing the trail and The Sisters) to a ledge 25 feet above the ground. Traverse right 30 feet to a bolt and piton belay. Next, climb right and over the overhang above the belay to easier climbing; traverse left to a bolt, and surmount a short, steep headwall. Traverse right a short distance to the north ridge.

GERTIE'S PINNACLE

THE HATCHET

128

Gertie's Pinnacle and The Hatchet as seen from the reservoir.

Deserted Valley

This seldom-visited valley is worth the trip, if only for its beauty. Deep canyons filled with magnificent rock formations are interspersed with juniper, gray pine and oak. The formation called Little Mustagh is an awesome display of elemental carving—a 90-foot boulder completely undercut for its entire circumference (not a recommended hangout during an earthquake).

The climbing in the valley, however, is limited. The climbs are rarely done and the few routes that exist are not highly recommended. Consider it an opportunity to escape the crowds if you wander up this way.

To get to the Deserted Valley, follow the perimeter of the northwest end of the reservoir until you come to the first obvious connecting stream bed on the right/northwest side. Follow the stream bed about a quarter of a mile until it runs directly in front of a distinct pinnacle on the left. This is Maniac's Delight.

131   **MANIAC'S DELIGHT – REGULAR ROUTE 5.7 R**   This route ascends the southwest ridge past a bolt. Avoid stemming up the boulder at the bottom for a 5.8 start. An assortment of medium Friends can be used to supplement the bolt.

132   **MANIAC'S DELIGHT – WEST SIDE 4th class**

photo: Kevin Kilpatrick

133 **THE KNEE – REGULAR ROUTE 5.5 R** This formation is uphill and west of Maniac's Delight. The climb starts on the uphill, shorter side. Climb just right of a water groove, using a slung horn for protection. Follow a right-slanting crack to a shoulder located halfway up. Climb the face on the left past a bolt to the top.

134 **THE KNEE – BLOWING CHUNKS 5.10b** This route ascends the large, northeast face past eight bolts. Begin climbing just right of the center of the face. A hard-to-see bolt is 15 feet up. Head up and slightly right to a second bolt, then up and left on a ramp past two more bolts. Climb straight up past three more bolts over a bulge to lower-angle rock. A bolt on a ledge to the left protects moves up to the shoulder on the **Regular Route**. Although this line wanders a bit, it has some entertaining climbing.

135 **NIT-WIT KNOB 5.7** This is the sharp spire uphill, left/south and closest to The Knee. Start on the uphill corner, traversing left to a bolt on the side facing The Knee. Follow a left-slanting crack to the top.

136 **LITTLE MUSTAGH 5.8 A2** This formation is located at the upper end of the Deserted Valley about 500 yards past The Knee. It is the largest formation in the area. The climb starts on the north side. Surmount a short vertical section to a cave-like ramp/ledge that traverses left to the north side of the rock (about 15 to 20 feet above the ground). A bolt ladder at the far left end takes you to easier fifth-class climbing and the summit.

Formations Southwest of Reservoir

This area is made up of a number of distinct formations spread out across the valley south of the reservoir. The massive formation furthest to the west is The Hand. The Thumb is the smaller pinnacle directly in front (north) of The Hand. Uphill and about 300 yards east is The Frog, a slightly smaller formation with a deep chimney/cleft in the middle. Between The Frog and The Hand is an even smaller rock called The Snail. Farthest east is a large pile of huge boulders called Crud and Mud.

To get to The Hand, The Snail and The Frog, hike around the north side of the reservoir until it becomes only a streambed. Follow the foot trail slightly up and right of the stream bed to join the old, overgrown Civilian Conservation Corps Road. Continue along this overgrown road until you reach the gully/streambed between The Hand and The Frog. Follow a trail that starts along the right side of the stream bed. This will take you directly to The Hand. To get to The Snail and The Frog, follow indistinct trails southeast from The Hand directly to both.

137 **CRUD AND MUD 3rd and 4th class** Once again, this hapless formation makes it into a Pinnacles guide. Never seeming to produce a route worth either the hike or reporting, Crud and Mud is only worth visiting if one is looking for a serious bush-whack.

The Frog

The Frog has been the scene of some very stimulating and bold routes. The majority of routes are characteristic of climbing at Pinnacles in the '70s; they're runout. It was during this time that climbers explored the possibility of leading on the steeper faces while placing bolts mainly from free stances. The result was the emergence of very sporty routes demanding resolve and focus.

To descend off The Frog, make your way to its southeast end and downclimb **South Side Shuffle**. There is a two-bolt rappel station on the southeast side of the

THE FROG

photo: Kevin Kilpatrick

northwest summit, which enables a rappel into the notch at the top of **MaGootchey Bird Chimney**. From there, easy scrambling along the ridge of The Frog gets you to the southeast side. Or you can also scramble down into **MaGootchey Bird Chimney** and rappel from bolts.

138 **SOUTH SIDE SHUFFLE 2nd class** Scramble up the gully near the southeast corner to the summit blocks. A rope is recommended for the summit block.

139 **EAST CHIMNEY 4th class** This is the southernmost chimney on the east face. Climb the chimney for 40 feet, reaching easier slopes and the summit.

140 **BIG SKY 5.8 R** This climb is loose.

141 **ATLAS SHRUGS 5.9 R ★★** This relatively long face climb is a lot of fun. Be ready for some pretty sporty runouts between bolts.

142 **MAGOOTCHEY BIRD CHIMNEY 5.5** Protection is scanty on this recessed chimney.

143 **TUFF 5.10c R** This steep chute is a little loose. There is no belay directly above the climb. Drop down and right about 15 feet to a good three-bolt belay over **Fear and Perspiration** and **Dirty Bird Crack**.

144 **FEAR AND PERSPIRATION 5.10a R+** The main drawback of this reputed death route is that the rock is insidiously bad. Other than that, a determined and masterful leader can creatively protect the bottom. Be aware that the crux is protected by cleverly placed nuts and camming units in and around loose flakes. A failure in protection will result in a very nasty groundfall.

145 **DIRTY BIRD CRACK 5.6 R** Very crumbly.

146 **PINCH GRIPPED 5.10a**

147 **SKI JUMP 5.8** ★ The first pitch of **Ski Jump** is a pleasurable knob hop on fairly good rock. The rock deteriorates slightly on the second pitch.

148 **LONESOME DOVE 5.5** This route starts off the toe of rock at the bottom of The Frog's northwest shoulder, approximately 50 feet to the right of **Ski Jump**.

149 **GETCHY-GETCHY BIRD 5.6** This climb is on the west side facing The Hand and The Snail. It makes its way up the main crack/chimney in the middle of the face. Climb a water chute to a bombay chimney. A bolt is on the left near the top of the chute. Make the crux move into the chimney, then easier climbing leads to the top.

Also in the area:

150 **SNAIL 5.7 R** ★ The Snail is the distinct 50-foot pinnacle between The Hand and The Frog. Climb the south ridge past a bolt to the top.

The Frog, Northeast Face

140 **BIG SKY 5.8 R**	144 **FEAR AND PERSPIRATION 5.10a R+**
141 **ATLAS SHRUGS 5.9 R** ★★	145 **DIRTY BIRD CRACK 5.6 R**
142 **MAGOOTCHEY BIRD CHIMNEY 5.5**	146 **PINCH GRIPPED 5.10a**
143 **TUFF 5.10c R**	147 **SKI JUMP 5.8** ★
	148 **LONESOME DOVE 5.5**

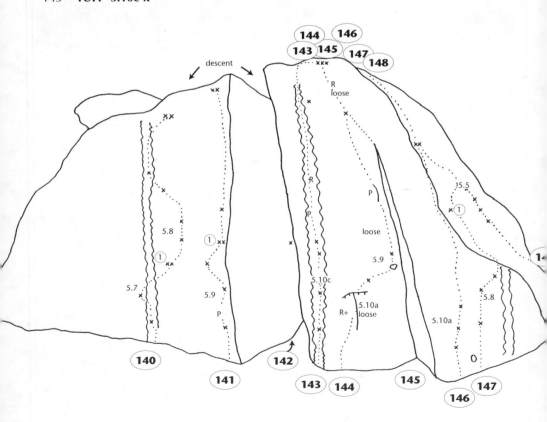

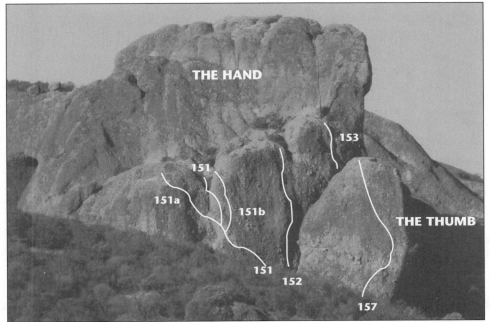

photo: Kevin Kilpatrick

The Hand

The Hand is the huge formation just right/west of The Snail. It has one of the best and boldest routes in the Monument. **Salathé** exemplifies the courage with which early first ascensionists approached the many rocks here. It is runout on a long traverse—on very steep rock—requiring a strong team. Although there are a few bolts on the line now, the climb originally was protected with pitons somehow.

The descent is made by rappelling 80 feet from bolts just below the large, dead pine into the notch between The Thumb and The Hand and scrambling down the gully to the base of the **Salathé**.

151   **SALATHE 5.6 R ★★★**   This spectacular climb starts in the notch between The Thumb and The Hand. To approach **Salathé** and the following four routes, scramble up third-class slabs to a ledge/corner and bush on The Thumb, then traverse left into the notch. The route traverses left out of the notch.

151a   **BURNETTE BOLT VARIATION 5.7 R ★★**   This a more direct finish to **Salathé**; very steep and sporty.

151b   **WILTS' BOLT VARIATION 5.6 R**

152   **LIFELINE 5.10a ★★**   **Lifeline** climbs past a line of bolts up an indistinct chute, straight up from the start of **Salathé**. This well-protected route is a lot of fun.

153   **CARPAL TUNNEL SYNDROME 5.10c ★★**   Climb from the notch between the **Thumb** and the **Hand** past a fixed pin and four bolts directly to the dead pine tree. Well-spaced bolts lend excitement to this airy line.

154 **BACK OF HAND 5.6 R** ★ Walk up and left around The Hand from below **Salathé** to the back/west side of the rock. From here, an obvious low-angle ledge gains access to the southwest arête. Traverse the ledge up and right to two closely spaced bolts. Move around the arête to another bolt. Diagonal upward to a two-bolt belay. Climb straight up easier climbing to the top. This is a very thrilling and exposed line.

155 **BOLT LADDER A1/A2** This archaic feat of engineering is located on the undercut west face. The bolts are old and crusty.

The Thumb

The Thumb is the obvious detached appendage on the north side of The Hand. There are two three-bolt belay anchors on top. There is one above the **Regular Route**, which requires only one rope to rappel back into the notch. There also is a bolt belay at the top of **Fifty Meter Must**, which, if used as a rappel anchor, requires two ropes to get back to the ground.

156 **REGULAR ROUTE 5.4 R** ★ This route starts at the point where the rappel from The Hand ends. A bolt down low protects the initial moves. Up above, move right past a second bolt to the top.

157 **FIFTY METER MUST 5.7 R+** ★ This Rupert Kammerlander route starts at the bush on the approach into the notch. This route is very severe for its grade. Characterized by long runouts, interspersed with crumbly rock, this thriller should be taken seriously. A strong leader will find this climb a handful.

Rubble Wall

This rarely visited area is a cliff band on the left/east side of the drainage several hundred yards southeast of The Hand. It might also be reached from above, off the Chalone Peak Trail. The large rock near the cliff's west end is Bicuspid. Just left and east of Bicuspid is Incisor, followed by the smaller Three Teeth. There is little known about these lines. You are on your own in this back forty.

158 **BICUSPID 5.4** Climb from a notch on the rock's east side, then up a fifth-class gully.

159 **INCISOR 5.7** As with many early first ascents at Pinnacles, the aim was solely to gain a summit. **Incisor** originally was climbed by somehow chucking a rope over the top, anchoring one end, and prusiking the other. This 50-foot pinnacle is separate from the main cliff and east of **Bicuspid**. Begin in the notch behind it and climb up past a bolt to the top.

160 **FIRST TOOTH 4th class** The sparse information on this pinnacle leads us to suspect a solo. The First and Second Tooth are the two lower rocks. The Third Tooth is above them.

161 **SECOND TOOTH easy 5th class** If you want an adventure, figure this one out. The route supposedly starts between the Second Tooth and the First.

162 **THIRD TOOTH easy 5th class** There is rumored to be a bolt on this pinnacle, leading to belay bolts on top.

Also in the area:

163 This isolated block is located several hundred yards further west along the right side of the old CCC road, past the cut-off to The Hand. Climb on the northeast side by two cracks, past a bulge, to a bolt. Third class to the summit. This obscure formation is reputed to be a solo.

The Hand

151   **SALATHE 5.6 R ★★★**
151a **BURNETTE BOLT VARIATION 5.7 R ★★**
151b **WILTS' BOLT VARIATION 5.6 R**
152   **LIFELINE 5.10a ★★**
153   **CARPAL TUNNEL SYNDROME 5.10c ★★**
154   **BACK OF HAND 5.6 R ★**

The Thumb

155   **BOLT LADDER A1/A2**
156   **REGULAR ROUTE 5.4 R ★**
157   **FIFTY METER MUST 5.7 R+ ★**

The Neglected Valley

As with the Deserted Valley, this valley is beautiful. Wonderful solitude will greet you in this almost never-visited corner of the Monument. There is decent climbing on some of the formations and high adventure to be found on many of them (notably The Mollusk, with its bouldering start). The Outcast and Knuckle Ridge have fairly good rock and a few exciting lines up a number of their faces. Neglected Valley is the main drainage/valley, just past the turnoff to The Hand. Head northwest up the valley, trusting that rock eventually will be reached. The Mollusk is the first formation you'll come to. It is on the left/west side of the drainage and definitely looks something like a sea shell.

164 **CHIMNEY SWEEP 5.10** ★ This three-bolt route lies on a formation immediately right/northeast of the start of the Neglected Valley drainage. Climb the prominent water streak in the middle of the wall. It is marked by a pine tree at the base.

165 **THE MOLLUSK 5.10** ★ Remember: This climb is quite a ways up the valley and can not be seen until you are almost there. Persevere! The Mollusk is the 40-foot boulder on the left side of the valley. Climb past one bolt, on the west/uphill face, to easier ground. Try this one for a challenging mantel problem.

166 **LITTLE FLATIRON 5.4 or 4th class** This slightly larger formation is located across the streambed and opposite The Mollusk. It looks somewhat like the Flatiron in the High Peaks area. Both routes are chimneys. The 5.4 slot originally was used to top out on the rock; that route has been overshadowed by the discovery of an easy fourth-class chimney just around the corner. Climb the uphill chimney-crack on the north side (5.4) or the easier fourth-class chimney about 15 feet away, on the right corner. Bolts with chains are on top.

167 **TOADSTOOL 5.9** This 50-foot rounded rock is 100 yards north and uphill on the same ridge from Little Flatiron. Climb a chimney on the north side. After about ten feet, the climbing becomes easy fourth class.

168 **TRIPLE DECKER 5.8 R** Friends, an assortment of Tri-cams and a fixed piton protect this challenging pitch. Pitons were used on early ascents. This formation looks like a severely leaning triple-decker ice cream cone. It is located approximately 200 yards directly up the valley from The Mollusk on the northeast slope. Start climbing from the southwest toe of the lowest "scoop." Climb straight up to a block where protection can be placed in a horizontal crack. Move left over the bulge onto the second "scoop," and climb to the top. Two bolts are on the top.

169 **LION'S HEAD 5.4** Bring long runners for slinging knobs. This formation is 100 feet upcanyon and north of Triple Decker. Starting on the north side, head up a third class slope to a steep and knobby headwall. Climb this, slinging knobs for protection. Two bolts are on top.

The Outcast and Knuckle Ridge

These two formations lie on top of the ridge at the head of the canyon. They are approximately 100 yards uphill and across the valley from Triple Decker and Lion's Head and are the most noticeable features in the valley. The Outcast is the farthest left of the formations. Knuckle Ridge continues uphill and north as a succession of five connected summits.

The summit of The Outcast has a marvelous view of the reservoir and the surrounding area. The rock actually is decent, providing a few worthwhile climbs. Although tricky to protect, the west face routes have enjoyable climbing up the long sweeping slab. There are bolts on top.

170 **THE OUTCAST – WEST FACE 5.5 R ★** On the west face of The Outcast are two crack systems. The original **West Face** line goes up the left hand crack, stepping right onto the face at its end. Knobs can be slung for protection on the upper face.

171 **THE OUTCAST – WEST FACE RIGHT 5.5 R** This is the right-hand crack. Follow it to its end and exit onto the face. Protection is the same as the regular **West Face**. It is important to take into account the scanty protection on these lines. They are definitely not worth the trouble if timidity is a factor.

172 **THE OUTCAST – SOUTH FACE 5.6 X** This route ascends the obvious chimney visible from the Neglected Valley below. Climb up the chimney until it becomes apparent that continuing upward will exceed 5.6. At that point, head right on substantial blocks for 25 feet, then climb straight up to the top. This route is loose and scary.

173 **THE OUTCAST – EAST FACE 5.7 R** Climb fourth-class up and left to a prominent shoulder and a bolt. Climb the 5.7 crux and scramble up a third class face to the top. This dicey lead will make you pause as you consider the date of the first ascent.

174 **THE OUTCAST – NORTHEAST RIB 5.7 R ★** This is one of the best lines on The Outcast. A bolt is located about a third of the way up and another about two-thirds of the way up. Failure in clipping into the second bolt could result in a groundfall.

174a **THE OUTCAST – BACK ALLEY DRIVER 5.8 TR ★** Toprope the north face of The Outcast.

Knuckle Ridge

175 **KNUCKLE RIDGE 4th or 5th class** This line of ridges can be climbed from right/north to left/south by way of the notches between them. It is neccessary to rope for fifth class climbing in a couple of spots when traversing the ridge. Most of the summits can be climbed fourth class on their west side.

175a **THE DARKNESS WITHIN 5.10a** Climb the most obvious crack to the left of **The Edge of Sundown** past six bolts. Additional protection: two medium stoppers, two medium camming units, two large camming units.

175b **THE EDGE OF SUNDOWN 5.9+** The information on this route is a little vague. Climb a rib on the left side of Knuckle Ridge past eight bolts. It is runout to last bolt up the headwall.

175c **CATATONIC STUPOR 5.8** This climb ascends the second rib from the left (as viewed from Neglected Valley), which at the bottom appears as a wishbone. Start on the right prong of the wishbone and ascend to the top.

175d **THE AGONY OF DEFEAT 5.10a** Climb the third knuckle. This route is a bit loose between fourth and fifth bolts. Knobs below the first bolt are also loose—don't PULL.

The Gargoyle and Piedras Bonitas Cliff Area

From the ridge by The Outcast and Knuckle Ridge a large wall can be seen to the west. This the Piedras Bonitas Cliff. The Gargoyle is the biggest free-standing formation east of that wall. One can also reach the area by descending the ridge behind (south) Goat Rocks past The Shaft and contour the drainage which feeds into The Gargoyle area. Be aware that raptors may nest in this area.

All routes in this area have been done "ground up" and in stance. Please respect this precedent and only establish first ascents in this style.

176   **THE GARGOYLE A1**   This large, pointed pinnacle is several hundred yards west of Knuckle Ridge and The Outcast. This formation was originally climbed by an amazing rope toss and a prusik. The free route ascends a crack. It is mentioned to validate the historical uniqueness of the monument in terms of rock climbing. At one time, "the summit" was everything.

176a   **THE GARGOYLE — QUE LASTIMA 5.10c R ★★**   Climb the northwest corner by stepping off boulders onto the steep face. Start just right of a vague corner that becomes a waterchute/wide crack above. Move past two bolts (5.9), then make increasingly difficult moves (5.10c) to get established in the chimney/chute. The crux is well protected by a #4 Friend or Camalot. Face climb, stem and wiggle up the wide crack, protected by a small camming device and a bolt, to a good stance. Finish with fun face moves up and left. Rappel the west face (one rope).

176b   **THE GARGOYLE — LA GRUNIGA 5.10d R/X**   Start atop a boulder leaning against the undercut base of The Gargoyle's northeast corner. Clip the first and possibly only bolt at the start, then boulder out very difficult moves (the crux) to easier but runout climbing above. There is decent rock down low, but not as good above. Rappel the west face (one rope).

Viva Zapatos Boulder

This large boulder lies just north of The Gargoyle. Rappel the north side from a two-bolt anchor.

176c   **VIVA ZAPATOS 5.8**   This short route ascends the east face past two bolts. The rock is a little loose.

176d   **LA MARGEN DE LA VIDA 5.9**   This sixty-foot route has some fun moves on okay rock. Climb up the west face more or less straight up past two bolts (5.9). Exit up and right with a challenging final sequence (5.8). Protection: three bolts supplemented with nuts and camming units.

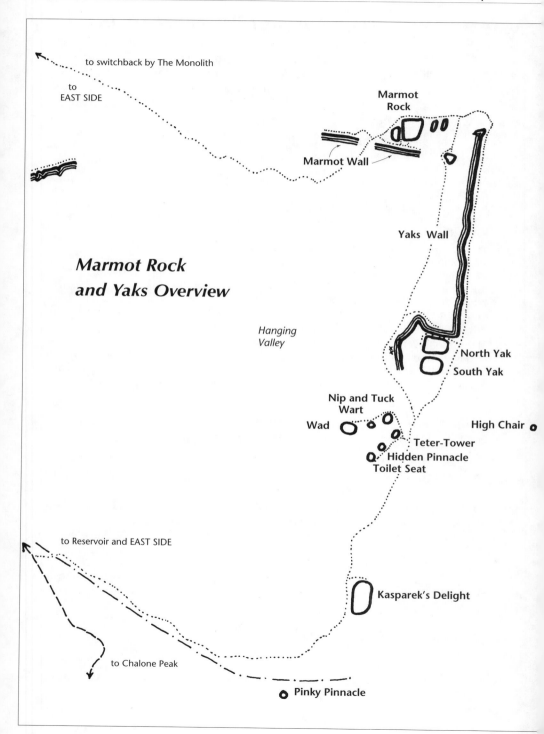

to switchback by The Monolith

to
EAST SIDE

Marmot
Rock

Marmot Wall

Yaks Wall

*Marmot Rock
and Yaks Overview*

*Hanging
Valley*

North Yak

South Yak

Nip and Tuck
Wart

Wad

High Chair

Teter-Tower

Hidden Pinnacle

Toilet Seat

to Reservoir and EAST SIDE

Kasparek's Delight

to Chalone Peak

Pinky Pinnacle

Marmot Rock and Yaks Area

Marmot Rock Area

Marmot Rock is the critter-like formation at the top of the ridge on the hill due east of The Monolith. Marmot Rock and the surrounding formations have a number of high-quality lines. By and large, the rock in this area is good. A number of bold lines have been put up here in the last ten years as climbers took on the vertical and sometimes overhanging lines with "ground up" ethics and hooks. Of note is the very improbable and imposing **Heretic** (5.10c), which surmounts the bulging north face of Marmot Rock. A hidden second bolt intimidates the mind into justified concern, as you blindly fire over the initial overhanging bulge. The awkward and surprising moves of **Wrinkle Remover** (5.10d) wind up the northwest shoulder of the pinnacle two formations uphill/east from Marmot Rock. Take on this route to get a taste of top-notch Pinnacles cragging.

Head up the lava flows that take off from the Moses Spring Trail as it bends around the northeast corner of The Monolith. Take care to stay to the right, avoiding the temptation to cut over left through one of the many notches. Follow the flows all the way up to near the top of the ridge, to a point where Marmot Rock can be seen directly to your left through a break in the lava flow. Descend a trail through this break directly to the formation.

177   **MARAUDER 5.7** ★   This is located on the north face of a large boulder 100 feet up the ridge, behind and to the left of **Wrinkle Remover**. Two bolts protect this moderate route.

178   **WRINKLE REMOVER 5.10d** ★★   One bolt on top. Good rock and interesting moves. Climbs the northwest side.

179   **ASLEEP AT THE WHEEL 5.10c** ★   This short line is a nice tidbit of climbing. The second bolt is difficult to clip.

180   **MARMOT WITH A HAND GRENADE 5.9 R**   Hard starting moves, then a runout to the second bolt.

181   **THE HERETIC 5.10c** ★★★   A spectacular line directly up the north face. The second bolt is hidden by a small ledge straight up from the first.

182   **LITTLE MARMOT 5.0**   This easy route ascends the obvious chimney/tunnel on the northwest face between the east and west summits of Marmot Rock. Climb up the hard-to-protect chimney to a secure ledge on the right (on the west rock). Chimney up ten more feet to the actual summit shoulder, staying over the ledge as you climb. This route is a little loose.

183   **BIG MARMOT 5.6**   From the west summit's shoulder, reach across to the east summit's west face to a series of five bolts that arch up and right to the top. Only the fourth bolt has a hanger.

184   **FURRY MARMOT SUBSTITUTE 5.9**   Climb the south face of the east summit of Marmot Rock past two bolts. Approach by walking around the uphill side of Marmot.

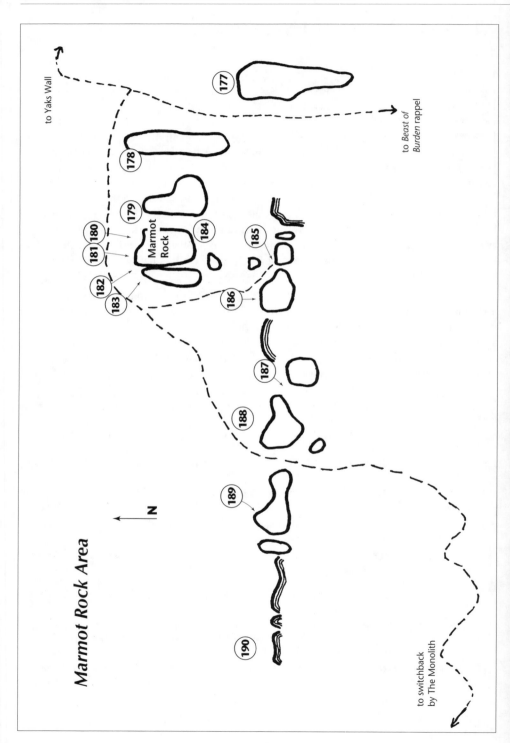

Marmot Rock Area

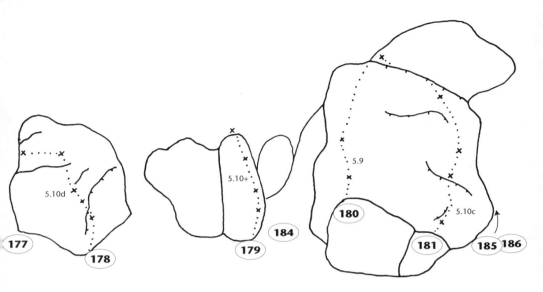

Marmot Rock Area: Right Side

177 MARAUDER 5.7 ★
178 WRINKLE REMOVER 5.10d ★★
179 ASLEEP AT THE WHEEL 5.10b ★
180 MARMOT WITH A HAND
     GRENADE 5.9 R

181 THE HERETIC 5.10c ★★★
182 LITTLE MARMOT 5.0
184 FURRY MARMOT SUBSTITUTE 5.9
185 MAKING PUPPIES 5.10a
186 ON A PALE HORSE 5.10a ★★

Also in the area:

185 **MAKING PUPPIES 5.10a**   This route is on the uphill of two formations situated
     directly behind Marmot Rock. Climb the right side of the formation, following a line
     of four bolts to the top. The fourth bolt has no hanger. Approach via the gully behind
     Marmot from the downhill/west side.

186 **ON A PALE HORSE 5.10a ★★**   This route is located on the right side on the lower
     of the two previously mentioned rocks. Follow a line of three bolts to the top. This is
     a thrilling and very sporty route.

187 **FRONTIERS OF CHAOS 5.10b ★**   The bouldering start is a little dangerous and
     needs a good spotter.

188 **MURKY BONG WATER 5.9 R ★**

189 **ONLY A LAD 5.10b R ★**

190 **THE TOM-TOM CLUB 5.8 R ★**   This route is located on a wide slab 200 yards
     downhill from **Only a Lad**.

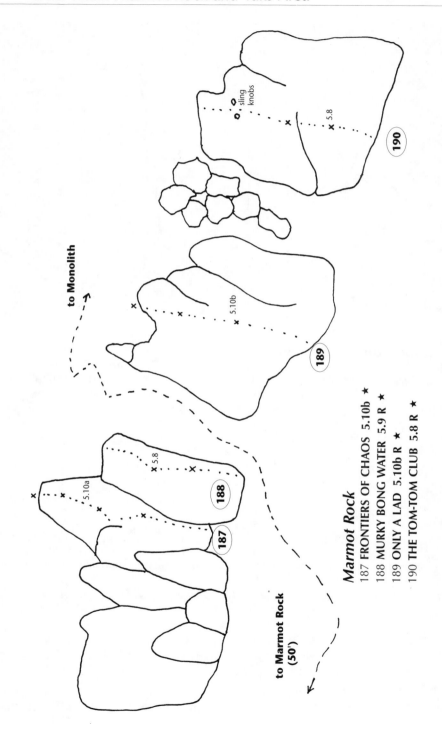

Marmot Rock

187 FRONTIERS OF CHAOS 5.10b ★
188 MURKY BONG WATER 5.9 R ★
189 ONLY A LAD 5.10b R ★
190 THE TOM-TOM CLUB 5.8 R ★

photo: Kevin Kilpatrick

The Yaks and Yaks Wall

This area is worth the hike. If you've mustered up the where-withal to seek out the Marmot area, dropping down to this immense and little-traveled area is a must. Not only is there the expected Pinnacles face climbing, there also are some long, moderate and decent crack climbing. **Liebacker's Lullaby** (5.8) is the long, sweeping right-facing corner that reaches to the skyline. There also is some rather eclectic "chute" climbing found here. **Shoot the Tube** (5.10a) climbs an almost tubular chute, giving one thoughts of fifth-class caving. Split Infinity is one of the most heroic 5.10 leads you'll ever do, considering the difficulty of this wildly overhanging chute. For the thrill of reaching a spectacular summit, the North Yak fits the bill. Perched up high on the wall's left end, this true pinnacle sports a wonderful 5.10a bolt ladder on excellent rock on the northwest face.

The Yaks area can be reached by two different approach trails (north and south). From the Marmot area (north), drop down over the saddle to the east side of the hill. Follow a semi-worn trail to the right/north end of the Yaks Wall. **Reach for the Sky** is the obvious right-facing arête on the wall's extreme right end. A trail skirts the base of the wall. The Yaks and the Yaks Wall also can be reached from the south by continuing up the gully past **Kasparek's Delight** to the ridge south of the Yaks. The ridge is a great vantage point for all the formations out past the reservoir, for the Hanging Valley (just below and west), and for the south face of the South Yak. One either can continue up the ridge to a rappel station above the notch between the Yaks pinnacles and the main wall or drop down to the trail to the east and below the Yaks Wall before getting to South Yak.

The Yaks—North and South

The Yaks are two very large, detached spires at the south end of the Yaks Wall. These rocks beckon climbers with their grandeur and position, as they loom high above the valley to the east. The **West Face** of the North Yak (5.10a) is delightful. Superb rock and a bolt ladder for protection classify this line as an absolute must.

As was mentioned in the general introduction to this area, there is a rappel station made up of several bolts at the top of the main wall northwest and across from the Yaks. One also can scramble up a fourth class gully between the North Yak and the Yaks Wall.

The North Yak originally was summited by a tyrolean traverse. Not strictly a climb in itself, this endeavor is mentioned as a possible adventure. The state of the South Yak's summit anchors is unknown. Likewise, the bolts on top of the North Yak should be scrutinized before engaging them in the high forces that a tyrolean generates.

191 **NORTH YAK – NORTHWEST FACE 5.10a or A1** ★★★ This classic route follows the bolt ladder on the northwest face. The bolts on this old aid line are well used and acquire safety through numbers. Some of the hangers require small gate carabiners.

192 **NORTH YAK – NORTH FACE 5.10+ or A2** This bolt ladder ascends the north prow of the **North Yak**, about 40 feet to the left of the **Northwest Face**, starting on top of a boulder leaning against the face. Follow several bolts and a fixed piton straight up. Veer left past several more bolts, moving around the corner and up onto the northeast shoulder, then run it out on loose rock to the top.

193 **SOUTH YAK – WEST FACE 5.7** Start on the far right side of the west face. Climb the face past a bush and a bolt to a corner. Step right and across the face, past another bolt, to the base of a chimney. Work up the chimney past two fixed pitons to easier climbing and the summit. The chimney reportedly also can be protected with nuts and camming units. As with all fixed pitons in the monument, try not to rely on them for your only protection.

194 **SOUTH YAK — SOUTH FACE 5.4 A1** This unfinished line ascends the south face. Climb the 40-foot apron past three bolts and a fixed pin driven straight down on top of a flake (5.4) to a ledge at the base of a long left-facing, left-arching corner system. Here, a bolt belay can be set up on the right-side or a slung chockstone placed to the left at the base of the corner. The second pitch looks unfinished, as a succession of about seven bolts in a ladder ends at two bolts doubled up. The first pitch, although crumbly in spots, is enjoyable enough to warrant a visit if you're in the area. The majority of hangers are swedged cables.

195 **BEAST OF BURDEN 5.10a** Follow a line of five bolts up the rappel route to the Yaks. This climb is loose.

196 **BULLRUN 5.10b** Follow a line of bolts up a steep chute on the wall opposite the **North Face Route** on the North Yak.

The Yaks Wall

The Yaks Wall is a 300-yard-long wall made up of a continuous line up of chutes and corners. Most of the routes can be done as multi-pitch climbs, but on many, only the first pitch is worth doing. One will find that the routes here are a wee bit sportier than some of the well-protected "clip-ups" in Bear Gulch. Primarily a menu of 5.10 climbing, 15-foot runouts are commonplace on this side of the

The Yaks and Yaks Wall

177	MARAUDER 5.7 ★
191	NORTH YAK – NORTHWEST FACE 5.10a or A1 ★★★
192	NORTH YAK – NORTH FACE 5.10 or A1
193	SOUTH YAK – WEST FACE 5.7
194	SOUTH YAK – SOUTH FACE 5.4 A1
195	BEAST OF BURDEN 5.9
196	BULLRUN 5.10b
197	SHOOT THE TUBE 5.10a ★
198	ORION 5.8+ R ★
199	WHITE PUNKS ON ROPE 5.11+
200	SPLIT INFINITY 5.10c ★★
201	SLIP STREAM 5.10b/c ★
202	TATO PANI (HOT WATER) 5.9 ★★
203	DANCE ON A VOLCANO 5.10b ★
204	NAKED LUNGE 5.9
205	LIEBACKER'S LULLABY 5.8 ★★
206	CRACK CLIMBER'S CONCERTO 5.9 ★
207	TERMINAL BUTTRESS 5.9 ★
207a	TERMINAL BUTTRESS – MCCONACHIE/BARBELLA VARIATION 5.9+ ★
208	VENUS FLY TRAP 5.10d R
209	REACH FOR THE SKY 5.10b ★★

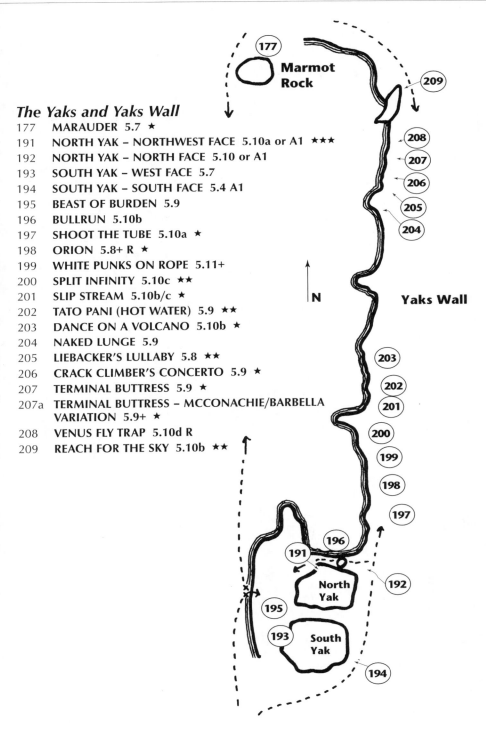

Yaks Wall—Left Side

192 NORTH YAK – NORTH FACE 5.10 OR A1
194 SOUTH YAK – SOUTH FACE 5.4 A1
197 SHOOT THE TUBE 5.10a ★
198 ORION 5.8+ R ★
199 WHITE PUNKS ON ROPE 5.11+
200 SPLIT INFINITY 5.10c ★★★

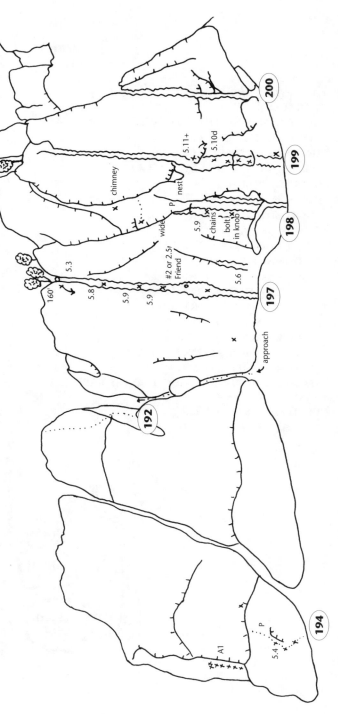

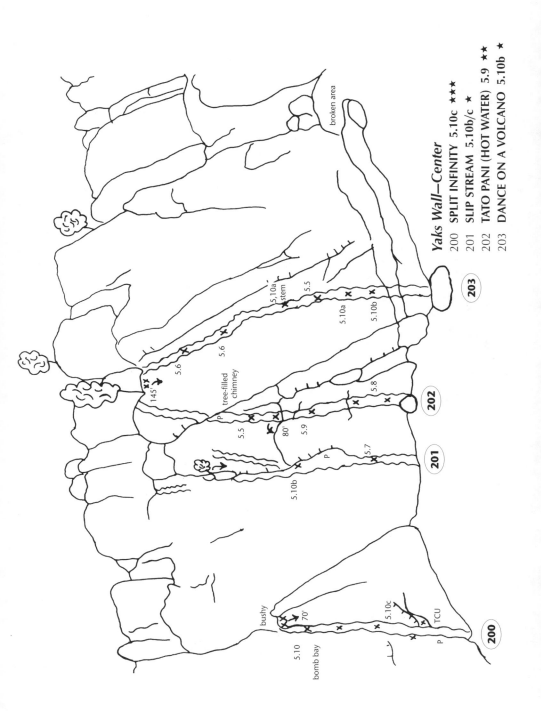

Yaks Wall—Center

200 **SPLIT INFINITY 5.10c** ★★★
201 **SLIP STREAM 5.10b/c** ★
202 **TATO PANI (HOT WATER) 5.9** ★★
203 **DANCE ON A VOLCANO 5.10b** ★

Marmot Rock

177 MARAUDER 5.7 ★

178 WRINKLE REMOVER 5.10d ★★

Yaks Wall – Right Side

204 NAKED LUNGE 5.9

205 LIEBACKER'S LULLABY 5.8 ★★

206 CRACK CLIMBER'S CONCERTO 5.9 ★

207 TERMINAL BUTTRESS 5.9 ★

208 VENUS FLY TRAP 5.10d R

209 REACH FOR THE SKY 5.10a ★★

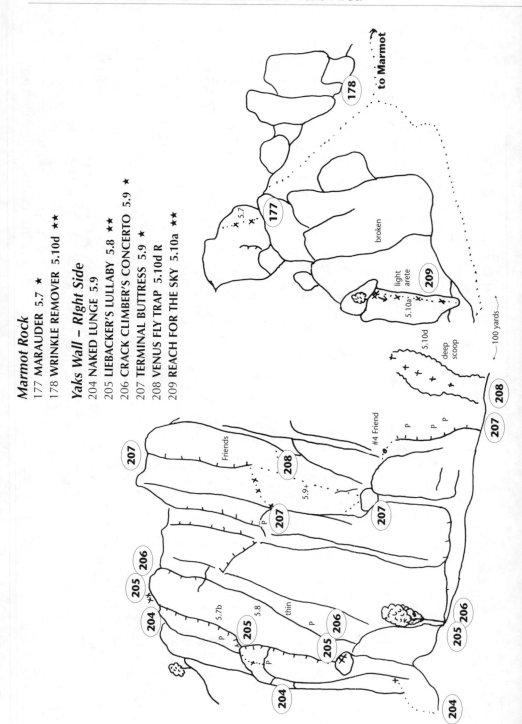

mountain. The other side of the coin is that a lot of the climbs are of moderate difficulty to a definite crux. For those of us spoiled by the proliferation of bolts, the Yaks Wall might be a good testing ground to see how we fare with less.

197 **SHOOT THE TUBE 5.10a** ★   Almost (literally) like climbing a tube. One bolt belay.

198 **ORION 5.8+ R** ★   Large protection is needed. This improbable-looking route is truly an adventure.

199 **WHITE PUNKS ON ROPE 5.11+** (unfinished) The last bolt is easy to locate because of the mass of slings that usually frequent it.

200 **SPLIT INFINITY 5.10c** ★★   Wild stemming takes one up this severely overhanging chute.

201 **SLIP STREAM 5.10b/c** ★   Originally an aid route, awkward free climbing takes one out of the bowl 30 feet up. Belay from a small tree. One can either rappel from the tree or continue to the top, although above the tree the route deteriorates quickly.

202 **TATO PANI (Hot Water) 5.9** ★★ Solid rock! One bolt at belay. Not recommended past first pitch.

203 **DANCE ON A VOLCANO 5.10b** ★   Hard climbing up a steep, undulating water streak. Rock around the second bolt may be a little unsound. A fall arrester or similar shock-absorbing protection is recommended to limit potential forces that may be placed on the bolt. Two ropes are necessary for the rappel.

204 **NAKED LUNGE 5.9**   Large protection is needed on this route.

205 **LIEBACKER'S LULLABY 5.8** ★★

206 **CRACK CLIMBER'S CONCERTO 5.9** ★   For those who don't want to lieback.

207 **TERMINAL BUTTRESS 5.9** ★   Many Friends are needed to protect this route

207a **TERMINAL BUTTRESS – McCONACHIE-BARBELLA VARIATION 5.9+**   Camming units can be used in pockets.

208 **VENUS FLY TRAP 5.10d R**   A face climb for those wanting to run it out on crumbly rock.

209 **REACH FOR THE SKY 5.10a** ★   A sweet route.

Also in the area:

210 **THE HIGH CHAIR 5.7**   This 30-foot rock is seen 500 feet below and to the east of the Yaks. It is an isolated boulder located between two large, gray gravel patches. Climb the north shoulder past a bolt down low.

The Hanging Valley

The Hanging Valley is yet another seldom-visited spot in the Monument. Regardless of the climbing, the area is scenic and quiet. It also is on the way to the Yaks and just past **Kasparek's**, so a visit here might be worth the adventure. All of the routes in this valley are more than 20 years old. First, the area can be thought of as a microcosm of Pinnacles climbing 20-plus years ago. If you are a climbing historian, have a blast visiting the past. Bolts are either very old or non-existent, so caution is necessary.

The Hanging Valley forms the higher end of the valley above **Kasparek's**. To get to this area hike up the valley past **Kasparek's** to the ridge above it (where the Yaks can be seen). The Hanging Valley is the little valley directly below the ridge and to the west. In other words it's just below you.

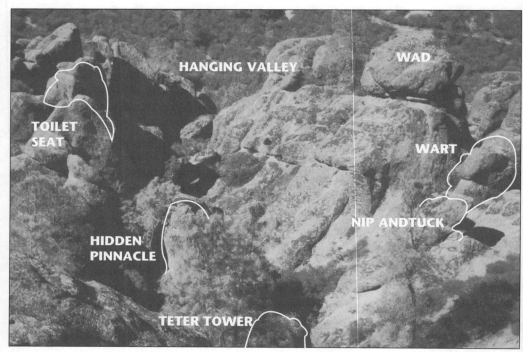

photo: Kevin Kilpatrick

211 **KASPAREK'S DELIGHT 5.9+ ★** Kasparek's marks the beginning of the Hanging Valley. It is reached by following the stream bed between the North Chalone Peak Trail and The Sisters. Make your way up the stream bed, staying to the right and out of the many deep gullies running up to the left, until it finally deadends in rock formations. Kasparek's is the largest formation uphill and to the north. Work your way around the right side to the uphill/northeast face. Climb the short 15-foot face past two bolts using man-made one-finger holes to low-angle slabs and the summit. An abundance of widely spaced bolts are on top. An aid route of unknown origin goes up a right-facing corner on the west face.

A historical note: The same year that Anton Nelson and Robin Hansen climbed Kasparek's, they also were part of the party that accomplished the first tyrolean traverse to Lost Arrow Spire in Yosemite.

212 **PINKY PINNACLE 5.5 X** Pinky Pinnacle is the 20-foot finger of rock just uphill and to the right/south from the point where the streambed deadends on the approach to the Kasparek's and The Hanging Valley. Climb the uphill side past one bolt down low that soon becomes worthless. There is one bolt on top.

213 **THE TOILET SEAT 5.5** As you come out onto the ridge past **Kasparek's,** this 20-foot boulder is just below you and the top bolt slings can be seen. The rock is located in the middle of three pinnacles. The 5.5 route climbs the uphill side.

214 **THE TOILET SEAT – THE DRAIN CHIMNEY 5.8** Starts around to the left and is 5.8 getting started.

Also in the area:

215   **HIDDEN PINNACLE 5.5 A1**   This 45-foot rock is the obvious spire 100 feet uphill and on the same side of the valley as The Toilet Seat. It is distinctly marked by a pine tree growing closely next to its east/uphill side. The route originally went up the pine tree and across to a bolt (using it for direct aid) to get started, then climbed past one more bolt to the top.

216   **TETER-TOWER 5.8**   This distinct formation is about 20 feet up the valley from Hidden Pinnacle. It is unmistakenly recognized by the balancing ball-like summit block. Once again, trees aid the ascent. Climb the southwest face using two pine trees to get started. Small nuts and TCUs may work in the bottom crack. Climb around either side of the "ball" to a rappel bolt on the right. A #2 and #3 Friend can be used for protection higher up.

217   **NIP AND TUCK 5.8**   If you circle counterclockwise (north to west, etc.) around the valley from Teter-Tower, the next, relatively small, boulder is Nip and Tuck. A bolt at the top protects this short lead, although the first ascensionists tossed a rope over the rock to gain an upper belay. The bolt may be hangerless.

218   **WART 5.8**   This is the next boulder, continuing counterclockwise (southwest) from Nip and Tuck. Ascents have been made by the classic rope toss and a precarious toprope. There is no rappel anchor on top.

219   **WAD – LEFT 5.9**   Wad is the last boulder in the U-shaped curve of boulders ringing Hidden Valley. It is 50 feet past Wart on our counterclockwise trek. The 5.9 route climbs the side facing Wart and Nip and Tuck. Start both **Right** and **Left Wad** by climbing 5.5 to a large, sandy area.

220   **WAD – RIGHT 5.5**   Climb up past a fixed pin near the top, to the right of the 5.9 route.

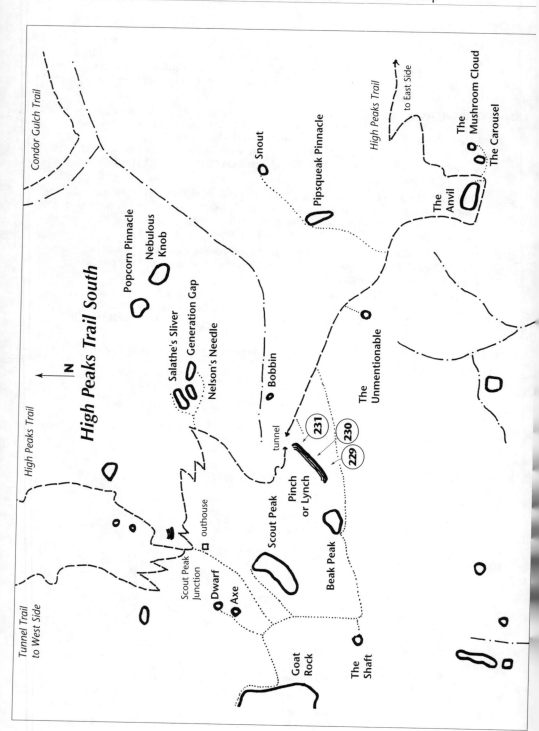

Condor Gulch Trail

High Peaks Trail

High Peaks Trail South

N

Tunnel Trail
to West Side

Popcorn Pinnacle

Nebulous
Knob

Salathe's Sliver

Generation Gap

Nelson's Needle

Snout

Pipsqueak Pinnacle

High Peaks Trail

to East Side

The
Mushroom Cloud

The Carousel

The
Anvil

Bobbin

tunnel

231

230

229

The
Unmentionable

Scout Peak

Pinch
or Lynch

Beak Peak

Scout Peak
Junction

outhouse

Dwarf

Axe

Goat
Rock

The
Shaft

HIGH PEAKS TRAIL SOUTH

The High Peaks Trail South area includes routes approached from the trail beginning at the point where it intersects the Rim Trail and going all the way to Scout Peak Junction. The isolated formations of The Mushroom Cloud and The Carousel rocks, The Anvil and Pipsqueak Ridge come into view approximately a quarter mile past the Rim Trail intersection and beyond several switchbacks. The magical formations of The Mushroom Cloud and The Carousel rocks are to the left. This cluster of mushroom-like rocks may have you scanning the scene for a hookah-smoking caterpillar. Across the trail to the right is The Anvil, looking remarkably like its namesake. Pipsqueak Ridge forms the skyline to the right of the Anvil. From this vantage, The Snout and Pipsqueak Pinnacle are obscured by the many rocks that line the ridge. These formations are easier to discern as you approach them from higher up the trail. The higher peaks in this area are described in the last part of this book, "The High Peaks."

As you leave the familiarity of Bear Gulch, you will enter an avenue of Pinnacles climbing history. Wandering among the little pinnacles along this trail, as well as along other trails leading to the High Peaks area, the importance of bagging summits becomes apparent. Old quarter-inch or Star Dryvin bolts seem to greet you everywhere, thwarting your intention of bagging their rock. A number of the climbs are simply backside walk ups, requiring only a move or two to gain the summit.

There are some very worthwhile climbs to be done along this trail. If you're looking for an excellent rock on which to toprope, Carousel is top notch. Problems ranging

THE ANVIL

THE CAROUSEL

A TRIP TO THE FAIR

photo: Kevin Kilpatrick

from easy fifth-class to hard 5.10 exist around this 18-foot boulder. Of particular note is the thrilling **A Trip to the Fair** (5.10b). It'll launch you from pocket to pocket on the south/uphill side of The Carousel. Farther up the trail, **The Unmentionable** (5.7) will stimulate your climbing senses as you surmount its distinct summit. Pipsqueak Pinnacle has two enjoyable lines at 5.5 and 5.8 which, combined with the two routes previously mentioned, could add up to a very memorable day of climbing.

221 **THE CAROUSEL 5.0 to 5.10+ TR** ★ This toproping area is on the largest rock in a cluster and lies uphill from the rest. Approach from an indistinct trail that leaves the High Peaks Trail just before the Anvil. There are four bolts on the southern highpoint of this rock that are used as an anchor. On the uphill side, starting just right of the chute between the two summits of Carousel is **A Trip to the Fair** (5.10b). This superb boulder problem is harder for shorter people and can be easily toproped.

222 **THE MUSHROOM CLOUD 5.8** This boulder problem is located down slope from all surrounding formations. On its uphill side, an interesting crank move gets you on top. Lower yourself off and drop.

223 **THE ANVIL 5.1 X** This distinct formation is just uphill and across the trail from The Carousel at the point where the trail curves back right toward the High Peaks. The Anvil is right next to the trail. There is no protection on this fairly casual solo. Surmount the multiple scoops up the east side, away from the trail. There are two bolts on top. One is hangerless.

224 **PIPSQUEAK PINNACLE – REGULAR ROUTE 5.5** ★ This formation is on Pipsqueak Ridge, which runs down from the right/northeast to meet the High Peaks Trail. An indistinct game trail located approximately a quarter-mile past The Anvil takes you up along the ridge to the pinnacle, which is the first formation you'll meet. A rock cluster

marks the trail intersection. Climb the west shoulder past two bolts to a two-bolt anchor. A TCU or a slider nut can protect the start if desired.

225 **PIPSQUEAK PINNACLE – RIGHTFOOT 5.8** ★ Start just right of the **Regular Route**, following four bolts to the top. It is a little far to the first bolt and a spotter might be useful.

226 **THE SNOUT 5.7** This formation is the most distant pinnacle along the ridge from Pipsqueak Pinnacle. Climb the front/west face past one bolt to the top. Two bolts are on top. You can't mistake this climb. It goes up the shortest side and is only about 15 feet long.

227 **THE UNMENTIONABLE 5.7** ★★★ This pinnacle looks more unmentionable from farther up the High Peaks Trail. This rock is located about 100 feet down a clearly worn trail opposite the rock formation that marks the approach to Pipsqueak Pinnacle and The Snout. Climb the uphill side of the formation past one bolt to a two-bolt belay. There is a belay bolt in the short saddle as you start the route. Good rock, juicy moves and an exciting location make this climb a must. Variations have been toproped to the left side of the regular route.

228 **BOBBIN A1** Mentioned out of a commitment to represent the entirety of Pinnacles climbing, this little spire is never climbed. The only recorded ascent was accomplished by, once again, a dynamic rope toss, fixing one end and prusik. To locate this beauty, follow the trail to where it enters a short man-made tunnel. Look downhill to your right and you will see this ten-foot " ball on a stick." As Chuck Richards put it in his guide: "It's a must for those determined to do every climb in the guidebook."

PIPSQUEAK PINNACLE

photo: Kevin Kilpatrick

THE UNMENTIONABLE

227

photo: Kevin Kilpatrick

photo: Tim Corcoram

Jeff Loris on **Ordeal**

Pinch or Lynch Wall

The trail levels out for about 100 yards on a ridge overlooking The Deserted Valley and Condor Gulch after passing The Unmentionable. As viewed from the ridge, Pinch or Lynch Wall is a large cliff band running across the hill, up and to your left. It is made up of a succession of cliffs and chimneys. About 100 feet before the tunnel, head up a grassy break in the slope directly to the right/northeast side of the cliff. **Pinch or Lynch** is located on a buttress at the cliff's northeast/downhill side. The start is marked by an isolated manzanita bush on a boulder, directly in front of the buttress and a left-facing corner (the start of the climb).

229 **ASSAULT AND BATTERY 5.10c** This crack/chimney climb is located 200 feet up and left from the lowest point of Pinch or Lynch Wall. It starts out with a bottomless offwidth. Climb up 40 feet and step right past a bolt on large knobs. Stem up a bottomless corner (fixed piton). Jam out a crack at the top of the corner, and then up a wide crack to the top. A 150-foot rappel returns you to the ground. This route has very continuous and varied crack climbing.

230 **POODLE WITH A MOHAWK 5.10a R** ★ This climb is the blackest water streak on the right side of the main wall. It is the first waterchute that goes all the way to the ground, located 50 feet uphill and right from the lowest point of the main wall. A scrub oak marks the start.

231 **PINCH OR LYNCH 5.6** This route is an interesting mix of face and crack climbing. Unfortunately, it is a little loose. Either rappel the route or walk off the backside to the main trail.

PINCH OR LYNCH WALL

photo: Kevin Kilpatrick

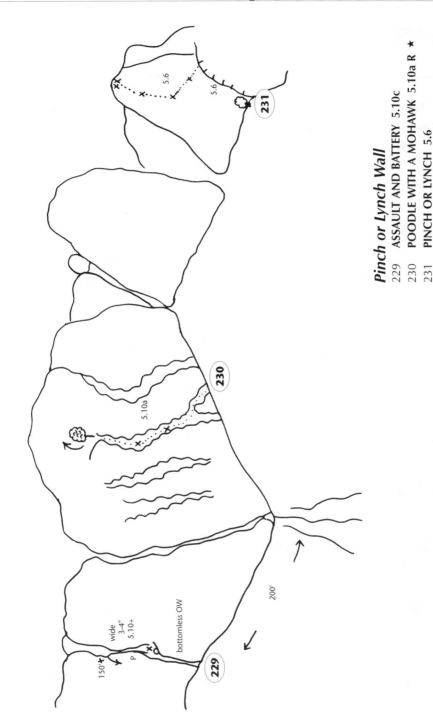

Pinch or Lynch Wall

229 ASSAULT AND BATTERY 5.10c
230 POODLE WITH A MOHAWK 5.10a R ★
231 PINCH OR LYNCH 5.6

Generation Gap Pinnacle

This pinnacle is on the right/northeast, beyond the man-made tunnel and just below Salathé's Sliver. It can be identified by a long left-curving chimney. Approach the formation from the end of the long switchback that takes one close to the base of Salathé's Sliver. Descend a rock gully to the right, between boulders, and skirt left around the base of the rock until the chimney is reached.

232 **GENERATION GAP 5.7** ★   Bring an assortment of camming units and nuts.

Pitch 1 Climb the chimney until it curves left, then step up and right to a spacious grassy ledge with a two-bolt belay. One bolt is on the ledge; the other is on the wall to the left. This actually is an enjoyable chimney. Careful climbing is needed to avoid loose rock in a few spots.

Pitch 2 Climb the face above, past a bolt to the top. Two bolts are on top.

233 **THIN MAN 5.8**   Rather than stepping right out of the chimney, continue along the chimney as it curves left to its end, and climb the bulge above, past two bolts. This pitch is 160 feet long.

234 **SALATHE'S SLIVER 5.7 R** ★   Look up from the man-made tunnel to the right/north. The two most distinctive rocks on the skyline are Salathé's Sliver (the larger one on the left) and Nelson's Needle (the smaller one approximately 15 feet to the right). The Flatiron can be seen behind these two closely spaced pinnacles. Walk up the trail, past the tunnel, to the point where it comes closest to the base of the rock and starts the first switchback. Clamber up a steep gully to the left of Salathé's Sliver to reach the shorter backsides of the formations.

Originally, the initial move up the **Sliver** was achieved by way of a committing shoulder stand. A delicate and dangerous move now commits you to an ancient fixed piton. Face climb past a bolt to the top and a magnificent view of the east side. This line is about 40 feet long. Two bolts are on top.

235 **NELSON'S NEEDLE – REGULAR ROUTE 5.6** ★   Climb up the north shoulder, staying just right of a small corner where nuts and/or TCUs can be placed. Continue up the face above, past a bolt to the top. This climb is a lot of fun. The rappel route offers some challenging toproping.

236 **NELSON'S NEEDLE – EAST FACE 5.6 R+**   Follow a rotten, unprotected crack up and left, past a bulge, to a loose ledge and a bolt. Climb up and right to the top.

SALATHE'S SLIVER

NELSON'S NEEDLE

GENERATION GAP

photo: Kevin Kilpatrick

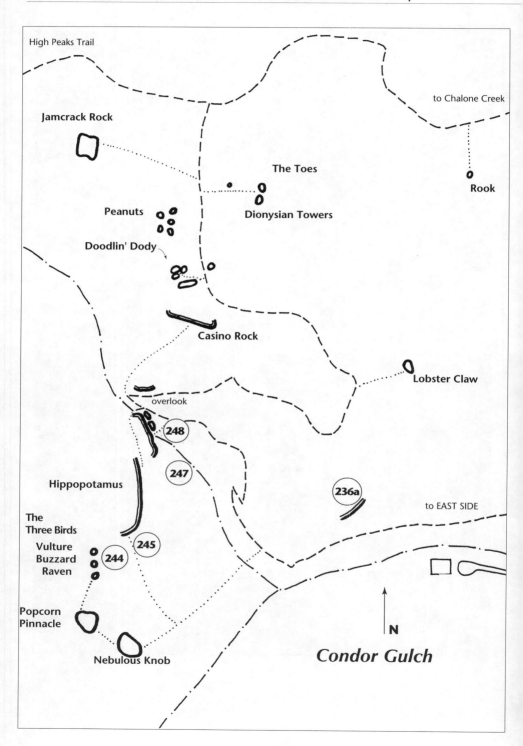

High Peaks Trail

to Chalone Creek

Jamcrack Rock

The Toes

Rook

Peanuts

Dionysian Towers

Doodlin' Dody

Casino Rock

Lobster Claw

overlook

248

247

236a

Hippopotamus

to EAST SIDE

The
Three Birds

Vulture
Buzzard
Raven

245

244

Popcorn
Pinnacle

N

Nebulous Knob

Condor Gulch

CONDOR GULCH AREA

The Condor Gulch area includes all routes approached from the Condor Gulch Trail. It also includes Rook, which is approached off the High Peaks Trail just north of the Condor Gulch and High Peaks Trail junction at the top of the ridge. Given the amount of rock situated in this drainage valley, there is a meager number of climbs.

The Condor Gulch Trail starts across from the Visitor's Center and heads up the wide valley to the northwest. Follow the trail up past the park buildings (on your left) to a point where the main valley on the left meets Condor Gulch proper. On the right/north slope of the adjoining valley, a series of pinnacles is situated up and right along the skyline. The one farthest down the slope is Nebulous Knob, followed uphill by Popcorn Pinnacle and the Three Birds: Raven, Buzzard and Vulture. A semi-brushless path can be seen from the Condor Gulch Trail leading up to Nebulous Knob. With clever navigation, a mostly painless path can be found.

Nebulous Knob, as well as the other formations in this group, can also be approached from the High Peaks Trail—South, just as you pass the rock marking the approach to Snout and Pipsqueak Pinnacle. From these formations, Popcorn Pinnacle clearly can be seen to the north as the pointed pinnacle with the long chimney running up its southwest face.

photo: Kevin Kilpatrick

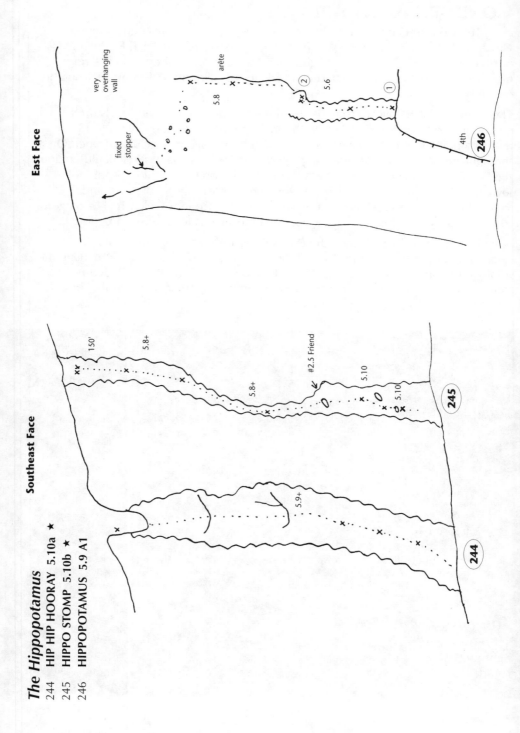

East Face

very overhanging wall

arête

5.8

② 5.6

①

fixed stopper

4th

246

Southeast Face

150'

5.8+

5.8+

#2.5 Friend

5.10

5.10

5.9+

245

244

The Hippopotamus
244 HIP HIP HOORAY 5.10a ★
245 HIPPO STOMP 5.10b ★
246 HIPPOPOTAMUS 5.9 A1

236a **CEMETARY GATES 5.10** Walk up the Chalone Creek trail until it switches back above the ranger's residence. Just ahead is a tall thin boulder overhanging the trail. One hundred yards uphill and to the right is a large formation with an obvious belay ledge. Climb past three bolts and a medium Friend placement to a two-bolt belay on the ledge. Route is visible from the trail.

237 **NEBULOUS KNOB 5.0** A small boulder next to the main rock marks the start of this route. The boulder is located on the uphill, short side. An initial unprotected move off the small boulder leads up to the southwest shoulder of the main rock. Climb up past a bolt to the top. One bolt with a ring is on summit. Be careful of the poison oak around the base.

238 **POPCORN PINNACLE CHIMNEY 5.6** This distinct pinnacle is about 100 yards uphill (northwest) from Nebulous Knob. The obvious, 60-foot chimney faces southwest toward the High Peaks Trail. This climb is hard to protect and there are no anchors on top. Protection is needed to 4½-inches, including Tri-cams. A rappel can be set up by fixing one end of the rope to a tree and descending off the opposite side.

239 **POPCORN PINNACLE — NORTHEAST CORNER 5.6** This climb is loose and dirty. The crux is getting started. The upper crack may be protectable.

The Three Birds

These three boulders—Raven, Buzzard and Vulture—actually have some interesting climbing on them. They are a curious hodgepodge of fifth-class climbing and intricate navigation. Once discovered, **Vulture**'s obscure line turns out to be an exciting adventure of route-finding on fairly decent rock.

The Birds are located in a line, starting 200 yards north and uphill from Popcorn Pinnacle. The first and most southern is Raven; Buzzard and Vulture follow.

240 **RAVEN 5.0 X** This unprotected route starts on the south side and winds around to the east face and continues to the top. There is one bolt on top.

241 **BUZZARD – NORTH FACE 5.6 R** A wedge-shaped block separates Buzzard and Vulture. Once on the uphill side of the formation, climb over a dead pine tree into the notch between the wedge and the north face. Loose climbing takes one up to a horizontal crack, where Friends can be placed. Surmount a small bulge and gain easier ground to the top. (There reportedly is a fourth-class route somewhere up the east face).

242 **BUZZARD – WESTSIDE LIEBACK 5.9+ TR** This strenuous, but short crack/flake may make negotiating the north face worth it.

243 **VULTURE 5.5 ★** From the uphill (west) side, tunnel underneath the wedge block, staying right next to Vulture until it is possible to chimney up between the two boulders. Work your way up until a crack, which leads horizontally onto the north shoulder, is reached. A large Friend and/or Tri-cams protect the entry moves onto the sloping east face of Vulture. Continue back left past one bolt to the top where there is a rappel bolt.

The Hippopotamus

The Hippopotamus is the largest cliff band 300 yards below and to the right/northeast of Nebulous Knob and Popcorn Pinnacle. It's about 200 yards southeast from the overlook on the right slope of the first drainage coming into

Condor Gulch and is approached in the same way as Nebulous Knob and Popcorn Pinnacle, contouring over to the cliffs left (uphill) end.

Hip Hip Hooray and **Hippo Stomp** are the two left-most waterchutes respectively. Both are enjoyable face climbs on decent rock. **Hippopotamus** is further right and downhill 150 yards on the northeast face, and is marked by a fourth-class, right-facing corner leading to a waterchute.

244   **HIP HIP HOORAY 5.10a**   An assortment of camming units supplement the few bolts. Care must be taken to place sufficient protection for the exit moves from the upper bowl.

245   **HIPPO STOMP 5.10c ★**   Coupled with **Hip Hip Hooray**, this route is worth the hike. An assortment of camming units and stoppers supplement the bolts.

246   **HIPPOPOTAMUS 5.9 A1**   This route has had very few ascents and the data on it is sketchy.

photo: Kevin Kilpatrick

photo: Time Corcoran

Coyote Ugly

Also in the area:

247   **DUTCH GOOSE 5.7 A2**   This never-done aid route is located at the very bottom of the worn water groove 150 feet below the overlook. A trail 50 feet before the overlook makes its way down the steep slope to the base of the waterfall chute. **Dutch Goose** is the 100-foot thin crack that turns into a chimney/gully about 20 feet from the bottom of the chute. Ascend a short flake at the bottom to reach the overhanging aid crack. This route is dirty and loose.

248   **DON GENARO'S WATERFALL 5.4 ★**   This fun two-pitch route follows the water course that starts at the base of the waterfall chute below the overlook. It is seasonally barred from usage due to cascading water, but this same water flow has cut and smoothed a very sound crack/groove and has scoured a good dry-month climb.

Pitch 1 Ascend the obvious chute 75 feet to the next ledge.

Pitch 2 This pitch would come recommended except that its path is blocked by a monstrous poison oak bush. Careful maneuvering can get you around the bush, but your rope will drag right through it. Finish just right of the overlook, or walk off the top of the first pitch.

DOODLIN' DODY

photo: Kevin Kilpatrick

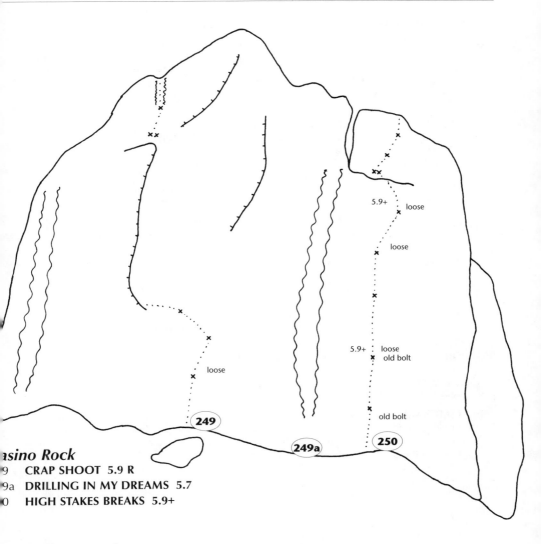

ısino Rock

9   **CRAP SHOOT 5.9 R**

9a   **DRILLING IN MY DREAMS 5.7**

0   **HIGH STAKES BREAKS 5.9+**

Casino Rock

Casino Rock is located on the hillside up and to the right of a switchback in the Condor Gulch Trail. The switchback is located at the overlook. Casino Rock is a large formation with a dark, black water streak on its lower right side. Hike directly up to the rock.

These routes are reportedly hair-raising leads on very questionable rock.

249   **CRAP SHOOT 5.9 R**

249a   **DRILLING IN MY DREAMS 5.7**   Ascend the water streak just left of **High Stakes Breaks** past five bolts.

250   **HIGH STAKES BREAKS 5.9+**

Also in the area:

251 **LOBSTER CLAW 5.4**   The 30-foot Lobster Claw is a distinct spire at the right/north-east end of a long jumble of rock formations to the east of Casino Rock. As you pass the overlook, the trail begins a long switchback east around the mountain. As the trail curves back northwest, the long jumble of rocks is to your right/east. Lobster Claw is the farthest away and on your left. A bolt and a small nut protect moves to a bolt on top.

252 **DOODLIN' DODY 5.7**   This 35-foot tall pinnacle is one of a cluster of three rocks to the left of the trail, just after it curves back right/north beyond the Lobster Claw. The cluster is opposite a lone rock located alongside the trail on the right, and to the west/downhill side of a larger formation on the same hillside. Start in the notch between Doodlin' Dody and the others in its cluster, spiral left (chocks may be used here) and up over two ledges, passing two bolts, to the top. There is a bolt on the summit. The other pinnacles have been climbed via fourth-class routes.

253 **PEANUTS**   This cluster of boulders is just left of the trail, a few hundred yards past Doodlin' Dody. The area has been used as a teaching area for belaying and practice moves.

254 **THE TOES 5.4**   This formation is part of the last group of boulders on the right, 200 feet before the Condor Gulch Trail intersects the High Peaks Trail. These two 30-foot boulders are situated downhill 100 yards, behind a group of smaller boulder/rocks, and from the trail they are slightly obscured from view. Both Toes have been led from the notch between them. The right/southeast Toe has a bolt to protect moves onto the front/west face. Originally, the other Toe was reached by a tyrolean from the southeast Toe.

255 **DIONYSIAN TOWERS 5.8**   On the way down to the Toes, you will notice several spires 100 feet to the south. Climb the largest pinnacle on its west face (visible from the trail) up third class ramps. A couple of fifth-class moves attains the summit and one bolt.

256 **JAMCRACK ROCK 5.6 A2**   This seldom sought-out rock is located in the southwest angle formed by the intersection of the High Peaks Trail and Condor Gulch Trail. From the same point on the Condor Gulch Trail where one would approach the Toes, head in the opposite direction to the top of the rounded ridge to the left. This lone rock is on the slope to the northwest. The route ascends the obvious vertical, bomb bay chimney on the downhill/south side. The aid is accomplished by a casual shoulder stand (if it was a bolt ladder it would be A1) to gain the chimney and a bolt above. Higher up, large protection can protect this 50-foot lead. Walk off the back side.

257 **THE ROOK – REGULAR ROUTE 5.7**   The Rook is two-thirds of the way from Condor Gulch and High Peaks Trail junction toward Chalone Creek picnic area. In other words, it is closer to the picnic area. It can be recognized by its resemblence to a rook (three battlements) from either the Chalone parking lot or from above the trail.

258 **THE ROOK – NORTH FACE 5.5**   This route ascends the uphill side. This, reputedly, is quite an enjoyable route. Unfortunately, the pinnacle is removed from the majority of Pinnacles climbing and sees little activity.

photo: Kevin Kilpatrick

The Toes

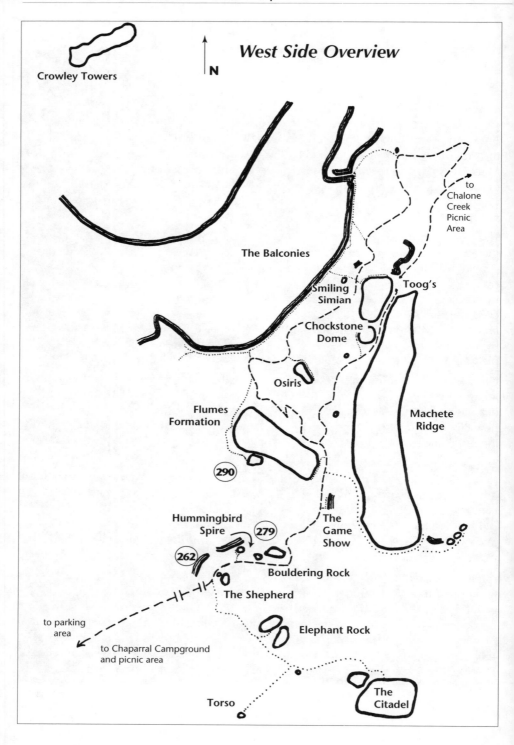

Crowley Towers

N

West Side Overview

The Balconies

to
Chalone
Creek
Picnic
Area

Smiling
Simian

Toog's

Chockstone
Dome

Osiris

Flumes
Formation

Machete
Ridge

290

Hummingbird
Spire

279

The
Game
Show

262

Bouldering Rock

The Shepherd

to parking
area

to Chaparral Campground
and picnic area

Elephant Rock

Torso

The
Citadel

WEST SIDE

The Pinnacles West Side area starts at the Chaparral Campground and Picnic Area and extends north along the Balconies Trail and/or the Balconies Cave Trail to the end of the deep valley formed by the massive walls of the Balconies and Machete Ridge. It includes all the formations approached from these trails. Several of the routes are located by counting the footbridges past the Chaparral Campground. In counting the bridges, do not include the one at the campground's north edge.

The West Side is utterly magnificent. As one drives into the Monument, glimpses of the formations only hint at the grandeur of this side. While the East Side is relatively spread out, the West Side is a compact valley of monolithic walls interspersed with smaller formations. The Balconies cliff is a colorful 200- to 500-foot face broken up by a succession of black water streaks. Occasionally, golden eagles and prairie falcons nest on the cliff and their piercing cries can be heard. Facing the Balconies is an equally awe-inspiring formation: Machete Ridge. This 700-foot wall is subdivided by several horizontal ledge systems that run the length of the cliff, providing a pleasing contrast to the vertical lines of the Balconies' water streaks.

Contrary to the beauty of this side is the general quality of the rock. Although there are a number of excellent routes, the rock is looser than on the East Side, but this has not slowed first ascensionists, whose tenacity has produced a wide array of new climbs. Climbing on the West Side can be a sure-fire test of your love of climbing at Pinnacles.

The West Side offers some of the longest routes in the monument. **Machete Direct** (5.8 A2 or 5.12) for many years has been a popular route for climbers practicing for a big wall. This route, combined with the **West Face**, offers six pitches of mixed climbing if done as an aid route (although the aid is a series of somewhat unsettling old bolt ladders). As a free climb, the first four pitches involve some very difficult and overhanging cruxes. On the Balconies, **Shake and Bake** (5.10a) and **Lava Falls** (5.9), both multi-pitch waterchutes, provide classic, water-scrubbed groove climbing.

On a shorter note, **Elephant Rock** (5.6) is an excellent adventure for the climber looking for a distinct summit. This spire stands as sentinel as you enter the depths of the valley. With good imagination and intense scrutiny, a long-nosed beast can be defined on this jutting rock. **Destiny aka Dos Equis** (5.8) is a wonderful, well-protected one-pitch waterchute on great rock. For the "clip and go" enthusiast, **Jeopardy** (5.12b/c), **Truth or Consequences** (5.12a) and the first pitch of **Machete Direct** (5.12a) will engage the inspired leader in some worthy cruxes.

The Shepherd Area

259 **THE TORSO aka The Cigar 5.9+ or 5.5 A2** From the Chaparral Campground, walk east up the ridge toward the high peaks. This isolated spire is just below (northeast), a few hundred yards up the hillside. From the ridgeline directly above the rock, make your way to the south side start. This route is notoriously crumbly. Follow discontinuous cracks until they lead to bolts on the upper bulge. Friends help supplement the bolts for protection. The original ascent used approximately 17 pitons, plus the bolts, to protect this devious pitch.

260 **THE SHEPHERD 5.11 or 5.4 A1** This formation often is overlooked as climbers hurriedly make their way to the more popular routes. Located just past the second footbridge at the junction of the climbers' access trail to The Elephant and The Citadel, it is just right of, and alongside, the Balconies Trail. On its trail side, a smaller 18-foot boulder juts up close to the main rock. The route starts on the boulder's south side and climbs 5.1 past several bolts to its top. Two closely-spaced bolts on the main rock protect climbing (5.11 or A1 off the boulder) to its south shoulder. There is one ⅜-inch bolt on top. An easy third class descent takes you off the back/east side to the stream bed behind. In spite of an abundance of lichen, this route has some challenging free moves.

261 **THE LAMB 5.0** This route follows the easy waterchute on The Shepherd's west side. There is one bolt near the bottom; this route's upper half is a solo. It would make a nice toprope for a beginner as the rock is fairly sound.

262 **PASSION PLAY 5.7 ★** This is a short water streak on a rock that rises out of the creek about 50 feet past the second foot bridge and opposite The Shepherd. Two bolts protect fun climbing up the streak to a mass of bolts (pre-dating the first lead) for the belay. A short walk off to the left, toward the campground, returns you to the **Balconies Trail.**

photo: Kevin Kilpatrick

Tom Davis on **Truth or Consequences**

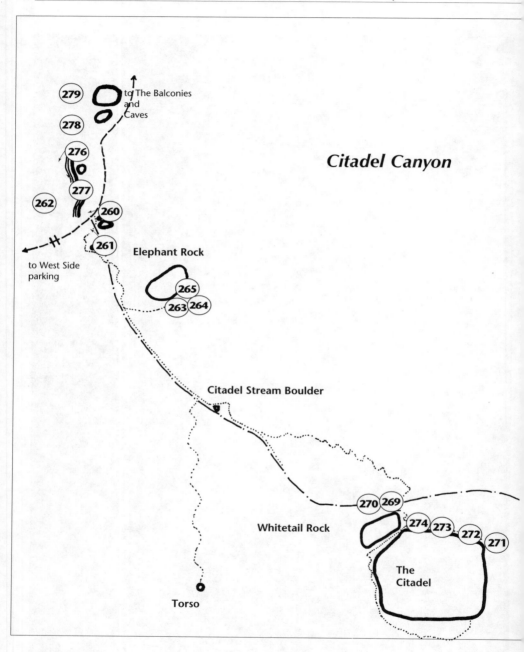

Citadel Canyon

279

278

276

277

262

260

261

to The Balconies
and
Caves

to West Side
parking

Elephant Rock

265

263 264

Citadel Stream Boulder

270 269

274 273

272

271

Whitetail Rock

The
Citadel

Torso

CITADEL CANYON

Elephant Rock

Many climbers have spent intense moments puzzling out the likeness of a pachyderm on the face of this large spire. Whether or not a likeness is discovered, the scrutiny undoubtedly will flex the creativity muscle. Besides its enigmatic name, the formation sports some nice climbing. The **Regular Route**, in particular, is a wonderful jaunt for a beginner or anyone wanting an exposed and lofty summit. There is, supposedly, an aid line of unknown difficulty going up the west face.

A designated access trail, just past the second footbridge, provides a direct path to the spire's south toe. Careful third-class climbing gets you into the notch on the rock's southeast, uphill side and the start of all routes.

263　**MOUSETRAP　5.10a TR**　This route follows the rappel line, providing an easy toprope.

264　**ELEPHANT CRACK　5.7 ★**　For an adventurous direct start.

265　**REGULAR ROUTE　5.6 ★★**　Small protection can be used in the thin crack after the initial chimney.

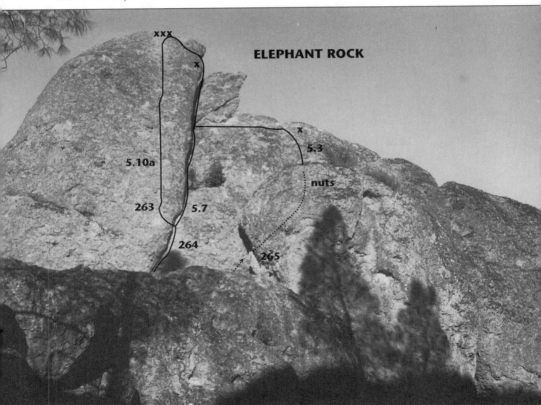

photo: Kevin Kilpatrick

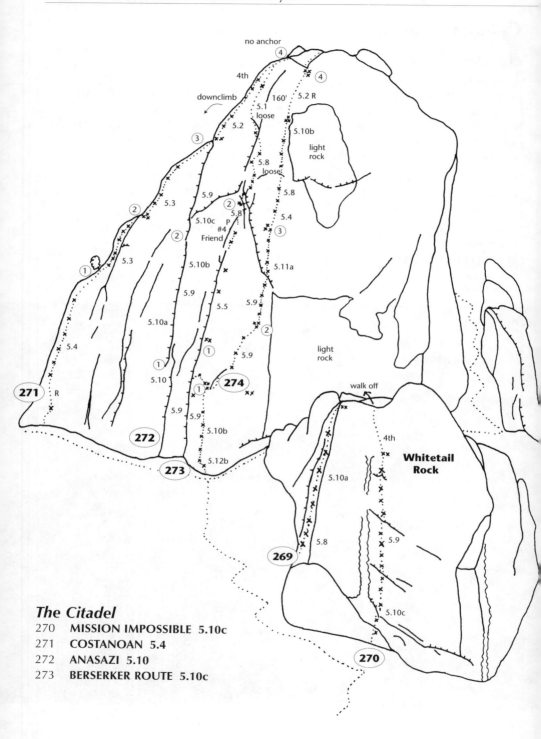

no anchor

④

4th

④

downclimb

160'   5.2 R

5.1
loose

5.2

5.10b

③

light
rock

5.8
loose

②

5.8

5.9

②   5.8

5.10c   P
#4
Friend   ③

5.4

②

5.3

①

5.3

5.10b

5.11a

5.9

②

5.10a

5.5   5.9

5.4

①   ①   5.9

5.10   ①   **274**

271   R

light
rock

5.9   5.9   walk off

272

5.10b   ×x

4th

273   5.12b   **Whitetail
Rock**

5.10a

269   5.8   5.9

5.10c

270

The Citadel
270   **MISSION IMPOSSIBLE 5.10c**
271   **COSTANOAN 5.4**
272   **ANASAZI 5.10**
273   **BERSERKER ROUTE 5.10c**

Citadel Stream Boulder

This boulder lies directly in the streambed alongside the trail to The Citadel, and is easily recognized by its scrubbed north face. Excessive scrubbing and unnecessary and damaging "trail maintenance" (sawn plant limbs and carved trails), from this boulder to The Citadel, stand as an example of the extreme efforts of a few climbers to gain notoriety. Acts like these very nearly imperiled the freedom climbers have enjoyed to climb when and where they will at Pinnacles.

266 **CITADEL STREAM BOULDER – EAST FACE 5.10** Two-bolt anchor on top.

267 **CITADEL STREAM BOULDER – NORTH FACE LEFT 5.10** An oak tree can be used for an anchor.

268 **CITADEL STREAM BOULDER – NORTH FACE RIGHT 5.9**

Whitetail Rock

This 100-foot formation stands directly below The Citadel's massive west face. Follow the obvious trail up Citadel Canyon until it passes directly under the rock's northwest face and the start of **Mission Impossible. Peon's Delight** is 50 feet uphill on the rock's north face.

269 **PEON'S DELIGHT 5.10a**

270 **MISSION IMPOSSIBLE 5.10c** A belay is recommended for the short fourth-class scramble to the top.

The Citadel

This massive rock, with its 400-foot wall, stands at the head of the canyon. The majestic formation is at the end of the worn approach trail, just uphill from Whitetail Rock. This is a great place to climb on a hot day, as all routes lie on the north face. One either can descend via a rappel down **Power Tools** or precariously downclimb off the uphill, southeast shoulder. Extreme care must be taken in the loose scramble down to the top bolts on **Power Tools**.

271 **COSTANOAN 5.4**

272 **ANASAZI 5.10**

273 **BERSERKER ROUTE 5.10c** This route is exceptionally loose and scary.

274 **POWER TOOLS 5.11a**

275 **POWER CORRUPTS 5.12b** Several of the initial holds may have been chiseled prior to the first lead.

Hummingbird Spire

This obscure spire is 100 yards downstream from the second footbridge on the Balconies Trail. Approach either by walking the streambed past **Passion Play** and scrambling up a break to the base of the spire, or continuing over the rise between **Passion Play** and **The Shepherd** to a trail on the left that makes its way down to the streambed and the break.

Buckwheats Bender starts on the lower south toe of the spire, just as you reach the rock. The **West Face** starts on the uphill side in the notch between the main wall and the spire. The **West Face** is approached by an easy fifth-class corner up the left/south side of the spire to the notch, or a third-class walk up the right side.

276 **WEST FACE 5.7** ★ This is a thrilling route. Chimney out of the notch to a bolt on the spire and step onto the spire itself. Face climb to the top.

277 **BUCKWHEATS BENDER 5.7 R** This route follows three bolts up the south shoulder. The first bolt is a long way up. Knobs possibly can be slung and TCUs placed on this serious lead on very loose rock.

Also in the area:

278 **BOULDERING ROCK 5.0 to 5.10+** ★ This fine practice area is located just over the rise past the second footbridge in an open area just left of the trail. Its long south face provides a whole array of climbing of varied difficulty on excellent rock. The overhanging north side offers more difficult climbing on slightly looser rock. Two bolts are on top of southwest face.

279 **THE ROOKIE 5.10+ TR** This 25-foot boulder lies next to and north of Bouldering Rock. An easy scramble up its south side enables one to set up a toprope on the northwest face. Three bolts are on top. Long runners needed to get over the edge.

The Game Show

This short wall offers two fierce clip-ups: **Truth or Consequences** and **Jeopardy.** Continue past The Rookie and the third footbridge to a short trail leading 30 feet downhill to this wall, which rises directly out of the streambed. A ten-foot roof with a crack splitting its right side caps the wall. A toprope can be set up by hiking up to a pine tree 50 feet above the wall and rappelling to the belay bolts directly above both routes and below the roof crack. If either climb is led, clip into the single bolt at the top of the route and traverse to the top bolt of the other route using both for a toprope anchor. There are several other possible topropes along this wall.

280 **JEOPARDY 5.12b** ★★ A spotter is recommended to the first bolt. This route packs a lot in for its length.

281 **TRUTH OR CONSEQUENCES 5.12a/b** ★★ Again, a spotter is recommended to the first bolt. A surprisingly difficult crux.

282 **VANNA 5.10+ TR** This climb is loose.

282a **CAME IN SECOND 5.10b** This is a five-bolt route 20 feet right of **Vanna**. It is a little loose. Closest belay tree is loose, use both trees.

282b **GLORIOUS 5.7 TR** Just right of Came in Second. Follow the obvious crevice and short face to the top.

Flumes Formation

This formation is to the left/west just after passing the fourth footbridge, and is marked by the obvious, deep chimney of **Flimsy Flume** on its left/south end. Most of the climbing on this formation involves loose rock with poor protection. Of recommendation is **Tilting Terrace**. This two-pitch route leads to a lush terrace that is perfect for a mid-climb picnic in the spring. This fun route is located halfway up the wall's north face. Continue up the Balconies Trail from the junction bridge (not into

THE GAME SHOW

xx

5.12a

5.11

5.12b/c

5.10+

282a

282b

280

281

282

the caves) and take the left branch at the third switchback. The travel-worn path of this route diagonals up and left.

Descend from all routes on the Flumes Formation by walking off the backside and skirting around the rock's northwest flank back to the Balconies Trail.

283 **FEEDING FRENZY 5.11a R** This loose route starts out of the cave-like grotto around the formation's southeast side. It is approached by skirting along to the left of **Flimsy Flume** and tunneling through to the amphitheater. **Feeding Frenzy** follows the rolling water streak out of the back/left side of the amphitheater for one pitch (5.9). The second pitch follows bolts in a water streak up and right (5.11a).

284 **THE GROTTO CHIMNEY 5th class** This chimney is just right of **Feeding Frenzy**. Little is known about this climb except that it was done. There are some bolts on this lead.

Flumes Wall

285 **FLIMSY FLUME 5.5 R/X** A hard-to-find bolt halfway up the chimney is the only protection on this route.

286 **FLAMES FACE 5.9 R** There is a double-bolt anchor with chains at the top of this route.

287 **DRIZZLY DRAIN 5.5 R** This route can be protected with nuts and slung knobs.

288 **DRIZZLY DRAIN – DIRECT FINISH 5.9**

288a **BITS 'N PIECES 5.9 ★** Start 50 feet left of **Tilting Terrace**. Climb past seven bolts to the belay on **Tilting Terrace**. One bolt protects the traverse to the belay.

289 **TILTING TERRACE 5.8 ★★** As described in the introduction to the wall, this climb is a lot of fun. Knobs can be slung on the second pitch to supplement protection.

289a **ADAM'S APPLE 5.9 ★★** This route heads right, up the corner from the terrace of **Tilting Terrace**. Seven ⅜" bolts protect the climbing and a long runout up the ramp at the top takes you to the belay. Fourth or easy fifth-class climbing up and left leads to the top of the formation. Descend down the backside.

289b **RUMBLING RAMPART 5.6** This route ascends the back, south side of the Flumes Formation, 40 feet left of **Once Around The Backside**, in the corridor. Follows the prominent waterchute. Very loose. Rock is slightly better on the left after the third bolt (crux).

290 **ONCE AROUND THE BACKSIDE 5.10 ★** This short route lies on the west face of an unobtrusive boulder on the back/west side of the Flumes Formation. The climb can be approached from the descent of any of the Flumes Formation routes. It also can be reached by hiking up the Balconies Trail to a point where the trail veers right towards the Balconies. A steep trail runs up along the formation's northwest shoulder. Follow this up and over the ridge and down the other side to this boulder. (This is also the descent trail for the Flumes Formation climbs.)

FLUMES FORMATION
NORTH FACE

FLUMES FORMATION: NORTH FACE, TILTING TERRACE AREA

288a **BITS 'N PIECES 5.9 ★**
289   **TILTING TERRACE 5.8 ★★**
289a **ADAM'S APPLE 5.9 ★★**

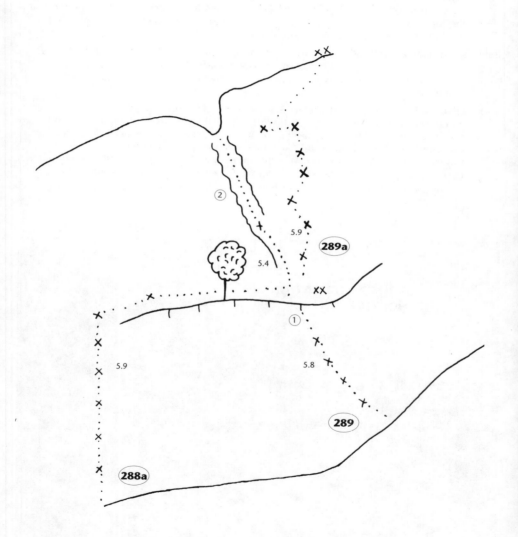

Follow four closely spaced bolts (originally used for aid) to gain a waterchute to the left. Two more bolts protect moderate climbing to several bolts on top. This route is a good mantel problem. Homemade hangers on the first two bolts, need small profile biners.

Crowley Towers

These formations are located on top and to the west of the upper tier of the Balconies Cliff. They are partially visible from the campground and easily viewed from the High Peaks. Although picturesque, the only known climbing on them is limited. All routes start on the backside and are listed from south to north. Follow game trails to the formations.

291 **CROWLEY TOWERS — TOWER 1 5.9**
From a ledge on the backside, climb the face past a bolt to the top.

292 **CROWLEY TOWERS — TOWER 2 3rd class**

293 **CROWLEY TOWERS — TOWER 3 5.5**
Twenty feet of crumbly climbing gains the summit. A downclimb is required to get off.

294 **CROWLEY TOWERS — TOWER 4 4th class** Either climb a few chimney moves or face moves to get started. Downclimb the route.

295 **CROWLEY TOWERS — TOWER 5 2nd class** The dominant chimney on the left side is easy (upon closer inspection).

295a **IF YOU BOLT IT THEY WILL COME 5.11a** ★ This is the left-hand of two parallel streaks on the upper west side tier of the Balconies—up and left of **Bongloadash**. See photograph on page 132.

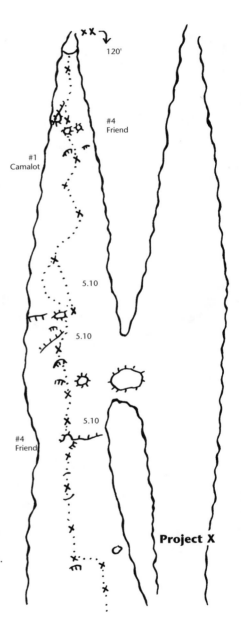

295a **IF YOU BOLT IT THEY WILL COME 5.11a**

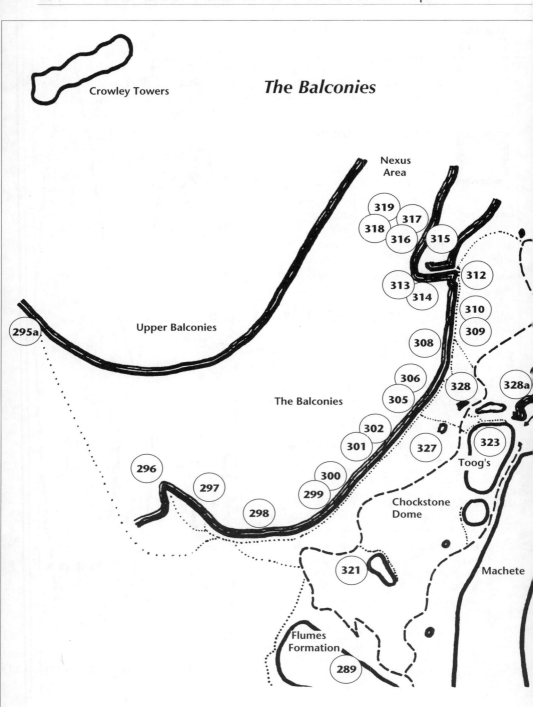

Crowley Towers

The Balconies

Nexus Area

319
318 317
316 315

313 312
314

310
309

Upper Balconies

295a

308

306
305 328 328a

The Balconies

302
301 327 323

Toog's

296

297

300
299

298

Chockstone Dome

Machete

321

Flumes Formation

289

THE BALCONIES AREA

The Balconies are a canvas on which climbers have painted a very unnerving picture. Its vertical chutes contain a handful of very sporty routes that relentlessly entice the leader farther and farther from security. This rap is not intended to thwart anyone's expectations. Rather, it's aimed at setting the foundation for the frame of mind needed to safely attack these lines. Most of the routes on the Balconies are marvelous examples of ingenuity and courage by climbers as they took on these long chutes. They just happened to have run a lot of them out in the process. When venturing on **Shake and Bake**, try to imagine Tom Higgins and Chris Vandiver rapidly scanning the vertical horizon for a no-hands stance on which they could drill while at least 20 feet out from the last bolt. **Lava Falls** is an amazing display of how moderate something so steep can be. At only 5.9, this long climb requires stern focus, as you master the gentle art of knob massage. The wild nature of the climbing, combined with the extraordinary beauty of this wall, provides an excellent opportunity for adventure.

One can't miss this south-facing wall, as it towers over the Balconies Trail. Follow the Balconies Trail until approximately even with the middle of the wall. A climbers' access trail, marked by a locking carabiner sign, leads up to the wall past **Smiling Simian**. Another access trail leads to the north end of the wall just past the **Even Coyotes Like it Doggie Style** formation (also marked by the carabiner sign). This trail also is the initial approach to all the climbs from **Knifeblade** through **Plexus** at the extreme northeast face of the Balconies. A single 160-foot rappel can be set up at the top of **Hook and Drill**.

296   **BONGLOADASH 5.8 R**   This scary and crumbly route lies in an obvious black waterchute immediately left of a chimney (which marks the beginning of The Balconies) at the Balconies' far south/left end. At the point where the trail turns away from the Flumes Formation, a gully runs directly uphill to an easy third-class slab leading to the base of the climb. Medium to large Friends in the bottom chimney make the lead a little safer. Above the chimney, four bolts provide protection to the top. There is a two-bolt anchor on top.

297   **PREMEDITATED 5.5 A4**   This serious aid route starts 30 feet right of **Bongloadash**, at the base of a horrendously loose-looking corner system. The intimidating reputation this route has earned makes one wonder if it really is so dangerous. On close observation, the need for a helmet becomes apparent on this long route. With the use of camming units, the route may be slightly more reasonable than with only pitons.

    Pitch 1   Climb 30 feet to a hidden bolt and move right into a very loose crack. Aid this for 60 feet to a two-bolt belay on a block.

    Pitch 2   Continue aiding up the crack a short distance, and either tension traverse or aid left to a left-facing book. Continue up to a large roof and a bolt belay 30 feet higher.

    Pitch 3   Continue aiding the roofs up and left to their end. Turn the roofs and continue up a rotten crack to a belay 35 feet higher.

    Pitch 4   More aiding and a few bolts gain the summit.

298   **WHERE THE BIRDS HANG 5.10 (incomplete)**   This obscure route ascends the low-angle apron on the Balconies' south shoulder. Start on the apron's left side, then diagonal up and right to the base of a dark waterchute at the top of the shoulder, about two-thirds up the wall. Supposedly, there are places to put Friends on this long pitch. Continue up to the chute at the top. This route is reported as incomplete.

photo: Kevin Kilpatrick

299 **PEREGRINE 5.12 or 5.9 A1** This climb is loose and scary.

300 **CONDUIT TO THE COSMOS 5.10d R ★★**

301 **PIPELOADS TO PLUTO 5.11c** This route is unfinished.

302 **LAVA FALLS 5.9 ★★★** Some #4 to #5 Rocks and slings to tie-off knobs augment the bolt protection on this route. The first 30 feet of the route are loose, but the rest is great.

303 **NO SENSE OF MEASURE 5.11b/c ★** Very steep.

304 **THE POWERS THAT BE 5.11b** The first pitch is loose. The second pitch is a quality lead. An improbable-looking line.

305 **ELECTRIC BLUE 5.11a R** Thin and sustained.

306 **SHAKE AND BAKE 5.10a R ★★★**

307 **ON THE THRESHOLD OF A SCREAM 5.10** Unfinished.

308 **BALCONIES — REGULAR ROUTE 5.10b** This historic route once was seen as a challenging aid route. Now, as a free climb, it remains a challenge, with its loose rock, bad bolts (at least the first pitch is a bolt ladder) and guano-laden corner system. This was the first route to successfully ascend the main, east face of Balconies. Beware of a large, loose block on the first pitch.

309 **DIGGER 5.10a R** This scary route is runout, dirty and loose. Hangers require narrow-gate carabiners.

310 **HOOK AND DRILL 5.9 R** This twin route to **Digger** is similar in nature.

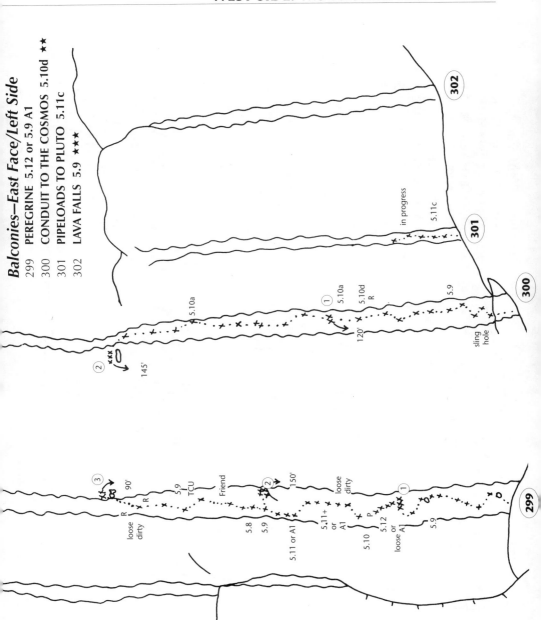

Balconies—East Face/Left Side

299   PEREGRINE 5.12 or 5.9 A1
300   CONDUIT TO THE COSMOS 5.10d ★★
301   PIPELOADS TO PLUTO 5.11c
302   LAVA FALLS 5.9 ★★★

Balconies—Right Side

300 CONDUIT TO THE COSMOS 5.10d ★★
302 LAVA FALLS 5.9 ★★★
303 NO SENSE OF MEASURE 5.11b/c ★
304 THE POWERS THAT BE 5.11b
305 ELECTRIC BLUE 5.11a
306 SHAKE AND BAKE 5.10a R ★★★
307 ON THE THRESHOLD OF A SCREAM 5.10
308 BALCONIES – REGULAR ROUTE 5.10b
309 DIGGER 5.10a R
310 HOOK AND DRILL 5.9 R
311 CRACK CLIMB 5.9 A1

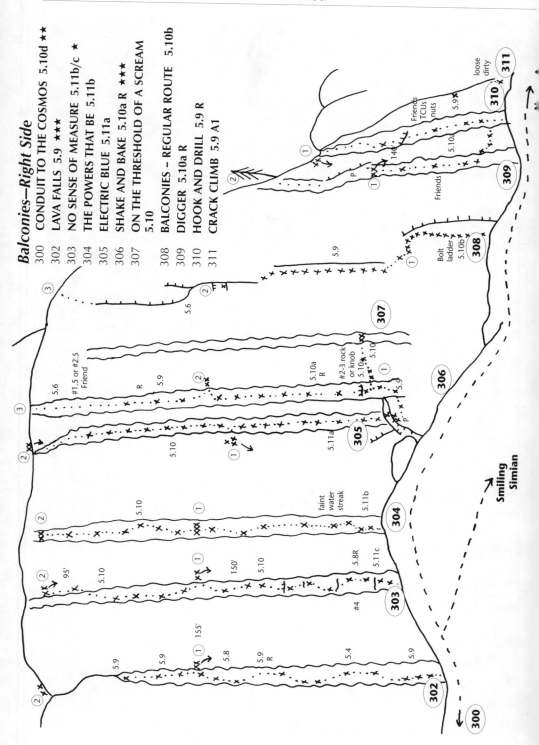

photo: Bruce Hildenbrand

Brian Sassone on **Twinkle Toes Traverse**

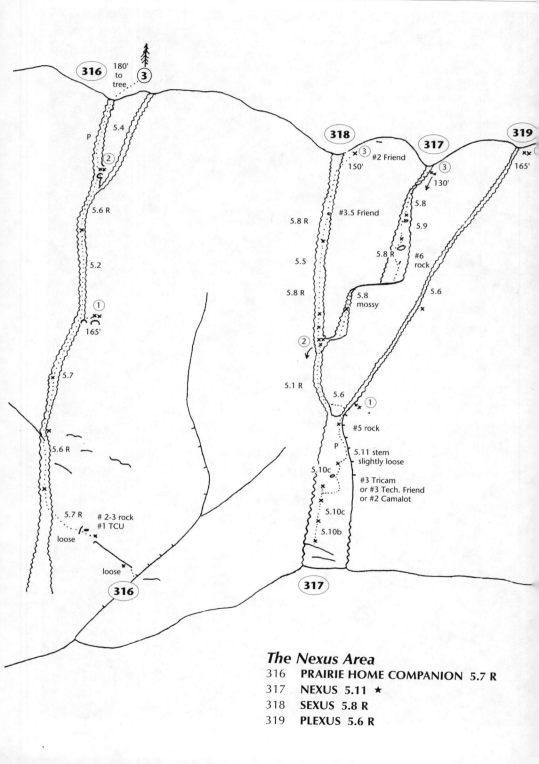

The Nexus Area

316 **PRAIRIE HOME COMPANION 5.7 R**
317 **NEXUS 5.11 ★**
318 **SEXUS 5.8 R**
319 **PLEXUS 5.6 R**

311 **CRACK CLIMB A3** This obscure route is rotten and dirty. It is unclear whether the route has gone beyond the third bolt. Due to the quality of rock, protection is poor on this climb. Although it has recently been climbed and given an A3 rating, this route is not for beginning aid climbers. Two sets of Friends (#1 to #4) and 20 pitons (Lost Arrows to 1½-inch angles) make up this aid rack.

312 **KNIFEBLADE DIRECT 5.8** This right-facing corner lies on the northeast shoulder of the Balconies formation. Follow the trail at the cliff's base to its far right/north end and drop down and left to the obvious corner. This crack takes one directly to the notch that separates The Knifeblade from the rest of the wall. This route is loose.

313 **THE KNIFEBLADE 5.5** This detached spire stands on top of the lower wall at the Balconies' north end. It can be approached directly by climbing **Knifeblade Direct** to the notch between it and the main wall, or by way of an intricate spiral to its back side. To approach the spire via the "spiral," continue along (northwest) the base of the Balconies, dropping down until one meets a huge and distinct boulder-filled corridor/cave. Scramble up the steep gully to a steeper mossy wall about 300 feet farther until it becomes necessary to traverse left (class three and/or four). Extreme caution is needed to avoid the thriving poison oak in this shaded haven. Pass a double-bolt anchor to the northeast ridge overlooking the Balconies Trail and **Hook and Drill.** Walk north along the ridge, passing a fifth-class gap, to a rappel station. Rappel 90 feet into the notch to the base of The Knifeblade. Climb up the exposed and sharp arête past one bolt to a two-bolt belay. One either can descend from the Knifeblade notch by climbing **Blade Runner** and reversing the "spiral" approach, or rappel (two ropes are necessary) from the notch down the northeast face.

314 **BLADE RUNNER 5.4** This two-bolt route ascends the face of the approach rappel into the notch below The Knifeblade.

315 **ECHOES 5.8** As one enters the corridor mentioned in the approach to The Knifeblade, a number of large chockstones fill the gully overhead. **Echoes** ascends the face beneath the largest chockstone, past two bolts, and continues out the large opening halfway up and past three more bolts. There is a two-bolt belay. This route can serve as an approach pitch to the **Nexus** Area. It also marvelously bypasses the poison oak.

The Nexus Area

This area lies at the head of the deep corridor mentioned in the approach to The Knifeblade. At the top of the gully, head up and right to a pleasant, grassy terrace with pine trees. **Nexus** is the obvious black waterchute rising out of the terrace's southwest corner.

Prairie Home Companion starts about 60 feet left of **Nexus**, diagonals up and left past several bolts on the low-angle part of the wall to a low-angle slab above. **Sexus** and **Plexus** start off the top of the first pitch of **Nexus**. Descend using the anchors on **Nexus**.

The **Nexus** Area is a wonderfully isolated and tranquil spot—a perfect place for a picnic. The climbing has potential, highlighted by the intimidating **Nexus** with its transparent bolts (almost impossible to see).

316 **PRAIRE HOME COMPANION aka Kachink 5.7 R** This climb is loose. The first pitch originally exited left along a ramp at the fourth bolt to the top of the east face of The Balconies.

317 **NEXUS 5.11 ★★** The rock is incredibly good on the third pitch. The first pitch is the most difficult lead at Pinnacles where bolts were placed from stance.

318 **SEXUS 5.8 R** Starts off the second pitch of **Nexus**.

319 **PLEXUS 5.6 R** Starts off the first pitch of **Nexus**.

The Front Row Area

The Front Row Area includes all routes and formations approached from the Balconies Trail, starting at the sharp right turn after the north face of the Flumes Formation and continuing to the end of The Balconies. These crags provide excellent climbing on some of the most sound rock on the west side. Smiling Simian is a wonderful little boulder with three fun routes of varied difficulty. All are easily toproped as well as led. **Toog's Trailside** will unnerve you with its steep, traversing start.

Osiris

Osiris is the first prominent formation on the right after the Balconies Trail curves away from the Flumes Formation and begins to parallel The Balconies. Its multi-layered mass provides one easy and one hard route. There are two bolts on top for belaying and for the rappel down the uphill side.

320 **REGULAR ROUTE 4th class** This long jaunt starts on the downhill side facing Machete Ridge. It begins at two pine trees and wanders up the sloping east face to the top.

321 **ESCAPE FROM SOLEDAD 5.10 R** ★ This challenging route starts on the right side of the uphill/northwest face. Follow three bolts up the steep face. It's a dangerously long way to the first bolt.

photo: Kevin Kilpatrick

photo: Kevin Kilpatrick

Upper Toog's Formation

These routes are located on the uphill side of Toog's, the large formation which slopes down from The Balconies Trail to the caves at the base of the north end of Machete Ridge. It is the next formation on the right, 200 yards after passing Osiris. To get off, rappel down the uphill/trailside face of **Toog's Trailside**.

322 **TOOG'S TERROR 5.2**   This is the easiest way to get to the top of Toog's. From the point where Toog's meets the Balconies Trail, head down and left 200 feet along the base of the formation until directly below a pine tree on the upper face. Start at an oak tree and climb the mossy slope. Above, move up and left to the pine tree. Climb the tree, then walk left and scramble up a short section to the summit.

323 **TOOG'S TRAILSIDE 5.10a R ★**   This sporty route starts on the uphill side of Toog's opposite the access trail leading past Smiling Simian to The Balconies. It follows a line of five bolts up the undercut face. Difficult entry moves over the initial bulge gain the main face. Move left and continue climbing 5.8 to the top.

323a **TOOG'S TRAILSIDE DIRECT 5.10c**   Climb past a bolt directly up to the second bolt on the original route.

Smiling Simian

This 30-foot boulder is located directly 50 feet uphill from Toog's and marks the designated central access trail to The Balconies. The rock is excellent on this formation; all routes are recommended. **Smiling Simian** and **Little Big Dog** are located on the uphill side facing The Balconies. See locator map on page 146.

324 **EASY ROUTE 4th Class** This line goes up the lower-angle, downhill northeast face. It is commonly used as an approach to set up topropes and as a downclimb.

325 **SMILING SIMIAN 5.8** ★ Climb up the middle of the northwest face past two bolts.

326 **LITTLE BIG DOG 5.10c/5.11a** ★ Fifteen feet right of **Smiling Simian**, the rock becomes undercut. Climb up the left side of the undercut to a bolt. Move up and right to a second bolt on the shoulder and continue to the top. It's a little far to the first bolt and the start is the crux. The route can be climbed to the left of the undercut (5.10c) to get to the first bolt.

326a **WINDMILLS 5.11c TR** Climb just right of the arête left of **No Smiles**.

327 **NO SMILES 5.10a R** ★ This bold lead surmounts the overhang 15 feet right and around the corner from **Little Big Dog**. Climb over the right side of the undercut and past two bolts.

photo: Kevin Kilpatrick

photo: Kevin Kilpatrick

327a **BAD APE 5.10+ TR** ★ Start in the overhanging chute to the right of **No Smiles**.

328 **EVEN COYOTES LIKE IT DOGGIE STYLE 5.10a** ★ This trailside formation is on the left, 100 yards past Toog's. This climb starts off the trail up the southeast face, past five bolts. The crux is the final bulge.

328a **STANCE DANCE 5.10 R** Climb past three bolts on the southeast side of the formation below **Even Coyotes Like It Doggie Style**.

Balconies Caves Trail

This section includes all formations—other than Machete Ridge—that are approached from the Balconies Caves Trail, starting at the intersection of the Caves Trail and the Balconies Trail at the fifth footbridge. It continues north to the far side of the caves. After emerging from the first section of the caves, a circuitous third-class scramble up and right enables one to avoid the black pit of the second section. See locator maps on pages 130 and 146.

329 **SOMBRERO 5.8** This is the 20-foot boulder up and right/northeast 50 feet from the junction bridge. It is perched above the trail and surrounded by oak trees. A two-bolt

route makes its way up the south face. A rappel can be set up off the oak which over-hangs the rock.

330 **WILD MEXICAN 5th class** This boulder problem is located to the left of the trail a short way past **Sombrero** and just before Chockstone Dome and the entrance to the caves. Climb the side facing the trail, starting on a small platform rock, and execute a few unprotected but easy fifth-class moves. Scramble to the top.

Chockstone Dome

Chockstone Dome is the large boulder wedged above the Caves Trail and marks the entrance to the caves. Two routes lie on the southwest side and are approached from either the Balconies Trail or the Caves Trail. All routes start off boulders leaning against the rock's west face. **Walk the Plank** is to the left and the **Regular Route** is to the right.

331 **WALK THE PLANK 5.6 ★★** Six bolts.

331a **OVERBOARD 5.8 ★★** Shares first bolt with **Walk the Plank**, then straight up past five more.

332 **REGULAR ROUTE 5.3 ★★** A thoroughly enjoyable romp. Two bolts.

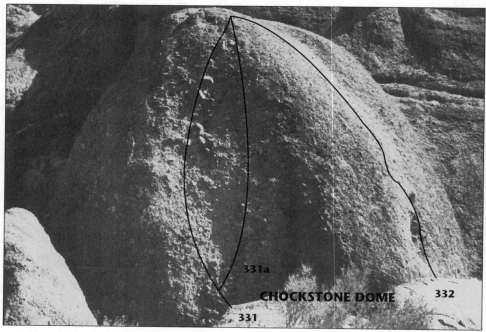

CHOCKSTONE DOME

331a

331

332

photo: Kevin Kilpatrick

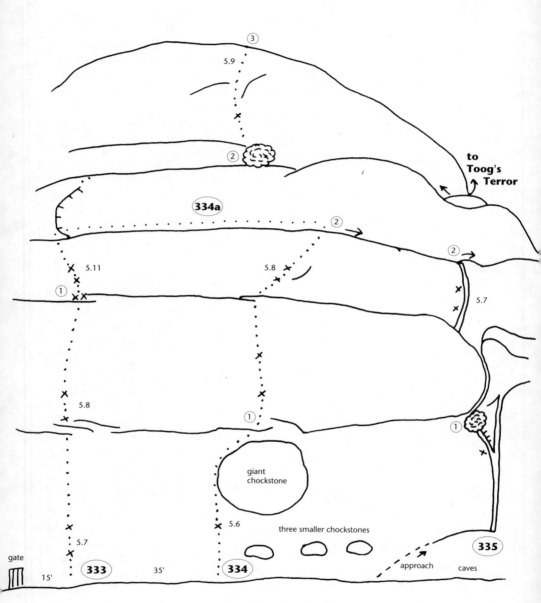

Lower Toog's Formation

333 **KAMIKAZE KOMMUTE 5.11a** ★
334 **TOOG'S GALLERY 5.7** ★
334a **TOOG'S GALLERY DIRECT VARIATION 5.9** ★
335 **TOOG'S ALLIGATOR 5.7** ★

Lower Toog's Formation

This formation is the lower, east toe of Toog's which forms the left/west wall of the caves. Several multi-pitch routes rise out of the caves, offering imaginative climbing from shadows into the sun. **Kamikaze Kommute** follows a faint water streak that rises about 15 feet beyond the caves' gate. **Toog's Gallery** starts about 35 feet right of the **Kommute** and climbs past the left side of the massive chockstone above. To get to the start of **Toog's Alligator**, enter the caves, pass under three low-lying chockstones and scramble up and left over boulders to the base of a chimney. For both **Toog's Alligator** and **Toog's Gallery**, one can either finish up the tree on **Toog's Terror** or traverse back left to meet **Kamikaze Kommute** on the final headwall. Take care not to knock off rocks on the hikers below.

333   **KAMIKAZE KOMMUTE 5.11a** ★   On top of the second pitch, belay by placing an anchor in a horizontal crack near a bush.

334   **TOOG'S GALLERY 5.7** ★   Assorted camming devices are needed for belays.

334a **TOOG'S GALLERY DIRECT VARIATION 5.9** ★   Follow **Toog's Gallery** to the second belay, traverse left to finish of **Kamikaze Kommute**. Two new bolts protect the direct finish (5.9). There is an added belay bolt just past direct finish.

335   **TOOG'S ALLIGATOR 5.7** ★   A varied climb, including everything from face climbing to the limb-devouring "Alligator Chimney."

336   **TOOG'S TARBABY 5.8+**   Start in a black water streak just right of the Alligator Chimney on the second pitch of **Toog's Alligator**. Climb (5.8+) past a bolt about ten feet up. Continue to a ledge, and belay at a bush. Traverse right five or ten feet, and climb over a bulge and a bolt. Scramble up the slab to a second belay.

337   **POWERSLAVE 5.9**   Follow a trail that begins about 50 feet beyond the final exit from the caves on the left—just in front of a large boulder—and you'll come to the west corner of the enclosed gorge. Take care to avoid the prolific poison oak that populates the gorge. An obvious, scrubbed, left-facing corner leads to the top of the wall. This is **Powerslave**. Three bolts protect various bulges on the climb. A standard rack will supplement the fixed protection.

338   **THUNDERING HERD 5.4**   This hard-to-locate route is on a formation north of the far end of Toog's. After exiting the caves, continue on the trail for a few hundred yards until the wall curves uphill and left. Skirt along the base of the wall to its north side, searching for a left-running ramp that leaves the ground under some oaks. Upon discovering this elusive ramp, follow a line of bolts for 60 feet. Eventually, the slope eases to third and fourth class, and a belay is found about 60 feet farther. The second pitch climbs 45 feet up the slope above—with some delicate initial moves—to a roomy ledge below the final summit. Scramble up and left to the trail.

339   **TUGBOAT 5.6**   This route lies on a lone rock north of the north junction of the Caves Trail and the Balconies Trail. From the intersection, walk north on the Old Pinnacles Trail several hundred yards; branch up and right/east along the hillside to this isolated formation. Starting on the left side of the west face, climb third class up and right to the base of a groove in the middle of the face. Two bolts protect climbing up the groove. From the second bolt, move right and climb 45 feet to the top. Rappel off the backside.

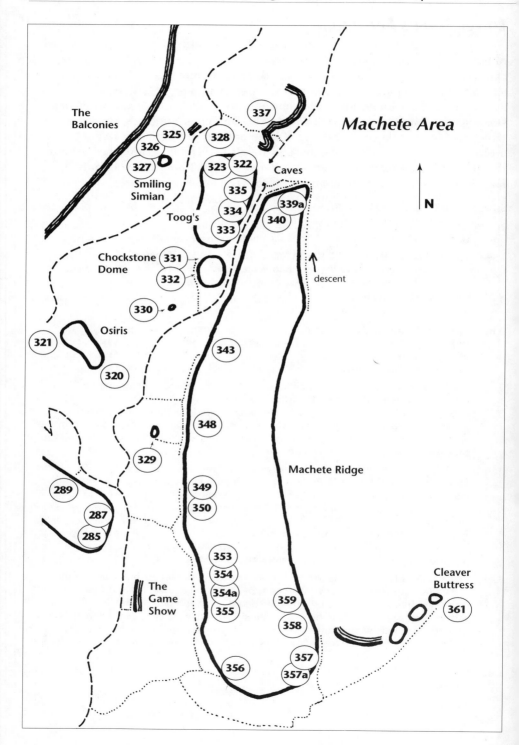

Machete Area

MACHETE RIDGE AREA

This magnificent wall rivals The Balconies in stature. Its sharp, angular ridge-line seems to score the sky, spires and turrets jut up along the edge. As with The Balconies, Machete Ridge provides a number of multi-pitch routes, as well as a handful of single-pitch climbs along the base. **Old Original** is an absolute must for those seeking an easy day-long adventure. Traversing the length of the ridge, this sidewalk in the sky is an airy multi-pitch excursion. Be sure to bring some edibles, as the final pitch ends at a merry picnic ledge. **Machete Direct** is a super free climb as well as an excellent practice aid climb. The first pitch, specifically, offers strenuous free climbing (5.12a) past the old aid ladder.

The descent for both the **West Face** and **Old Original** is made by rappelling off a series of bolts and a block into the gully just to the east (at the routes end). Follow a steep and dangerous third-class trail down the gully, traversing over some treacherous slabs. There are optional rappels available, off trees, to avoid the most treacherous sections. This descent takes one to the north end of the caves.

All routes ending on Badman Mezzanine descend via rappel anchors at the top of **Bandits in Bondage** (two 165-foot ropes needed).

339a **CUIDADO! 5.10+** ★★ Although this route is reportedly sound, there is still loose rock on it. It is recommended that one bring a stuff sack and haul the rock out to avoid dropping any on the Cave Trail below. This climb should only be climbed on weekdays and a "sentry" posted to warn people of the climbing above. Climbers should also be prepared to pause while hikers pass below. To approach the climb go past the metal gate and the two chockstones at the base of Toog's. Cutback right, third or fourth class, to grass bench with an oak tree. The tree is the belay for the first pitch. See topo page 148.

340 **TIBURCIO'S AMBUSH 5.2** Little is known about this route, except that it gets you from one side of Machete to the other. Approach by scrambling over boulders up and right at the first exit from the caves, and follow an indistinct trail to Machete's north end and the traversing ledge. One also can get to the ledge by way of **Ambush Cutoff.** Several pitches with possible bush belays lead to the pine tree on the left side of Badman Mezzanine.

341 **AMBUSH CUTOFF 5.7 R** Assorted nuts and camming units are needed. This route goes above the trail.

342 **FLIES ON A PILE 5.9** This route goes above the trail.

343 **MACHETE DIRECT 5.12a or 5.8 A2** ★★★ The second pitch is runout.

344 **MY MISTAKE 5.8 X** This variation is very dangerous.

345 **WEST FACE 5.12+ or 5.7 A2** This bolt ladder, when originally freed, was humbly rated 5.11c. In a committed attempt by the author and a friend, it was decided that it is definitely 5.12 climbing past desperate bolt-ladder clips. This route is a long traverse to the top of the fourth pitch of **Machete Direct**, where you can gain access to the north towers on Machete. To start the route walk uphill 100 feet past **Destiny** to a prominent waterchute/gully that leads back up and left. Follow the chute until it dead-ends at a headwall above **Destiny**, where two aid bolts on the right lead to the traversing ledge.

346 **TOWER BYPASS VARIATION 5.6** Poor protection and loose rock.

347 **SWANSON'S CRACK 5.10** The second pitch is unfinished.

348 **THE ARCH** This significant formation shelters numerous possibilities of traversing and bouldering.

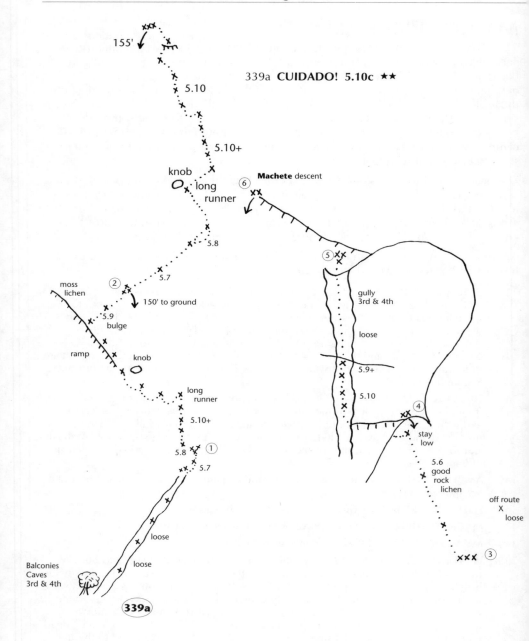

339a **CUIDADO! 5.10c** ★★

155'

5.10

5.10+

knob

long runner

Machete descent

⑥

5.8

5.7

② 150' to ground

moss lichen

5.9 bulge

ramp

knob

long runner

5.10+

5.8 ①

5.7

loose

loose

Balconies Caves 3rd & 4th

339a

⑤

gully 3rd & 4th

loose

5.9+

5.10

④

stay low

5.6 good rock lichen

off route X loose

③

349 **ALIAS BANDIT BENCH 5.8**   This route is located 100 feet up and right of The Arch and is identified by a short, right-facing corner with a bolt up and left at the top of the corner. The first bolt can be backed up by Friends in the arching crack to the right. Supposedly, there is an alternate first pitch, two-bolt belay on the left side of Badman Mezzanine.

350 **BANDITS IN BONDAGE 5.11a** ★★   Very sporty. Two ropes are needed to rappel off the double-belay bolts.

351 **UPPER BANDIT BENCH 5.10a R** ★   Although relatively easy, falling from the upper section of this pitch may result in hitting Bandit's Bench.

352 **BILL'S BAD BOLTS 5.7 A1**

352a **BILL'S BAD BOLTS DIRECT FINISH 5.8 R**   From the top of the first pitch continue directly up the top of Machete Ridge. Little is known about this route.

352b **YOUNG IN DEED 5.6 R**   Start directly below the top of the first pitch of **Twinkle Toes Traverse**. Climb straight up the face past two bolts to **Twinkle Toes** belay. Can be started from the beginning of **Twinkle Toes Traverse** for a safer lead.

353 **TWINKLE TOES TRAVERSE 5.6** ★★   The moves out of the corner on the first pitch can adequately be protected with nuts and camming units.

354 **DESTINY aka Dos Equis 5.8** ★★★

354a **CRACKAPHOBIA 5.10c**   A full crack rack is needed for this pitch.

354b **PIGEON CRACK AID ROUTE**   Little is known about this route except that it follows the obvious corner system which goes diagonally up and right on the main face.

355 **SON OF DAWN WALL 5.11b A1** ★   This route starts 100 yards uphill from **Destiny** and under several oaks. The first pitch is a bolt ladder and an excellent free pitch.

356 **DESPERADO CHUTEOUT 5.10 or 5.6 A1 R**   This long route is on the southwest shoulder of Machete and begins off the highest boulders against that side. Wander up and right from **Destiny** along the base of Machete. Intricate scrambling gets one up to the starting boulders. The hardest free moves are climbing past the bolt ladder at the beginning of the first pitch. Except for the start, all pitches of this climb are some-what loose.

357 **DENNY-COLLIVER FINISH 5.7** ★

357a **SERPIENTE DE CASCABEL 5.9 A1 or 5.10c**   Start right of a long overhanging water-chute and left of a huge rotten book (left of **Derringer**). Climb four pitches and then link up with **Desperado Chuteout**. See topo.

358 **DERRINGER 5.5-5.7 R** ★   This route runs up a series of waterchutes on Machete's southeast shoulder (facing The Citadel) and ends on the summit at the top of the first pitch of **Old Original**. Wind around the upper east side of Machete just below the start of **Old Original**, where a series of five pine trees grow along the base. Traverse left about 80 feet, just below the first pine tree, to a big pothole in a waterchute – and two bolts. Bolts have been added to this route (at the first ascensionist's request) making the lead a more reasonable endeavor. This line, combined with **Old Original**, would make a great day.

358a **DERRINGER – DIRECT START (BULLSEYE VARIATION) 5.5**   Start in a talus pile directly below the first belay. Starts atop a bomb bay chimney (hike around to right, do not climb chimney).

Machete Ridge

329 SOMBRERO 5.8
331 WALK THE PLANK 5.6 ★★
331a OVERBOARD 5.8 ★★
332 REGULAR ROUTE 5.3 ★★
340 TIBURCIO'S AMBUSH 5.2
341 AMBUSH CUTOFF 5.7 R
342 FLIES ON A PILE 5.9
343 MACHETE DIRECT 5.12a or 5.8 A2 ★★★
344 MY MISTAKE 5.8 X
345 WEST FACE 5.12 or 5.7 A2
346 TOWER BYPASS VARIATION 5.6 ★

347 SWANSON'S CRACK 5.10
348 THE ARCH
349 ALIAS BANDIT BENCH 5.8
350 BANDITS IN BONDAGE 5.11a ★★
351 UPPER BANDIT BENCH 5.10a R ★
352 BILL'S BAD BOLTS 5.9 A1
353 TWINKLE TOES TRAVERSE 5.6 ★★

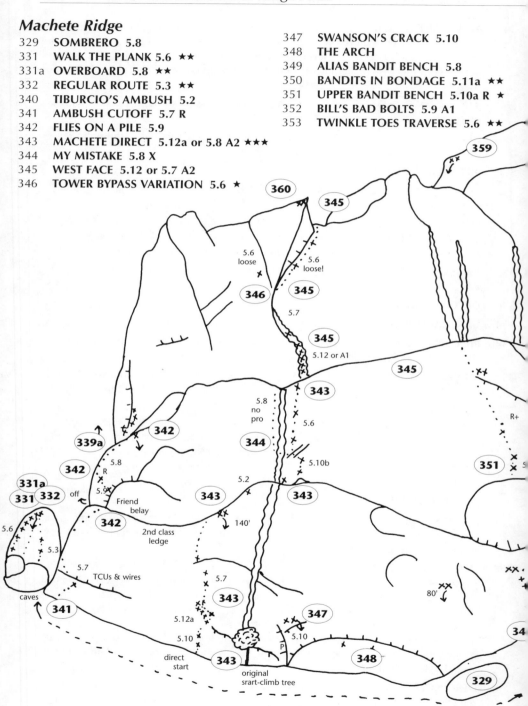

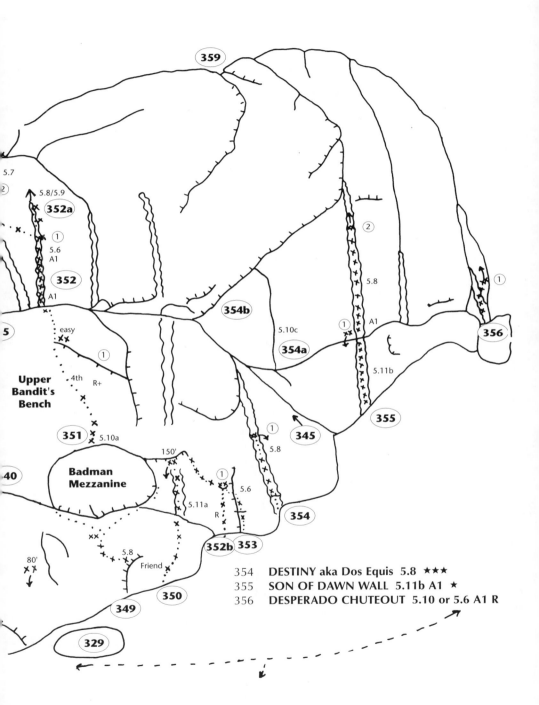

359

5.7

2

5.8/5.9

352a

1

5.6
A1

352

A1

2

5.8

1

A1

1

356

5.10c

354a

5.11b

5.8

354b

355

5

easy

Upper
Bandit's
Bench

1

4th   R+

1

5.8

345

351   5.10a

150'

40

**Badman
Mezzanine**

1

5.6

354

5.11a

R

352b   **353**

80'

5.8

Friend

350

349

329

354   **DESTINY aka Dos Equis 5.8 ★★★**
355   **SON OF DAWN WALL 5.11b A1 ★**
356   **DESPERADO CHUTEOUT 5.10 or 5.6 A1 R**

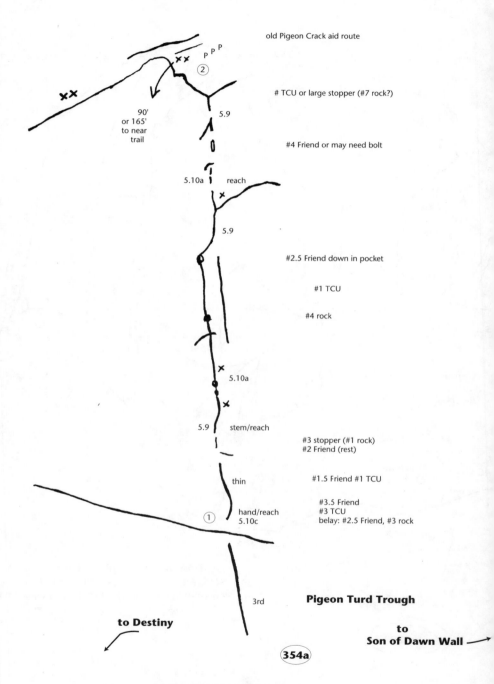

old Pigeon Crack aid route

TCU or large stopper (#7 rock?)

#4 Friend or may need bolt

#2.5 Friend down in pocket

#1 TCU

#4 rock

#3 stopper (#1 rock)
#2 Friend (rest)

#1.5 Friend #1 TCU

#3.5 Friend
#3 TCU
belay: #2.5 Friend, #3 rock

90'
or 165'
to near
trail

5.9

5.10a reach

5.9

5.10a

5.9 stem/reach

thin

hand/reach
5.10c

3rd

to Destiny

Pigeon Turd Trough

**to
Son of Dawn Wall** ⟶

354a

354a **CRACKAPHOBIA 5.10c**

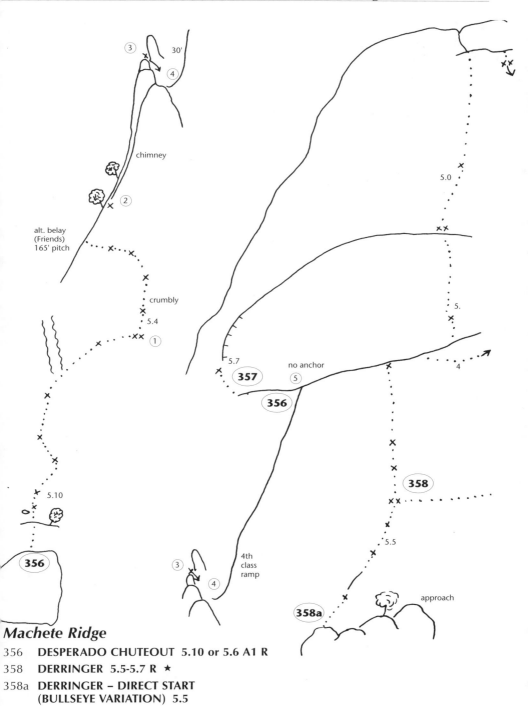

Machete Ridge

356   **DESPERADO CHUTEOUT 5.10 or 5.6 A1 R**

358   **DERRINGER 5.5-5.7 R ★**

358a   **DERRINGER – DIRECT START
        (BULLSEYE VARIATION) 5.5**

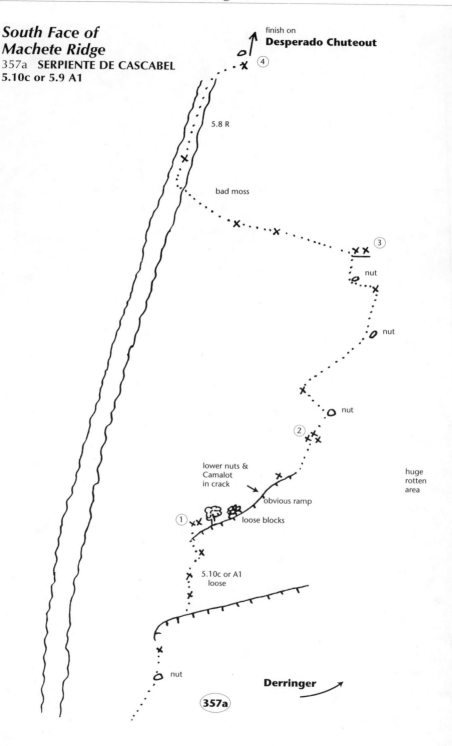

*South Face of
Machete Ridge*
357a **SERPIENTE DE CASCABEL**
5.10c or 5.9 A1

finish on
Desperado Chuteout

4

5.8 R

bad moss

3

nut

nut

nut

2

lower nuts &
Camalot
in crack

huge
rotten
area

obvious ramp

1

loose blocks

5.10c or A1
loose

nut

Derringer

357a

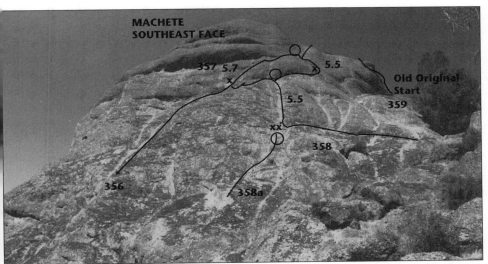

MACHETE
SOUTHEAST FACE

357 5.7

5.5

5.5

Old Original
Start
359

358

356

358a

photo: Kevin Kilpatrick

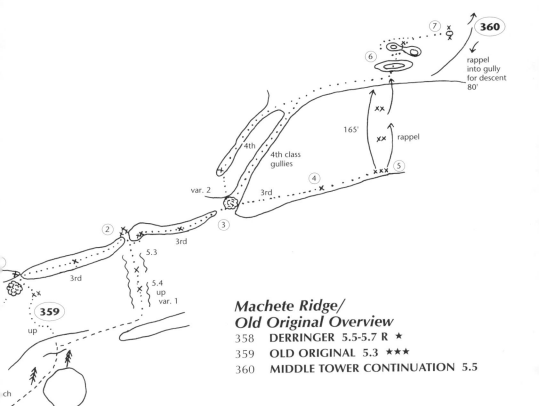

360

rappel
into gully
for descent
80'

7

6

xx

165'

xx rappel

4th

4th class
gullies

5

var. 2

3rd

4

2

3rd

3

3rd

5.3

5.4
up
var. 1

359

up

ch

Machete Ridge/
Old Original Overview

358 **DERRINGER** 5.5-5.7 R ★
359 **OLD ORIGINAL** 5.3 ★★★
360 **MIDDLE TOWER CONTINUATION** 5.5

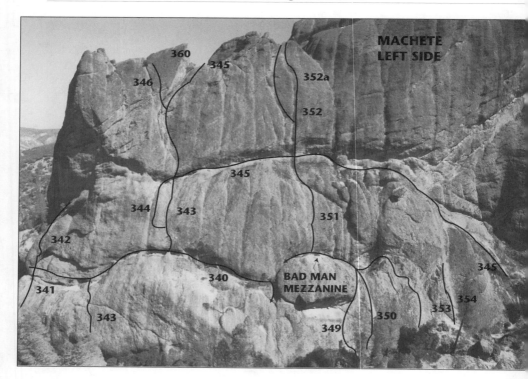

359 **OLD ORIGINAL 5.3** ★★★ This classic starts on the uphill east face of Machete. Approach as for **Derringer**, and continue all the way around to the uphill/east side to two pine trees. Scramble out of the notch between Machete Ridge and the lower boulders in the saddle. Both an overview map and a description are given for this horizontal route. See page 155 for map.

Pitch 1 Climb an unprotected slab (5.3) up and to the left to the actual ridge. Two bolts toward the top provide an interim belay and a rappel station back to the notch if needed.

Pitch 2 From the top of the ridge, walk north along the edge until it drops down into the next notch with belay bolts.

Pitch 3 Traverse around the bulge (5.3), pass a bolt, and continue down the ramp for 40 feet, passing another bolt, to a flat area. Climb up through the six-foot notch, and belay from a manzanita bush.

Pitch 4 Continue walking along the ridge for a full rope length to the first rappel station and three bolts.

Pitch 5 Two 165-foot ropes enable one to make a single rappel northwest to the ridge below. Two intermediate rappel stations exist to facilitate single-rope rappels, although the anchors are not nearly as good. From the bottom of the rappel, walk over a small rise to the base of twin towers with a U-shaped notch between them.

Pitch 6 Climb through the notch (5.3) and fourth-class down the other side. A bolt is just on the other side of the notch. Walk to the base of the next pointed tower,

photos: Kevin Kilpatrick

which marks the top of the **West Face**. A three-foot block with a bolt on either side marks the final descent rappel station.

Variation 1 – The Hideout 5.4 ★ At the start of the initial approach pitch to **Old Original**, walk 50 feet down and right. Staying close to Machete, walk past a pine tree into a narrow corridor. A sound waterchute leads up to the belay at the end of the third pitch. Two bolts protect this fun alternative.

Variation 2 – Rappel Bypass 4th class Two fourth-class gullies descend down and to the left from the manzanita at the end of the third pitch, offering a way to avoid the rappel. The right-hand gully is the obvious one leading down from the bush. The left-hand gully starts about 30 feet over the rise behind the bush. A bolt protects the entry moves into the gully. Follow both gullies down and right to the base of the double spire. It is advised to stay roped for these alternatives.

360 **MIDDLE TOWER CONTINUATION 5.5** ★ Two bolts protect interesting climbing up the middle tower just north of the final rappel station. There are bolts on top. Continue (fourth class) to the final tower (where a register is located) for a complete traverse of the ridge. Rappel off the **Middle Tower** bolts to the base.

360a **MIDDLE TOWER ARETE 5.9 TR** ★ An interesting and exposed toprope problem can be done on the arête just left of the standard middle tower line.

Also in the area:

361 **CLEAVER BUTTRESS 5.7** This seldom-visited pinnacle is located farther up on the saddle, past the start to **Old Original** and **Derringer**. To approach, don't hug the base of Machete Ridge when hiking up. Instead, head up and right around the large pinnacle toward the drainage. Continue up the hillside to the highest formation in the series of pinnacles just east of Machete. A 30-foot waterchute draining from the base of a cleft splitting the pinnacle marks the start of the route.

Pitch 1 Climb the waterchute past two bolts to a small tree at the base of the chimney.

Pitch 2 Climb the chimney above past two very elusive bolts. Climb down and around the prow of the buttress, and back up to another bolt. Head up and slightly left to the fourth bolt. Easy climbing above leads to the summit. Scramble down the backside to get off.

Variation 1 From the second bolt on the second pitch, continue straight up onto the buttress.

*uce **Hildebrand** on **The Shaft***

photo: Bruce Hildebrand Collection

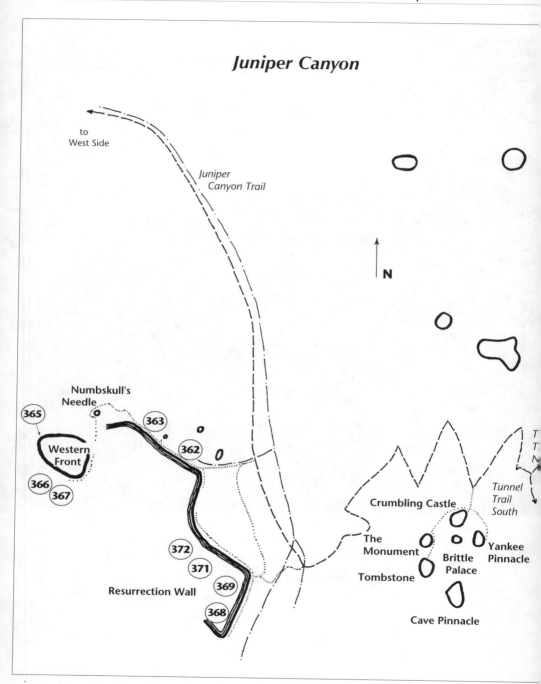

Juniper Canyon

to
West Side

*Juniper
Canyon Trail*

N

Numbskull's
Needle

365

363

362

Western
Front

366

367

372

371

369

368

Resurrection Wall

Crumbling Castle

The
Monument

Tombstone

Brittle
Palace

Yankee
Pinnacle

Cave Pinnacle

Tunnel
Trail
South

T
T
N

JUNIPER CANYON

Juniper Canyon is the deep canyon running southeast from the West Side parking lot. This section includes all routes approached from the Juniper Canyon Trail to its intersection with the Tunnel Trail.

The Canyon is one of the most lush areas in the monument. In spring, a stream winds its way past many junipers down the canyon. The head of the canyon appears to be an impenetrable wall of chaparral, an effective deterrent to climbing activities on the rocks trapped within.

The dominant climbing feature in the canyon is the 500-foot Resurrection Wall. Several multi-pitch routes wander up the imposing face. Highlighting the bill is the **Regular Route** (5.11a). This long climb sports an airy bolt ladder (freed) on decent rock sandwiched between sparsely protected pitches of moderate climbing.

362　**CASPER／5.8**　This right-facing corner is located on the 200-foot northwest-facing wall several hundred yards right/northwest of Resurrection Wall. A streambed runs directly up to and below the face. Follow this to the base of the climb. The route is an obvious right-facing corner at the cliff's lower left/north end. This climb is loose at the end of the corner, where face moves (protected by TCUs and nuts) lead to a two-bolt belay. Rappel the route.

363　**DOG DO AFTERNOON 5.7**　This route lies on the southeast face of the fourth formation uphill, on the opposite side of the streambed from **Mama Don't**. Three bolts protect the 40-foot face.

364　**NUMBSKULL'S NEEDLE 5.8**　This distinct pinnacle lies at the very top of the ridge, at the head of the little canyon. Three bolts protect moves up the rolling, loose and broken-up southeast face.

photo: Kevin Kilpatrick

The Western Front

This large formation can be seen straight up the canyon to the east, on the right side of the ridge just before the final left-hand turn to the West Side ranger station. **I.C.B.M.** is the obvious waterchute facing the road. Three routes have been reported on this long-ignored rock. The approach is the same as for the preceding three routes. From the top of the ridge, hike up past **Numbskull's Needle** and contour down and right a few hundred yards to the uphill side of the formation. **I.C.B.M.** follows a right-slanting chute/gully up the southwest face. **Life's Still Scary** and **Ready for Lift Off** follow parallel water streaks on the right side of the southeast face.

365 **I.C.B.M. 5.8**   A tied-off block and some Friend placements are required for the final belay

365a **Y.F.T. 5.5**   Climb the chute to the right of **I.C.B.M.**

366 **LIFE'S STILL SCARY 5.9+**   A mid-size Tri-cam placement in a hole can protect moves getting to the first bolt.

367 **READY FOR LIFT OFF 5.8 TR**   A good warm-up.

photo: Kevin Kilpatrick

THE WESTERN FRONT

The Western Front

365   I.C.B.M. 5.8
365a Y.F.T. 5.5
366   LIFE'S STILL SCARY 5.9+
367   READY FOR LIFT OFF 5.8 TR

Southeast Face

West Face

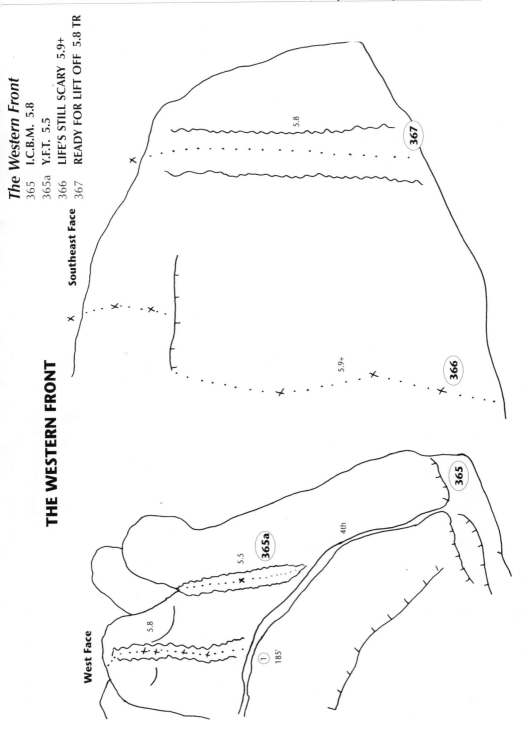

Resurrection Wall

The shadowed north face of this huge wall overlooks Juniper Canyon. **The Regular Route** can be distinguished by the faintly worn second pitch in the middle of the main north wall.

To approach the wall, head up a streambed at the final left-hand turn on Juniper Canyon Trail, just before it starts on its steep uphill trek to the high peaks. The streambed winds its way up to the left/east end of the wall. Careful trailblazing is necessary to avoid the groves of poison oak along the base of the wall. **The Great Spectacular** is the obvious arching right-facing corner—the beginning of the under-cut right side. **Regular Route** starts just left of the corner.

368 **HERCHEL-BERCHEL 5.10c R** This route is runout and loose. It follows the long green slab, up and left, along the left side of the northeast face.

369 **RESURRECTION WALL – THE REGULAR ROUTE 5.11a ★★** The second pitch is worth the effort.

370 **REINCARNATION VARIATION 5.10a** This variation requires clever protection placements.

photo: Kevin Kilpatrick

Resurrection Wall

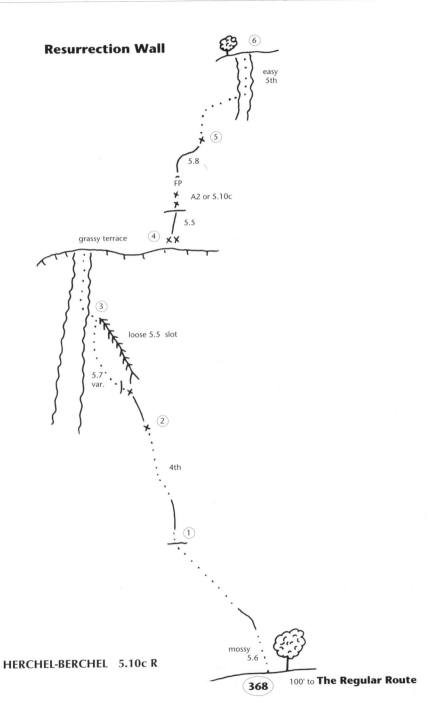

6

easy
5th

5

5.8

FP

A2 or 5.10c

5.5

grassy terrace   4

loose 5.5 slot

3

5.7
var.

2

4th

1

mossy
5.6

368   HERCHEL-BERCHEL   5.10c R

368   100' to **The Regular Route**

Resurrection Wall

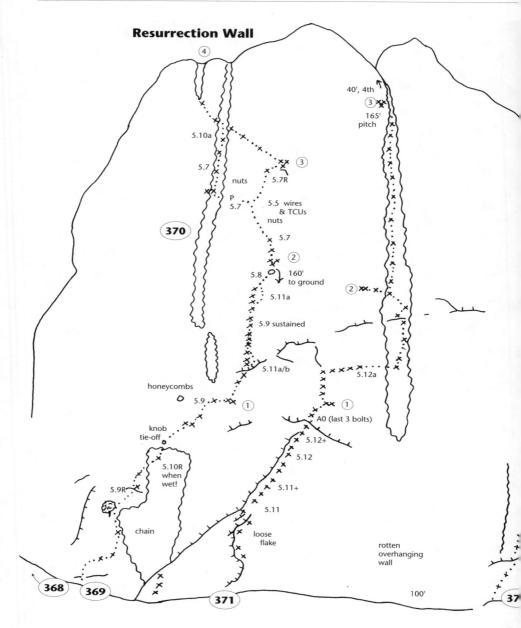

Resurrection Wall

371 **THE GREAT SPECTACULAR   5.12+ A0**   The overhanging corner is an intimidating jaunt. Only for those accustomed to Pinnacles rock. Slightly loose.

372 **WHAT IF 5.11d A0**   A #3 or 4 Friend is needed after the second bolt. Climb a short face to an overhanging bulge 100 feet right of **The Great Spectacular**, just north of a huge rotten alcove.

373 **CRUMBLING CASTLE – REGULAR ROUTE 5.7 R**   As the Juniper Canyon Trail switchbacks uphill, Crumbling Castle is on the right and downhill. It lies just off the trail a few switchbacks before its intersection with the Tunnel Trail. Descend down the slope where the trail comes closest to the formation's north side. The route starts on the north/uphill face, and eventually makes its way to the west/right summit, which has a multi-layered top. Start on the right side of the north face; diagonal up and left past bolts to the saddle separating the two summits and another bolt. Climb the shoulder back right to the first of two summit bulges. Protect the first bulge by installing medium to large, hard-to-place protection in the horizontal crack at its base. A fall from this bulge (5.7) lands one firmly on the shoulder below. The second bulge is easier on its low left side. This route, if carefully protected by a strong leader, is very enjoyable. There are rappel bolts on top.

374 **CRUMBLING CASTLE – ORIGINAL ROUTE 5.7**   The **Original Route** avoided the face and climbed a chimney to the left. An aid piton was used to mount the saddle leading to the main formation on the right. Proceed along the saddle, passing a bolt for the second, and join the **Regular Route**. If done free, getting to the saddle is 5.6.

374a **CRUMBLING CASTLE – DIRECT FINISH 5.10a** Follow three bolts straight up 15 feet right of the start of Crumbling Castle **Regular Route**. One can get a Friend between the second and third bolt.

375 **MONUMENT 5.5 ★** Slightly downhill and right of Crumbling Castle. Climb past one bolt on the northwest/uphill face.

376 **TOMBSTONE – REGULAR ROUTE 5.2 R** This is the next pinnacle slightly left/east and downhill of Monument. Start climbing at the northwest corner and head up and right past a large hole and out onto the west face to a bolt. Continue back left, up unprotected, loose rock to the top. There are two bolts on top.

377 **TOMBSTONE – DOC HOLLIDAY DIRECT 5.8 R+** This more direct alternative heads straight up the groove/chute at the start of the **Regular Route** past one bolt on fairly good rock. This route has a dangerous runout.

Also in the area:

378 **CAVE PINNACLE 4th class** This pinnacle is downhill and left/east of the large east face of **Tombstone.** Climb the south face, on very loose rock. This climb ascends a 10-foot wide face directly between an arête (to the right) and a chimney to the left.

379 **BRITTLE PALACE 4th class** This pinnacle lies about ten feet directly behind the southwest face of Crumbling Castle. Hideous thrashing, bushwhacking and chimney-ing out of the choked corridor between the Palace and the Castle allows the explorer passage to the lump's right edge. One hangerless bolt on top. One can also approach from around the west face of Crumbling Castle and thrash to the base. There is one hangerless bolt for protection.

380 **YANKEE PINNACLE 5.5 A2 or 5.10+** This is the next pinnacle southeast and 200 feet downhill from Crumbling Castle. The original ascent was made by a tyrolean tra-verse from a nearby cliff. The route goes up the east face from the notch. Twenty-five feet of aid or free climbing leads past a crusty aid ladder on crustier rock, up to a right traverse and a short crack that leads to the summit.

381 **JUBILATION PINNACLE 5.3 A3** This large pinnacle is located partway up the streambed that runs through Juniper Canyon, and can be seen by looking southeast up the canyon, as the trail begins switchbacking up the hillside. The pinnacle is dwarfed by a much larger formation on its southwest side, and careful observation is needed to distinguish it from the larger rock. Climb out of the notch between the two formations, past a series of aid bolts. It's a crumbly scramble to the top. The ladder supposedly is in tatters, with bad bolts and missing hangers. A sky hook and hero loops might come in handy on this obscurity.

photo: Bruce Hildebrand Collection

Climbers on **Photographer's Delight**

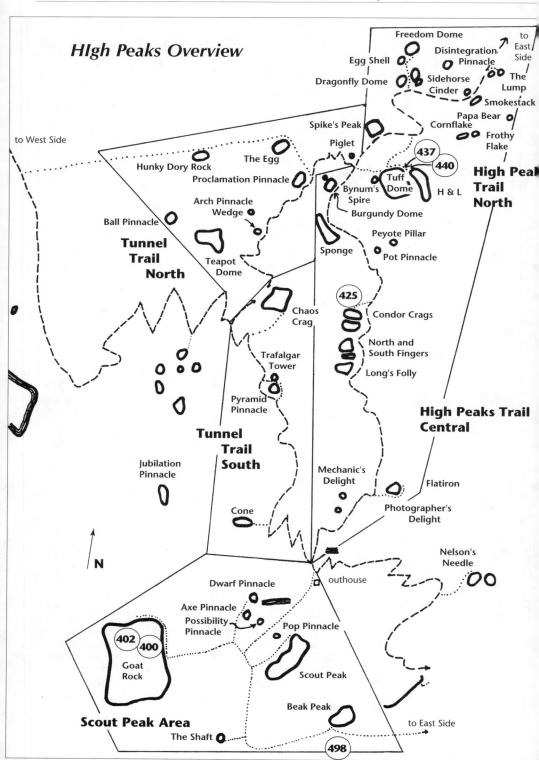

HIgh Peaks Overview

Freedom Dome

Egg Shell

Dragonfly Dome

Disintegration Pinnacle

to East Side

Sidehorse Cinder

The Lump

Smokestack

Spike's Peak

Papa Bear

Cornflake

Frothy Flake

Piglet

437

440

High Peak Trail North

Hunky Dory Rock

The Egg

Proclamation Pinnacle

Bynum's Spire

Tuff Dome

H & L

Arch Pinnacle Wedge

Burgundy Dome

Ball Pinnacle

Peyote Pillar

Tunnel Trail North

Sponge

Pot Pinnacle

Teapot Dome

425

Chaos Crag

Condor Crags

North and South Fingers

Trafalgar Tower

Long's Folly

Pyramid Pinnacle

High Peaks Trail Central

Tunnel Trail South

Jubilation Pinnacle

Mechanic's Delight

Flatiron

Cone

Photographer's Delight

Nelson's Needle

N

outhouse

Dwarf Pinnacle

Axe Pinnacle

Possibility Pinnacle

Pop Pinnacle

402

400

Goat Rock

Scout Peak

Scout Peak Area

Beak Peak

to East Side

The Shaft

498

HIGH PEAKS

This area is a complex assortment of spires and formations approached from sections of the High Peaks Trail and the Tunnel Trail as they circumvent the ridge top separating the east and west sides of the park. This area will be subdivided into segments defined by trail intersections and will be in the following sequence:

Tunnel Trail South: Intersection with Juniper Canyon Trail to intersection with the south end of the High Peaks Trail at the outhouse.

Scout Peak Area: Area south of the intersection of the High Peaks Trail and Tunnel Trail–South.

High Peaks Trail Central: Intersection with the south end of the Tunnel Trail and the north end of the Tunnel Trail.

High Peaks Trail North: From intersection with north end of the Tunnel Trail to intersection with the Condor Gulch Trail.

Tunnel Trail North: From its intersection with the Juniper Canyon Trail to its north intersection with the High Peaks Trail.

The entire park can be viewed from the High Peaks. To the north are the disruptive workings of the San Andreas Fault. Twisted and broken hills adorn the vista—evidence of a lively earth. To the southwest, the Salinas Valley separates the Coast Range from the drier inland mountains. Both the east and west sides of the park can be scrutinized from here.

The High Peaks are a day-long adventure for climbers. A strenuous hike from either side starts the day off, providing a cardiovascular workout so often missed in the relatively static movement of rock climbing. Many of us have, at some point, been thrashed by some perverse approach march, making us connoisseurs of the curbside belay. A committed expedition to "the high country" brings you to a wide assortment of excellent climbs. A whole day spent in the High Peaks will reward the climber with numerous summits and fantastic picnic areas (it doesn't have to be all about the numbers).

TUNNEL TRAIL SOUTH

382   CHAOS CRAG 5.5   Although this monolithic rock faces the Tunnel Trail North (which tunnels through it), it is approached from the Tunnel Trail South, just past the intersection with the Juniper Canyon Trail. From the intersection, walk south on the Tunnel Trail until it comes near the gully along the back/southeast side of the crag. Head up the gully until boulders impede the easy approach. Climb the knobby left-hand wall past two bolts. A wide crack opens above the second bolt. Climb the crack to its top and back down its opposite side and belay. Climb up the steep chute above past two bolts to the top. Return via the route. The roundabout nature of this route can be confusing.

383   **PYRAMID PINNACLE 5.6** ★   This towering pinnacle looms over the trail a few hundred feet south of Chaos Crag. The climb ascends the uphill/north face. Follow steep

PYRAMID
PINNACLE

TRAFALGAR
TOWER

photo: Kevin Kilpatrick

trails up either side of the rock to get to the start. Follow a ledge up and left, 30 feet past several crux scrub oaks, to a point where it is easy to move up and right to a bolt. Continue straight up past another bolt to easy slopes and the top. Rappel the route.

384 **TRAFALGAR TOWER A1** This short, pointed spire is alongside the trail and 100 feet left/northwest of Pyramid Pinnacle. The summit of this finger of rock has been gained by the infamous mighty rope toss and prusik.

385 **THE CONE – REGULAR ROUTE 5.3 ★** This isolated rock is downhill and southwest, at the end of the long switchback after Pyramid Pinnacle. It stands on the right, alone on the hillside, after passing Pyramid Pinnacle. The **Regular Route** passes two bolts on the uphill/east side. Originally, the lead was unprotected.

386 **THE CONE – WANDERLUST 5.6 X** This uninviting route follows a crack on the downhill/northwest side. Head up the crack until it becomes necessary to move left onto the face. Continue unprotected to the top.

THE CONE

385

photo: Kevin Kilpatrick

Scout Peak Area

This area includes all routes and formations approached from the Tunnel Trail South and High Peaks Trail intersection. Approach these climbs from the intersection by following a trail south along the ridge to the high point a few hundred yards farther. From this ridgetop, Goat Rock can be seen to the southwest, its large northeast face cleaved by several long chimney systems. Scout Peak is the large mound sharing the ridgetop, southeast and to the left a couple hundred feet. The Shaft is just southeast of Scout Peak; a lone pinnacle jutting up from the hillside below. Possibility Pinnacle is the dominant spire closest to the right/west, overlooking the backside of Axe Pinnacle. Although Dwarf Pinnacle is not approached from Scout Peak Area, it is included in this section since its location is identified by its relation to Axe Pinnacle. Some of the smaller and lower formations in this area are described in the East Side section of this book, under High Peaks Trail South.

By and large, the rock in this sector is good, which along with its great vantage point, makes the area worth a visit.

387   **AXE PINNACLE – REGULAR ROUTE 5.7 A1**   From the Tunnel Trail South/High Peaks Trail junction, Axe Pinnacle can be seen as a separate spire at the right/west end of a larger wall of rock 100 yards to the west. Approach from the ridge behind it. Start the climb in the notch between the pinnacle and the main wall. Several aid bolts and some free moves lead to the summit.

388   **JAM IT! 5.9**   This is a handcrack on the wall approximately 80 feet below and left from **Axe Pinnacle**. It faces the bench by the outhouse.

389   **DWARF PINNACLE 5.2 X**   This obscure little spire is located just below Axe Pinnacle on the outhouse side. Approach from the switchbacks on the Tunnel Trail facing it. Climb the uphill/east corner (unprotected) to the top. Two bolts are on the summit.

390   **POSSIBILITY PINNACLE 3rd class ★**   Climb the south shoulder up good rock to a magnificent view. There is no anchor on top, so the route must be downclimbed.

391   **POP PINNACLE 5.7**   This small formation lies between Possibility Pinnacle and Scout Peak, just right of the approach to Scout Peak. Climb the uphill side by surmounting the initial shoulder, climbing it directly (or up the small corner to the left) to the final face and a bolt. Continue up and right through shaky rock to the top, where there are bolts.

Scout Peak

This is the highest point in the southern High Peaks area. It is the large, bulbous formation immediately to your left as you hike over the top of the rise south of and behind the outhouse.

392   **SCOUT PEAK – REGULAR ROUTE 5.5 R**   Climb the north-facing chimney/chute to a fixed piton at its end. Climb up and left to a second chute, past a bolt and a piton, to its end. A climb up a short, unprotected section of face gets you to two belay bolts. An assortment of Friends can be used in the initial chute. Two bolts on top of the **Regular Route** allow a rappel down the north face.

393   **SCOUT PEAK – TRACKER 5.6 R**   From the uphill side, hike around the northeast face to a short, steep chute. Climb up and left on good rock past one bolt. From the shoulder above, climb left into another chute and follow it unprotected to the higher shoulder. Scramble up and left to the summit proper.

394 **SCOUT PEAK – SOUTH FACE 5th class** An unnerving chimney has been climbed on the south face. Chimney at your own risk.

395 **SCOUT PEAK – LEONARD-HORSFALL ROUTE 5.3** From the eastern-most point of Scout Peak, at the base of **Tracker**, go around the south face taking care to go out on a broad series of ledges. The route starts on the ledge, entering into a guano-filled chimney with a bolt. From the top of the chimney go up and right on a ramp past a fixed pin. Protects with medium and large pieces.

POSSIBILITY PINNACLE

AXE PINNACLE

As seen from The Bench

photo: Kevin Kilpatrick

SCOUT PEAK

392

THE
SHAFT

photo: Kevin Kilpatrick

Also in the area:

396 **THE SHAFT 5.10a** ★ This 70-foot spire is located a few hundred yards directly south and downhill from the saddle between **Goat Rock** and **Scout Peak**. Climb past nine bolts on the uphill side to the top. **The Shaft** originally was climbed by a prusik up a rope tossed over the top.

397 **BEAK PEAK – REGULAR ROUTE 3rd class** This is the second-to-last big outcrop to the east of Scout Peak. Intricate scrambling on the west side leads past a bush to knobby climbing and the summit. See photo in East Side Reservoir Area on page 78.

398 **BEAK PEAK – SUBTLE SLOPES 5.8** Walk up and right from The Shaft for 200 feet to the low-angle southwest slabs of Beak Peak. There are two arch-like formations on its right side. Ascend the face between the arches for 15 feet to a bolt. Continue past a block, then step left and climb the steep groove with a bolt on the left to a steep bulge with a bolt. Move right, then back left to another bolt. The rock here is very steep. Stay focused and surmount the bulge to lower-angle slopes, which lead to a belay bolt. To descend, walk west and downclimb third-class terrain to a grassy notch. A gully leads to the bottom. This route is a full 165 feet. There are a total of six protection bolts on this climb.

photo: Bruce Hildenbrand Collection

Bruce Hildenbrand on **St. Valentine's Day Massacre, Condor Crags**

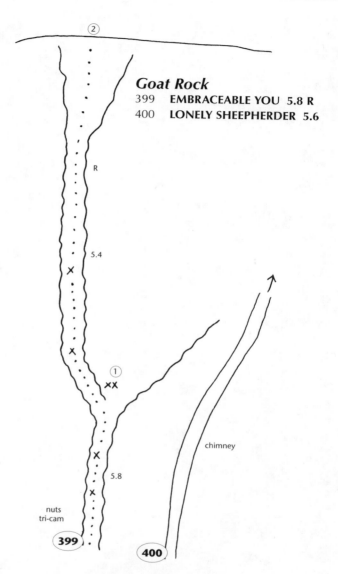

Goat Rock

399   **EMBRACEABLE YOU**   **5.8 R**

400   **LONELY SHEEPHERDER**   **5.6**

HIGH PEAKS TRAIL CENTRAL

Goat Rock

This huge formation sports a few routes that make their way up the impressive chimney systems dominating the northeast face. From "outhouse junction," the northeast face can be seen the southwest, behind Axe Pinnacle. To get to the formation, continue down the ridge south of the junction, heading directly to the north face.

399   **EMBRACEABLE YOU 5.8 R**   Start in the chimney/chute just left of **Lonely Sheepherder**.

400   **GOAT ROCK – LONELY SHEEPHERDER 5.6**   This chimney climb ascends the main chimney in the middle of the north face. Start left of the overhanging bottom and traverse up and right past a bolt. Continue up the chimney for 140 feet, past two more bolts, to a belay ledge with bolts. A second 50-foot lead finishes up the chimney.

401   **GOAT ROCK – PIECE OF EWE 5.7 R**   From **Lonely Sheepherder**, walk almost to the right corner of the northeast face.

Pitch 1 This pitch is fourth class and bypasses the loose bottom chimney-and-crack systems by climbing up and right 60 feet in a gully to the large ledge on the corner of the rock.

Pitch 2 Climb the arête for 50 feet, passing a bolt. A small crack provides protection for the 40-foot traverse to the belay—a three-inch crack at the base of a steep water groove.

Pitch 3 Climb up moderate rock for 25 feet to an overhang that may or may not be protected by a bolt (crux). A fall here could be disastrous. Continue up easier ground to the top.

402   **GOAT ROCK – RETURN OF PIECE OF EWE 5.9 X**   This chimney is on the right side of the northwest face (facing the Chaparral parking area). Start on a ledge just right of the chimney. A strenuous and dangerous boulder start (the crux) past an uncooperative oak gets you into the chimney. Continue up the chimney until you can exit out left to easier slopes above. The start is unprotected, loose and has a terrible landing.

photo: Kevin Kilpatrick

Also in the area:

403   **PHOTOGRAPHER'S DELIGHT – REGULAR ROUTE 5.2 ★★**   This popular spire is just left/west of the trail, 500 feet past the outhouse. Climb past one bolt on the uphill/trail side.

404   **PHOTOGRAPHER'S DELIGHT – NORTHEAST CORNER 5.8 R+**   This dangerous climb starts just down and right of the Regular Route. Climb over a loose overhang to a bolt. Climb up and right (runout) to the top.

405   **MECHANIC'S DELIGHT 5.11b or A1 ★**   This bolt ladder ascends the northeast shoulder of the pinnacle downhill and to the right/north of Photographer's Delight. The overhanging entry moves provide challenging free climbing up the old ladder.

photo: Kevin Kilpatrick

photo: Kevin Kilpatrick

High Peaks from the West Side parking lot

The Flatiron

As one walks north past Photographer's Delight, the trail makes a sharp right turn, then sharply switchbacks to the left 100 feet further. The Flatiron is straight ahead at the point where the trail switchbacks. Go right from the switchback and follow another trail under the brush, directly to the rock.

The climbing on The Flatiron is varied and on decent rock. In the spring, the lower grassy slope is a pristine setting for a base camp. The **Regular Route** (the easiest way to the summit) is a powerful succession of moves over the summit bulge. **Silent Running** either can be toproped or led, and is slab-like in its edging. The easier approach variations to the **Regular Route** offer marvelous alternatives for beginners. All routes start on the northeast face (the side facing Condor Gulch), except for the **Original Route**, which climbs up and right along the obvious ramp on the south side.

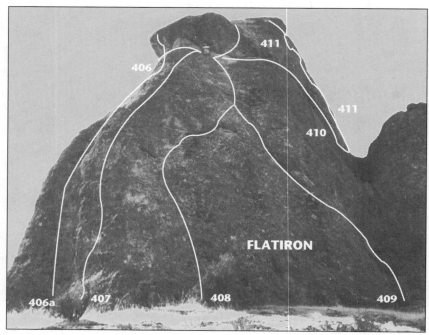

photo: Kevin Kilpatrick

South Face

406 **FLATIRON SOUTH FACE – ORIGINAL ROUTE 5.10a or 5.4 A1** ★ Climb the easy south face ramp up and right, past a hangerless bolt in a block, until the ramp curves around the upper shoulder to belay bolts on the northeast face. Finish up the bolt ladder free or aid.

406a **BURTON'S BELOW 5.8+** Climb the waterchute left of **Lost Fortune** past four bolts. Continue straight up the easy face pat two more bolts. A final bolt protects the nice, moderate, thrilling overhang move to the summit.

Northeast Face

407 **LOST FORTUNE 5.9** Goes up the northeast corner.

408 **FLATIRON NORTHEAST FACE – REGULAR ROUTE, VARIATION 1 5.10a or 5.4 A1** ★★ An excellent direct approach to the bolt ladder. Can be done in one or two pitches.

409 **FLATIRON NORTHEAST FACE – REGULAR ROUTE, VARIATION 2 5.10a or 5.4 A1** ★ A little loose in places but still fun.

409a **MUNGY BULGY 5.9** The obvious deep grove/chute right of **Variation 2**. Protection for the last moves has been achieved by hanging a long sling from a bolt at the top of the chute. According to the first ascent party the rock was too poor to provide an adequate bolt placement in the chute.

410 **REGULAR ROUTE – VARIATION 3 5.10a or 5.4 A1** ★ From the start of **Silent Running**, head up and left along the ramp, past a bolt, to the belay below the bolt ladder.

411 **SILENT RUNNING 5.10a** ★ A pleasant alternative to the bolt ladder.

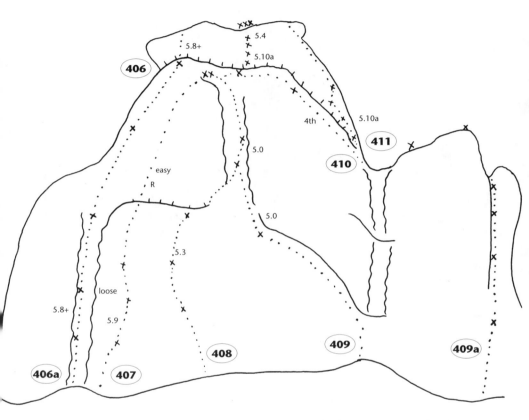

The Flatiron

406 **ORIGINAL ROUTE 5.9 or 5.4 A1** ★
406a **BURTON'S BELOW 5.8+**
407 **LOST FORTUNE 5.9**
408 **VARIATION 1 5.9 or 5.4 A1** ★★

409 **VARIATION 2 5.9 or 5.4 A1** ★
409a **MUNGY BULGY 5.9**
410 **VARIATION 3 5.9 or 5.0 A1** ★
411 **SILENT RUNNING 5.10a** ★

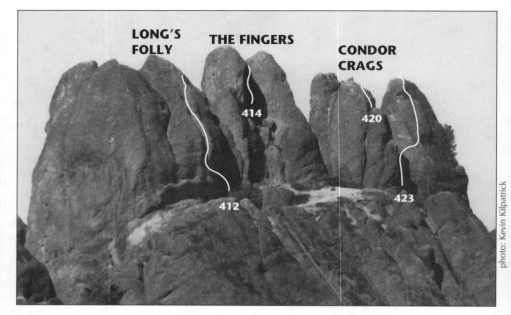

LONG'S FOLLY · THE FINGERS · CONDOR CRAGS

414

420

412

423

photo: Kevin Kilpatrick

Long's Folly, The Fingers and Condor Crags

After passing the Flatiron cut-off, the trail works its way down and around a jumble of formations (past a series of metal railings), finally making its way up and left to a wide gap and a view, again, of the west valley. At this point, the trail becomes an awkward, carved staircase that leads up and right to large ridgetop formations. Long's Folly, the bomb bay squeeze chimney that quaintly resembles a derriere, is on the southern-most of these formations, and faces the High Peaks Trail. North and South Finger are the next two highest spires to the north, and are separated by a chimney/corridor. Condor Crags is the next formation down the trail and to the north, and is recognized easily by the deep, recessed notch separating the two summits. A large, healthy pine tree marks the start of the climbing.

412 **LONG'S FOLLY 5.8 R** ★ Although the chimney is a little easier than the moves getting into it, it is slightly runout. There are two sets of belay anchors on the route. The first and lower set allows a single-rope rappel to the ground. The higher summit set requires two ropes to reach the ground. There is some respectable bouldering on two boulders at the base of the route.

413 **SOUTH FINGER – REGULAR ROUTE 5.5** ★ After climbing the approach corners, continue down through the corridor to a wide crack on the left. Follow the crack to its end, where a series of four bolts located up and to the left nicely protect the face climbing to the top. Rappel the front face, where a single 165-foot rope barely delivers you back to the ground.

414 **SOUTH FINGER – EARTH MAGNET 5.12a TR** ★ Climb the right arête immediately left of the notch for 15 feet, then move up and left onto the main face.

415 **NORTH FINGER – REGULAR ROUTE 5.5** No pro. Continue through the corridor just past the crack on the South Finger. Chimney a short ways up the corridor until it's possible to step right, onto the main face. A few fifth-class moves bring you into a fourth-class gully and scrambling to the top. Rappel the south face to the start of the South Finger.

Long's Folly, The Fingers and Condor Crags

412 LONG'S FOLLY 5.8 R ★

413 SOUTH FINGER – REGULAR ROUTE 5.5 ★

414 SOUTH FINGER – EARTH MAGNET 5.12a TR ★

415 NORTH FINGER – REGULAR ROUTE 5.5

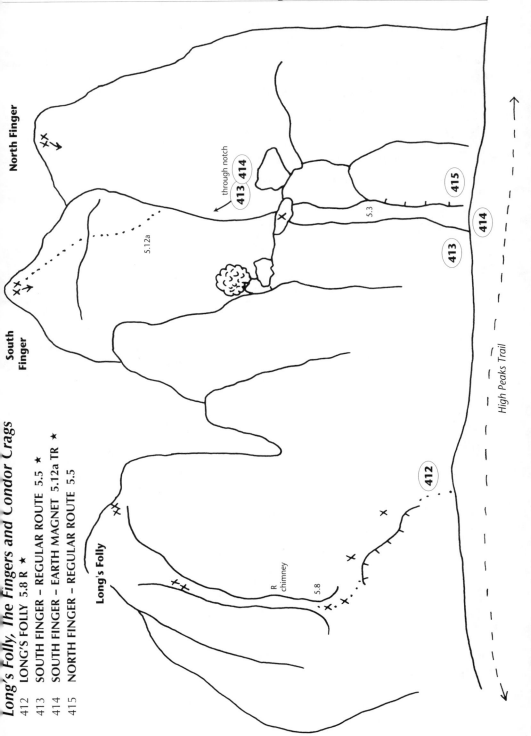

North Finger–Northeast Face

Just around the corner from the preceding routes is a scooped-out face. The **East Edge** goes up the obvious left-hand arête. **Slippery People** starts 15 feet to the right of the **East Edge**, and heads up the waterchute in the middle of the face and then right, out to the northeast prow. **Monga Bonna Memorial Route** starts just around the corner from the prow.

416   **NORTH FINGER NORTHEAST FACE – EAST EDGE 5.7**   Bad bolts, bad rock and pointless runouts makes one wish this climb was on granite.

417   **SLIPPERY PEOPLE 5.9+**   The crux is slightly loose.

418   **MONGA BONNA MEMORIAL ROUTE 5.10a ★**   A fun route.

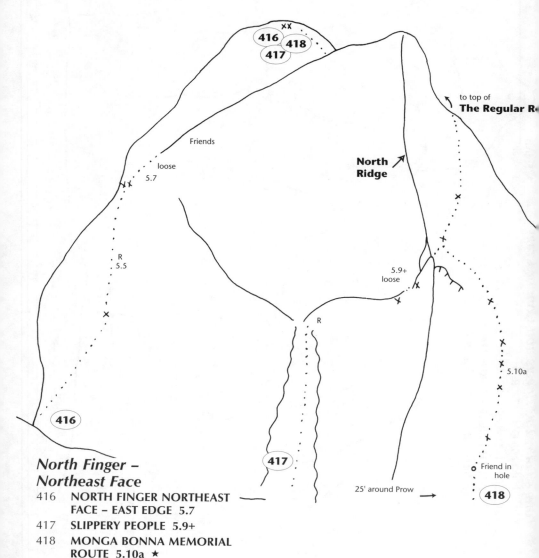

North Finger – Northeast Face

416   **NORTH FINGER NORTHEAST FACE – EAST EDGE 5.7**

417   **SLIPPERY PEOPLE 5.9+**

418   **MONGA BONNA MEMORIAL ROUTE 5.10a ★**

photo: Kevin Kilpatrick

Condor Crags: North and South Summits

The Condor Crags are just north of the North and South Fingers. All routes up both summits climb the initial thin crack leading into the notch between them (except for **For M.E.** and the **Denny–Colliver Route**, which traverse immediately right at the base of the rock on a third-class ledge). Both **St. Valentine's Day Massacre** and **For M.E.** hover over the trail at various points and require caution; be careful not to pelt an unsuspecting hiker with a rock. A double-rope rappel will get you all the way down to the trail from either summit. There are two rappels with a single line; use the oak at the top of the fingercrack as the second anchor.

These summits were the scene of the first roped climbing in the Monument.

Condor Crags South Summit

419   **CONDOR CRAGS SOUTH SUMMIT – ORIGINAL ROUTE 5.7**   From the top of the first pitch, continue back through the notch until it is possible to climb fourth class up to the top.

420   **CONDOR CRAGS SOUTH SUMMIT – SOUTH TRAVERSE 5.7** ★★   From the top of the first pitch, traverse straight left past several bolts to a shoulder below the top. One more bolt protects summit moves. This is the best route on the wall.

Condor Crags North Summit

421 **CONDOR CRAGS NORTH SUMMIT – ORIGINAL ROUTE 5.7** From the top of the first pitch, wander (third class) up and around to the back side and scramble to the top.

422 **ST. VALENTINE'S DAY MASSACRE 5.7 ★** From the top of the initial thin crack, face climb up and right through the scoop to the east arête/shoulder. Climb around to the right side of the shoulder and straight up to the top. A little loose.

423 **FOR M.E. 5.10+** This climb is loose.

424 **DENNY-COLLIVER ROUTE 5.7 R** An assortment of Tri-cams and camming units can be used in the initial chute. The route goes to the top of the north summit above the chute.

Condor Crags North Face

425 **CONDOR CONDOM CONDIMENT 5.8 ★ Condor Condom Condiment** starts off long boulders, approximately 100 feet down the north face from the trail.

426 **CONDOR CONDUIT – REGULAR ROUTE 5.7** This four-pitch route climbs a series of chimney systems up the north face of **Condor Crags**. To get started, skirt around the north side of the formation past the start of **Condor Condom Condiment**. It may be necessary to make a short rappel down a small cliff at the base of **Condor Condom Condiment**.

Pitch 1 Climb 100 feet up the narrow chimney using tied-off chockstones for protection (the original ascent also used tied-off horizontal pitons). Belay at the start of an easy fourth-class gully. This pitch is the crux.

Pitch 2 Scramble up the gully until it branches into two chimney systems.

Pitch 3 Climb the right-hand chimney/groove (5.6) then traverse left ten feet into a long chimney. Follow the chimney until it ends. Easy face climbing leads to the incredible hanging meadow.

Pitch 4 Climb up the left wall, pass a bolt (5.6) and continue climbing up the rib separating the right gully from **The Great Chimney** to the left. This pitch soon turns to fourth class. At a small tree, drop down into **The Great Chimney** and scramble third class to the top.

427 **THE GREAT CHIMNEY 5.7 A2** Catch **The Great Chimney** where it branches left at the top of the second pitch of the **Regular Route**. A point of aid was used at the bulging headwall on the original ascent.

Also in the area:

428 **POT PINNACLE 5.5** As one continues past Condor Crags to the descending chiseled steps, Pot Pinnacle and Peyote Pinnacle are straight across the saddle to the north. Both are slightly above and right of the bend before The Sponge. Climb up a steep chute on the uphill/north side, past a bolt. Exit left to a rappel anchor at the top.

429 **PEYOTE PINNACLE 4th class** From the start of Pot Pinnacle, walk northeast to the next pinnacle, which has a chimney cleaving it in two. Climb the chimney to the top.

425 **CONDOR CONDOM CONDIMENT 5.8**

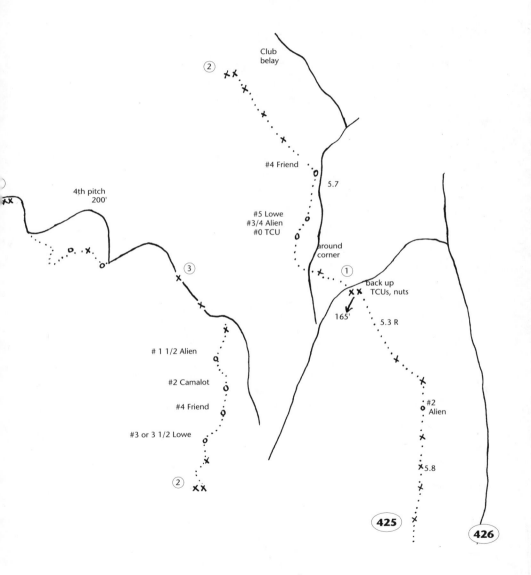

Club belay

② ✕✕

4th pitch
200'

#4 Friend

5.7

#5 Lowe
#3/4 Alien
#0 TCU

around corner

①

back up
TCUs, nuts

165'

5.3 R

③

1 1/2 Alien

#2 Camalot

#4 Friend

#2
Alien

#3 or 3 1/2 Lowe

✕ 5.8

② ✕✕

425

426

The Sponge

The Sponge borders the trail. It is on the left, about 200 yards beyond the Condor Crags steps. Its trailside face is heavily pockmarked and resembles Swiss cheese. The rock is very sound and the routes are excellent. The **Direct Northeast Face** is a superb climb on "Swiss cheese" holds. The **Regular Route** is a pleasant romp up the northwest shoulder. The rappel requires two 165-foot ropes.

430 **THE SPONGE – DIRECT NORTHEAST FACE 5.6** ★★ Start up a short apron of rock on the left side of the north/trailside face.

431 **HOLES 5.6 X** ★ The route is 15 feet right of **Direct**. Although this route has been soloed, it can be set up as a fun toprope.

432 **THE REGULAR ROUTE 5.2** ★★ Climb up 20 feet to the saddle below the north-west shoulder. Follow the shoulder to the top.

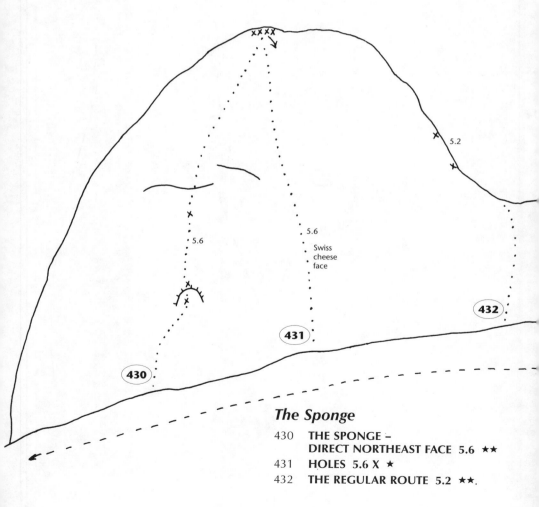

The Sponge

430 **THE SPONGE –
DIRECT NORTHEAST FACE 5.6** ★★
431 **HOLES 5.6 X** ★
432 **THE REGULAR ROUTE 5.2** ★★.

Larry Arthur on Burgundy Dome **Rappel Route**

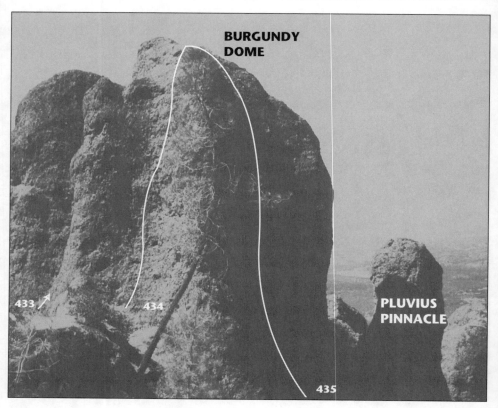

photo: Kevin Kilpatrick

Burgundy Dome

This distinct pinnacle is on the left about 50 feet before the High Peaks Trail intersection with the Tunnel Trail. It is identified by the concave scoop on the right of the trailside face of the **Rappel Route**. The **Rappel Route** is a marvelous climb that ascends the vertical chute using "thank God" pockets. **Vin Ordinaire** follows an excellent line but, unfortunately, it may have bad bolts.

433   **BURGUNDY DOME – ORIGINAL ROUTE 4th class**   Climb a short face to the obvious chimney left of the **Rappel Route**.

434   **BURGUNDY DOME – RAPPEL ROUTE 5.7 ★★★**   Follow a line of three bolts in the scoop.

435   **BURGUNDY DOME – VIN ORDINAIRE 5.8 R ★**   Around the corner, to the right of the **Rappel Route**, is another chute on the north face. Run it out up the scoop to a fixed Lost Arrow on the right. Continue up and left to a bolt. A #2.5 or #3 Tri-cam can be used between the first two fixed pieces. Climb straight up the steepening chute to the final bolt, #2.5 to 3 Friends and Tri-cams can be used in pockets in the runout section to the final bolt. Belay on top of the **Rappel Route**.

Also in the area:

436   **PLUVIUS PINNACLE A2**   This is the finger of rock behind and downhill from Burgundy Dome. Its distinct summit was attained by the ever-popular "Pinnacles rope chuck" and a desperate prusik.

436a **PIGLET PINNACLE 5.8 ★**   This little, pointed pinnacle is located in the northwest angle formed by the junction of the Tunnel Trail and the High Peaks Trail North. It's right behind a larger boulder that borders the High Peaks Trail. Two bolts protect sound face climbing on the right/northeast corner facing the larger, uphill rock.

436b **THE SOW – EAST SHOULDER 4TH CLASS**   The Sow towers right over Piglet Pinnacle on its east side.

436c **THE SOW 5.6**   Southeast face has a one-bolt climb.

HIGH PEAKS TRAIL NORTH

Tuff Dome

At 2,658 feet, Tuff Dome (known on government maps as Hawkins Peak) is the highest point in the High Peaks. The Regular Route (5.6) is a Pinnacles classic. The rock is worn down to solidity from so many ascents.

From the High Peaks/Tunnel Trail intersection, continue north to the sharp left turn at the top of the ridge, just before the trail goes downhill past Dragonfly Dome. Follow another trail up and right/south to the highest point on the hill. This is Tuff Dome. Bynum's Spire is just right/southwest, surrounded by a beautiful meadow (especially so in the spring, with its carpet of flowers). The **Regular Route** starts on the northeast face and makes its way into the obvious notch at the top. **Aliens Ate My Buick** starts on the opposite side, facing Bynum's Spire.

437 **TUFF DOME – REGULAR ROUTE 5.6** ★★★ It is advised to belay from the notch to the actual summit, up and right.

437a **TUFF DOME – DIRECT START 5.7**

438 **TUFF DOME TRAVERSE 5.6 R**

438a **TUFF DOME – PRELUDE 5.10c R** On the west face is an obvious left-facing corner. Climb the corner past a fixed piton. At the top of the corner, move up and right past a bolt and continue to the top.

438b **TUFF DOME – ADAGIO 5.11a** ★ Fifteen feet right of **Prelude**, climb past a series of bolts to a two-bolt belay.

439 **TUFF DOME – ALIENS ATE MY BUICK 5.10c** ★ Follow a line of five bolts ten feet right of **Adagio** and opposite **Bynum's Spire**. Although a little loose in spots, the climb is worth doing.

photo: Kevin Kilpatrick

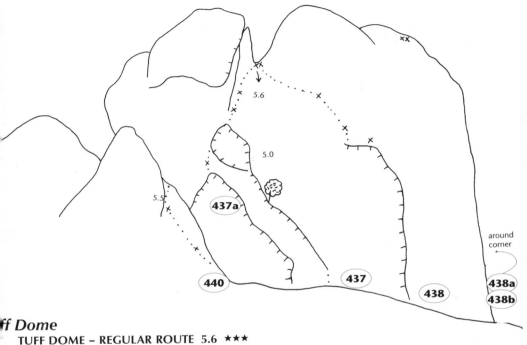

ff Dome

TUFF DOME – REGULAR ROUTE 5.6 ★★★

a **TUFF DOME – DIRECT START**

TUFF DOME TRAVERSE

a **TUFF DOME – PRELUDE**

b **TUFF DOME – ADAGIO**

TUFF DOME – ALIENS ATE MY BUICK

H&L DOME – REGULAR ROUTE

Also in the area:

440   **H&L DOME – REGULAR ROUTE 5.5 ★★★**   Directly across from the **Regular Route** on **Tuff Dome** is this excellent little climb. Belayers literally can stand back to back for both rocks. Climb the sloping face past a bolt to a final bulge. Surmount the steep face past one more bolt to a bolt belay on top. Continue southeast along the top of the ridge (fourth class) for another 50 feet to another belay and gain a second pitch.

440a   **CATCH ME 5.3 X**   This is the second formation north of H&L Dome. If you are standing at the base of **Tuff Dome – Regular Route**, it's the second dome formation left of H&L. Climb unprotected 15 feet up the northwest face to top. There are two bolts on top.

441 **H&L DOME – FEATHER CANYON 5.8** This climb winds up the long east face of H&L Dome. Start way down in the canyon to the east, at the overlook on the Condor Gulch Trail. Looking west from the overlook, the east side of H&L Dome is a massive fractured face dominating the head of the canyon. The climb starts in the huge, curved chimney that splits the rock in half. Thrash uphill through the chaparral and along the stream bed – some steep talus climbing and boulder hopping is needed to get to the base of the chimney. Twenty-five feet of easy face climbing gets you into the huge chimney. Walk right/north along the chimney until it begins to descend. Here, begin the first fifth-class lead.

Pitch 1 Chimney diagonally up and left, over the approach chimney, toward a giant chockstone resting on top about 70 feet away. Four bolts protect this lead. Belay beside the chockstone.

Pitch 2 From the top of the chockstone, climb (5.8) into the deep chimney above, passing a bolt. The climbing soon eases as the route becomes a scree-filled trough. Branch right, from the back into a third-class gully, and climb it to the top.

Pitch 3 From the top of the gully, climb up and left into a water chute with two bolts (5.6); it's a short ways to the top.

Pitch 4 A rope-length walk with some third-class scrambling brings you around the right side of a short pinnacle to the ridge crest.

Pitch 5 Continue roped climbing along the ridge, passing over two rises (with a bolt on top of the second) and around the right side of a third. Here, the ridge ends below a face.

Pitch 6 Ascend the face past a bolt, to a ledge that diagonals to the right. This ledge leads to another with a bolt. Climb the final moves to the second summit of H&L Dome.

Bynum's Spire

Bynum's Spire sits higher on the hillside, but is overshadowed by the larger Tuff Dome to its left/northeast. In the spring, Bynum's Spire (more like a lump) rises out of the green meadow that surrounds it, creating a pleasing contrast. The rock is good, and here at Pinnacles where good rock is treasured, that means the routes also are good.

Both **Rock Steady** and **Chocolate Face**, which face Tuff Dome and **Aliens Ate My Buick**, are worthwhile topropes. **Rock Steady** is the obvious right-facing corner; **Chocolate Face** is to the left. The **Regular Route** climbs the low-angle west face.

442 **CHOCOLATE FACE 5.9 TR**

443 **ROCK STEADY 5.7** ★★ Climb past three fixed pitons. Great rock.

444 **REGULAR ROUTE 5.2** ★★ Climb the west face past one bolt.

Also in the area:

444a **BEGIN IT NOW 5.4** Ninety yards west of Bynum's Spire is a long formation running south (uphill side) to north (downhill). As you look at the formation from the east, there is a waterchute just right of a larger spire marking the middle of the formation.

Pitch 1 Climb the waterchute past two bolts. Belay from small trees.

Pitch 2 Move south and up onto a small shoulder. From there, go across and up onto the main formation, passing one bolt.

photo: Kevin Kilpatrick

445   **SPIKE'S PEAK 5.6**   The "peak" in the formation's name is misleading, as there isn't any actual peak. The large formation is a blocky tier of rocks 100 yards north of the High Peaks intersection with the Tunnel Trail. Walk north on High Peaks, past the intersection, to the point where the trail curves right. Spike's Peak is immediately to the left. Climb up the brushy cleft facing the trail past a bolt somewhat hidden under tree branches. Climb up and left to the large ledge above. A short, steep headwall takes you to the top. There are two bolts on top. Rappel to the start.

445a   **LITTLE JAVELINA 5.9**   Climb down and left below Spike's Peak, toward West Side parking lot, from the switchback just above Dragonfly Dome. Climb straight up past eight bolts next to a small corner to a two-bolt belay. The bottom is loose. Walk off the top.

446   **DRAGONFLY DOME – REGULAR ROUTE 5.6 R ★★★**   This dome is the first distinct formation on the left after starting the switchbacks downhill from Spike's Peak. Its inviting and lofty summit is just off the trail. This great route goes directly up the east face, starting on the right side of the bottom flake. Climb the flake (which can be protected) to a bolt 20 feet up. Climb up and left to another bolt, and the final bulge to the top anchors.

447   **DRAGONFLY DOME – SCHOOL DAZE 5.9 TR ★**   After doing the **Regular Route**, this climb is easily toproped. Climb the shallow groove left of the start of the **Regular Route**, moving up and right to join it at the second bolt.

448 **SIDEHORSE 5.10a** ★ This formation, with its distinct summit block, is immediately right of Dragonfly. Initial fifth-class moves on the trail side of the rock lands you on an easy walk over to the final bulge and the crux. A sketchy boulder problem (and a bolt) puts you on the summit 10 feet higher. There are two bolts on top.

449 **EGG SHELL 5.8** ★ Follow a trail down the gully between Sidehorse and Dragonfly Dome; it'll take you directly to this formation 100 feet below. Egg Shell is the 30-foot rock with a pine standing close to the southeast corner. The climb starts in this corner. Climb past three bolts to the top.

Freedom Dome

This formation is immediately downhill from Egg Shell. The **Regular Route** starts on the southeast shoulder, which is marked by several closely spaced bolts close to the ground. **Preferred Freedom** ascends the corner 30 feet right of the **Regular Route**.

For years, the **Regular Route** was considered only 5.8. However, this meandering route sports a solid 5.9 headwall mantel. Worn mostly clean of loose rock from numerous ascents, this route is worth the hike.

450 **CAPTAIN CRUNCH 5.10a** This climb is horrendously loose.

451 **REGULAR ROUTE 5.9** ★★

452 **PREFERRED FREEDOM 5.9 R** ★

Also in the area:

453 **DISINTEGRATION PINNACLE 5.6** This pinnacle is just past Dragonfly and Sidehorse, down (northeast) and to the right. It is approximately 100 yards east of Freedom Dome. The rappel anchors are seen easily from the trail. Climb past two bolts from the notch on the west side.

454 **CINDER 5.7** ★ This 20-foot pillar is on the left side of the trail after it swings to the left about 100 yards past Sidehorse. One bolt protects climbing on the trail side face. Although short, the climb is solid and challenging.

Smokestack

This formation is opposite (to the east of) Cinder. It looms above the smaller rock in front of it. There are three routes on Smokestack. The original fourth-class route climbs the chimney/crack system on the left/north side. **Swept Away** (5.9) climbs directly up the middle of the northwest face past a small oak. **Clean Sweep**, although a bit loose, is the best line on the rock. It makes its way up the south shoulder.

455 **SMOKESTACK – ORIGINAL ROUTE 4th class** Climb up cracks and ledges on the left/northeast shoulder to the top.

456 **SMOKESTACK – SWEPT AWAY 5.9** Climb up the middle of the north face (the side facing the trail) past two bolts and a tied-off tree. A little loose at the top.

457 **SMOKESTACK – CLEAN SWEEP 5.9** Climb up the southwest shoulder past three bolts.

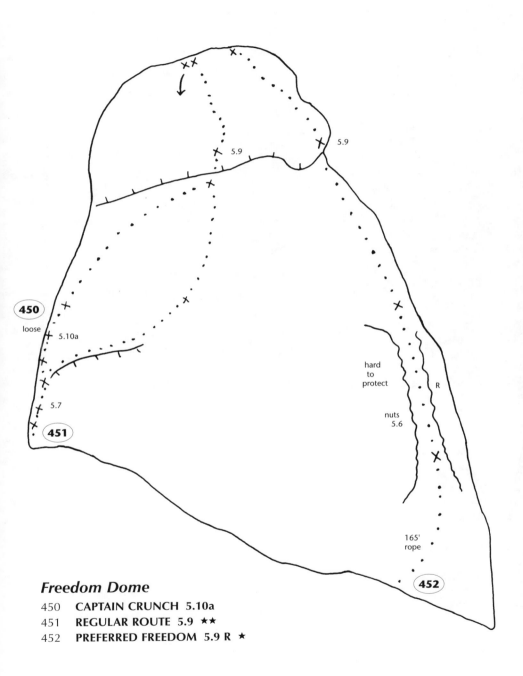

Freedom Dome

450   **CAPTAIN CRUNCH 5.10a**
451   **REGULAR ROUTE 5.9 ★★**
452   **PREFERRED FREEDOM 5.9 R ★**

FROTHY FLAKE · CORNFLAKE · SMOKESTACK · 456 · 455

photo: Kevin Kilpatrick

Also in the area:

458 **CORNFLAKE 5.3** This climb—and the following climb—surmount the pinnacles facing Smokestack and the trail. These pinnacles have vertical, pink faces and, viewed from the north, are on the hillside above and to the right of Smokestack, or below Tuff Dome. Cornflake is the summit on the right. Approach by roundabout gullies, reaching the uphill side to climb to the top. This climb is very exposed.

459 **FROTHY FLAKE 4th class** It's to the left of Cornflake and also is climbed from its uphill side. Easy, but loose.

460 **THE BIG STEP 5.6** Until now, this route appeared only in Steve Roper's 1966 guide to the Pinnacles. Hike north on the trail about 50 feet past **Smokestack,** then head left/downhill to the most prominent and nearest pinnacle. Climb the uphill side to the exposed summit ridge past one hangerless bolt for protection. The original descent description advises anchoring one end of the rope to the ground and rappelling down the opposite side. There is one old bolt on top. This climb is loose.

461 **PAPA BEAR – REGULAR ROUTE 5.2** After passing Smokestack, head down the hill to the left and southeast, where you will find this semi-isolated pinnacle. Flanking it slightly uphill are Mama and Baby Bear. Climb a crack on the uphill face to a shoulder. A bolt protects moves to the top.

462   **PAPA BEAR – APRIL FOOL'S ROUTE 5.10a**   This steep line climbs out of the notch on the north side past two bolts.

462a   **BABY BEAR 5.6**   Climb past one bolt on a formation ten away from Papa Bear. One bolt anchor.

462b **MAMA BEAR 5.7**   Climb past one bolt on the west face of a formation 20 feet east of Papa Bear. This route is about 20 feet long. One bolt anchor.

463   **THE LUMP 5.6**   A boulder sits on the right side of the trail with a lone pine opposite it. It is 100 feet north of, around the bend from, Smokestack. Walk up and around the north side of the boulder to a second boulder behind it. Start up north face and move up and over to west face past two bolts.

463a   **PEACE OF HEAVEN 5.8**   As one walks out to Squareblock Rock along the saddle of the trail, several 40- to 50-foot pinnacles sit on the right, slightly east of the crest of the saddle. These are one-third of the way from the trail to Squareblock. Fifty feet southeast of the largest formation, slightly downhill, is a thin, steep pinnacle. The downhill side has the only weakness due to its lower angle. Climb past two bolts to the top.

Squareblock Rock

Viewed from the trail near Smokestack, Squareblock Rock is the immense formation to the north with a lone pine tree between it and a left-leaning pinnacle on its west side. Shortly after passing Smokestack, contour along the brushy ridgeline, following indistinct brush paths to the rock. To get off, either rappel (two bolts) the south side or downclimb a third-class chimney (just right of **Buzzard's Breakfast**) on the north side.

464   **SQUAREBLOCK ROCK CRACK 5.5**   Climb the obvious chimney/crack on the south side facing the High Peaks Trail.

     Pitch 1   Climb the crack to its end. There is a bad belay bolt that can be backed up by a tree further back at the top of the third class gully.

     Pitch 2   Climb the face to the highest summit. Two belay bolts on top.

465   **BUZZARD'S BREAKFAST 5.6**   Climb the left of two chimneys on the opposite/north side of the rock, opposite **Squareblock Rock Crack**. At the top of the chimney head over to **Squareblock Rock Crack** and continue to the top.

TUNNEL TRAIL NORTH

Teapot Dome and Lower Teapot Dome

After passing through the tunnel and crossing the bridge, the trail contours left several hundred yards along the slope to Teapot Dome. Immediately to the right is the alien-shaped Wedge. Teapot is identified by the chimney splitting the trailside face. The **Regular Route** ascends the chimney. A double-rope rappel is required for a safe landing.

The lower dome is reached by using the **Regular Route** as an approach pitch.

465a **TEAPOT DOME – SCANDAL 5.9 R ★** This route features good climbing on some-times suspect rock. Begin twenty feet left of the **Regular Route** (east face), just left of a right-leaning wide crack. Climb a shallow corner for twenty feet past fixed pins (R at the start). Place a #1.5 Friend in a pocket and move up and left to a good stance on the southeast corner. Clip a bolt, then step right onto the main face (5.8). Climb up and right past two bolts (5.9), then clip a fixed pin in a thin crack. Move left, placing an excellent #4 in an obvious pocket, then climb straight up past a final bolt to a slab (5.7). Fourth class for 50' with no protection to the summit. Rap the route with two ropes. [A 5.10-a variation climbs straight up past he third bolt to the #4 Friend place-ment.]

466 **TEAPOT DOME – REGULAR ROUTE 4th class** There are fifth-class moves on the route, but they're the entry moves into the chimney. At the top of the chimney, cross over to rappel bolts on the left.

467 **TEAPOT DOME CRACK 5.6** This long left-facing corner/crack is about 40 feet around to the right of the **Regular Route**. Follow the crack to its end, and climb unprotected to the top of the right-hand summit. Drop over the other side and belay from a manzanita bush.

467a **TEAPOT DOME – GREEN DOLPHIN ST. 5.10** This two-pitch route ascends the north face of Teapot Dome. Climb a right-facing corner for the entire climb.

Pitch 1 Climb a 5.10 fingercrack (the crux) to join the corner. Continue up the corner (5.8) past two bolts to a sling belay with Friends.

Pitch 2 Continue (5.7) moving left at a crack at the top. Descend via the **Regular Route**.

468 **LOWER TEAPOT DOME 5.8** This summit originally was attained by way of a tyrolean traverse. An aid climb later was established, and more recently, the route was freed. From the top of the **Regular Route**, walk down the backside to the notch between the two summits. Walk around to the right (to the north face) to reach the "ivy crack." Follow the crack to a tree where unprotected climbing leads to the sum-mit. This climb is loose and protected from climbers by poison oak.

469 **BALL PINNACLE 5.6** This photogenic spire is directly behind and downhill from **Lower Teapot Dome**. It is the tantalizing, pointed spire with the mystical bush grow-ing out of the summit block. It can be seen by those hiking up the Juniper Canyon Trail. Although most sides of the formation look insurmountable, the uphill side facing Lower Teapot Dome is mostly third class with some fifth-class climbing. The mystical bush is the rappel anchor. Climb third class left, then up for 100 feet to a notch with a bolt. Circumvent the first bulge by traversing either left or right to the final bulge. A bolt protects this move, another bolt is found 20 feet higher. Approach down the west side of Teapot Dome.

470 **THE WEDGE 5.5 A2** This bizarre-looking pinnacle makes one mutter thanks that they are not on top during a big quake. Definitely a wedge, this rock looks like a trail-side guardian. Located just right of Teapot, climb a bolt ladder on the overhanging west side.

470a **WEDGIE 5.9 TR** This route ascends the northeast face of The Wedge. Loose.

471 **DISINTEGRATION POINT 4th class** This little pinnacle is just north/uphill of The Wedge. Anyone looking to bag all the fourth-class summits in the park can climb up the north side of this rock.

472 **ARCH PINNACLE 5.6** This formation is the northernmost of the trio of pinnacles formed with the two preceding routes. This rock has another slab leaning over it to the right. The route goes up to the left of the slab, past a bolt, to the top.

TEAPOT
DOME

THE
WEDGE

465a | 466

photo: Kevin Kilpatrick

473 **THE GROOVE 5.7** This unnerving route follows a right-slanting groove/corner 40
feet south (downhill) of Proclamation Pinnacle. It rises off the opposite of the trail.
Loose rock, a hard-to-protect crack and disconcerting bolts relegate this climb to the
"know what you're getting into" list.

Proclamation Pinnacle

Proclamation Pinnacle is the large, split pinnacle on the left/west side of the
trail just before the final switchbacks leading to the High Peaks/Tunnel Trail intersection. It's also right below Burgundy Dome. The two original routes (ascending the
north and south summits) – and a newer line, **Adrenaline Junkies** – are on the side
facing the trail. **Emancipation** starts around the corner, to the right and slightly
downhill from **Adrenaline Junkies** and angles up and right to a wide crack above.
There are rappel anchors on the shoulder at the top of **Adrenaline Junkies**.

474 **PROCLAMATION PINNACLE – SOUTH SUMMIT 4th class or 5.5** This infrequent-
ly visited summit is climbed by going through the slot between the summits to the
northwest shoulder. Climb the shoulder fourth class to the top. The obvious slot facing the trail, just left of the fourth class start, has been climbed and has a 5.5 start.

474a **PROCLAMATION PINNACLE – NORTH SUMMIT CRACK** 5.7   The chimney that splits the north and south summits may be climbed from the back/downhill side. Start up a crack just left of the chimney. Follow the crack until it merges with the chimney. Continue up the chimney past the bolt on **North Summit**. This route has been done in two pitches.

475 **PROCLAMATION PINNACLE – NORTH SUMMIT** 5.6   Climb the right-hand chimney to near its top. Step left past a bolt and climb to the summit.

476 **PROCLAMATION PINNACLE – ADRENALINE JUNKIES** 5.10c ★   Follow a line of six bolts up the prow to the right of **North Summit**. Thrilling climbing on okay rock leads directly to the rappel anchors.

477 **PROCLAMATION PINNACLE – EMANCIPATION** 5.9   This climb is on the northeast face. Creative and skillful protection placements are required to safely climb this route.

477 PROCLAMATION PINNACLE—EMANCIPATION 5.9

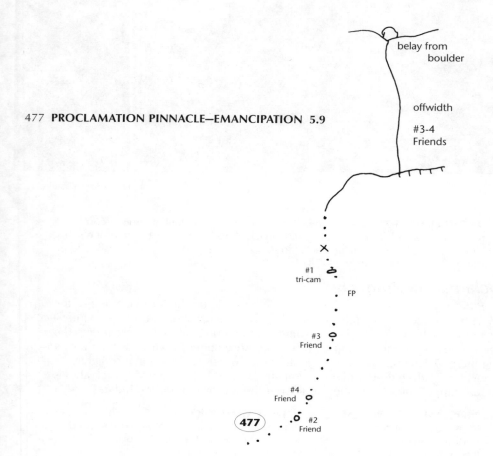

PROCLAMATION
PINNACLE

474   475   476

477

The Egg

This triple-layered formation is located a couple hundred yards behind, downhill and northwest from Proclamation Pinnacle. It can be seen by looking past the north face of Proclamation Pinnacle. See the photo on page 181.

Follow a small trail, starting about 20 yards up the main trail from Proclamation Pinnacle, directly over to the rock. The **Regular Route** is the inviting and obvious waterchute on the left side of the north face. **Sunny Side Up** starts downhill on the west face and follows the obvious waterchute on the left side of that face. The first two pitches ascend the lower angle apron below the main formation of The Egg.

478   **THE EGG – REGULAR ROUTE 5.9** ★   Climb the waterchute past a bolt ladder to an anchor. The first bolt is missing. Continue fourth class to the top.

479   **THE EGG – SUNNY SIDE UP 5.10 A1 or 5.10+**   The first pitch starts about 100 yards downhill and to the right/south of the main rock on a low angle slab. A three-foot block marks the start.

The Egg
478   **THE EGG – REGULAR ROUTE 5.9** ★
479   **THE EGG – SUNNY SIDE UP 5.10 A1 or 5.10+**

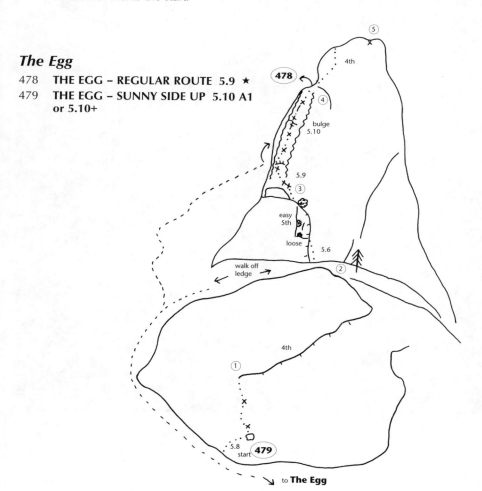

Hunky Dory Rock

This rock is the next largest formation downhill and southwest of The Egg. It can be approached either by descending the slope from The Egg or hiking directly from below, off the Juniper Canyon Trail. Both routes ascend the west/downhill face.

480 **HUNKY DORY 5.8**

481 **HALLOWEENIE 5.7** This route is very loose.

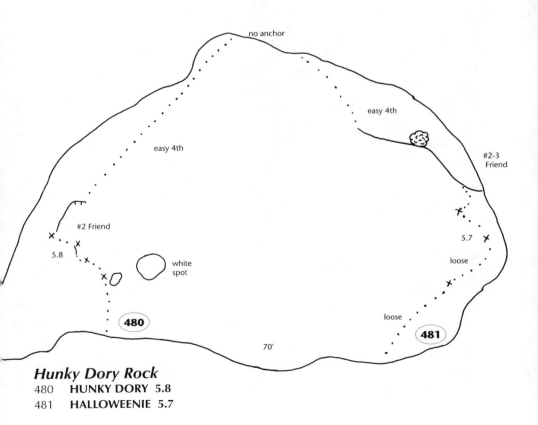

Hunky Dory Rock
480 **HUNKY DORY 5.8**
481 **HALLOWEENIE 5.7**

Bret Bernhardt on Shake and Bake

FIRST ASCENTS

NOTATION:
FA = First Ascent
FFA = First Free Ascent
FL = First Lead of a toprope route
tr = Toprope
?? = Obscure route (available information is either minimal, unclear or very old).

NOTE: All routes have been done ground up except where noted as a rappel route. Occasionally, bolt types will be noted where it is fairly clear that a first ascentionist consistently used the same type of bolt. **Do not take the bolt data as the absolute truth**, but rather as another possible gauge to measure the security of protection. Style will not be noted where there is uncertainty. "Bolts placed from stance" means that the leader was able to drill the bolt standing in balance. "Bolts placed from aid" means that the bolt was placed after securing a point of aid and then weighting it, whether from a skyhook, tied-off knob, a nut or camming unit.

The purpose of including the bolting information is to enlarge the data available to climbers leading in an area where bolts make up the primary form of protection and where there is an abundance of old bolts. Hopefully, this data might prevent someone from the rude awakening of encountering a bad or inadequate bolt. This index is a start and far from being complete. As further additions are published, current bolt status will be added. Please inform me of any retro-bolting you do or know that needs to be done. For guidelines in replacing a bolt refer to the section on bolting. Also, if you do a route marked with the **??** symbol and find the description either accurate or not, please let me know so that I can update the guide.

1   **Bat Cave** FA: Dave Haller, Dave Crough, Rick Gustafson, 6/73. FFA: Larry Martin, Sam Davidson, 1984. Bolts: ¼", no bolts on top.

1a   **Bat Cave—Direct Finish** FA (tr): Kelly Rich, 1990.

2   **Contraband Crack** FA: Jeff Vance, Kent Kaiser, Dave Robertson, 6/73, ??

3   **Delusion Overhang** FA: Jim Bridwell, Craig Little, 6/64, ??

4   **Delusion Overhang—Right** FA: Jeff Vance, Kent Merlie, 6/73. FFA: Unknown. ??

5   **Anchor Scream** FA: David Rubine, Eric Topel, 2/90. Bolts placed from aid. Bolts: ⅜" x 3¾" wedge anchors.

6   **This Bolt's For You aka The Price** FA: David Rubine, Tom Davis, Tim Reid, 10/90. Six bolts placed from aid, one from stance. Bolts: ⅜" Rawl torque bolts, wedge anchors.

7   **Triangle Skirt** FA: Dave Haller, Dave Crough, Chuck Richards, 1/73, ??

7a   **Angstrom's Away** FA: Ken Lowe, Carey Zumpano, 8/1/92.

8   **Rat Race** FA: Unknown.

9   **Happy Married Bachelor** FA: Tim Kemple et al., mid-1980s, ??

10   **Thrill Hammer** FA: Tim Reid, Eric Topel, David Rubine, 10/90. One bolt placed from stance, rest placed from aid. Bolts: ⅜" x 3" wedge anchors.

11   **Pastie** FA: Unknown.

12   **Nipple Jam** FA: Unknown.

12a   **Wild Berry Crack** FA: Jon McConachie, Kelly Wells, 10/27/91.

13   **Steve's Folly** FA: Jack Davis, Jim Broadhurst, 11/57. Bolts: ¼"

13a   **Chunky Monkey** FA: Clint Cummins, Chris Bellizzi, Dave Woodin, 4/1/92. Bolts ⅜" Rawl. Bolts placed from aid.

14   **Flip-a-Coin Chimney** FA: Unknown

14a   **Sport Climber's Terror** FA: Clint Cummins, Chris Donahue, 4/1/92.

15   **Heffalump** FA: Don Evers, Floyd Burnette, Bob Swift, Ray DeSaussure, 10/51.

16   **December Shadows** FA: Paul Gagner, Robert Renfer, 12/78. FFA (tr): James McConachie, 9/86. FFA (lead): Barry Bates, 10/87.

17   **Daddy Long Legs** FA (tr): Mike Carville, 11/86. FL: Tom Davis, 4/88. Bolts placed from aid. Bolts: ⅜" Rawl.

17a   **Time Stands Still** FA: Peter Nielsen, Chris Cooke, Spring 1993. Bolts: ⅜" Rawl. Bolts placed from aid.

18   **Tarantula** FA (tr): Mike Carville, 9/86. FL: Chris Bellizzi, David Rubine, 9/89. Bolts placed from aid. Bolts: ⅜" Rawl torque bolts and wedge anchors.

19   **No Holds Barred** FA: Jim Bridwell, Larry Kilmer, 11/61. FFA: Jim Bridwell, 1965.

19a   **No Holds Barred Direct Finish** FA: Jim Bridwell, 1965.

20   **Overhang Chimney** FA: Chuck Pratt, 1960, ??

20a   **This Spud's For You** FA: James McConachie, Jon McConachie, 1/1/88.

20b   **Nothin' Beats A Spud** FA: James and Karl McConachie, 3/1/92.

21   **Pillbox Crack** FA: Al MacDonald, Jim Buckley, Bob Clune, Bob Klose, Jeff Foott, Joe McKeown, Dave Gaunt, Gary Skelton 1959.

22   **Nailbox Crack** FA: Will Piper, John Armitage, 5/65. FFA: Barry Bates, Drummond Hoffman, 12/70. Bolts: first belay stance includes two ⅜" wedge anchors.

23   **Coffin Nail** FA: Paul Gagner, Chris Bellizzi, 1989. Bolts placed from aid. Bolts: ⅜" split shaft.

24   **Mustache** FA: Tom Rohrer, Ben Robinson, 12/67. First clean ascent: Pete King, May 1995.

24a   **Racing Stripes** FA: Tom Davis, Kelly Rich, 6/1/91. Bolts: ⅜" Rawl torque. Bolts placed from aid.

24b   **Melvin** FA: Kelly Rich, David Rubine, Tom Davis, 6/1/91. Bolts: ⅜" Rawl torque. Bolts placed from aid.

25   **Between a Rock and a Hard Place** FA: Tom Davis, Kelly Rich, David Rubine, Chris Bellizzi, 1/90. One bolt placed from stance, rest placed from aid. Bolts: ⅜" Rawl torque bolts and wedge anchors.

25a   **Labor of Love** FA: Jeff Dopp, John McCoy, early '90s. Bolts: ⅜" Rawl torque.

26   **Portent** FA: Andrew Emery, Steve Roper, 12/65. Bolts: ⅜" split shaft, ⅜" Rawl torque bolt.

26a   **Fat Lip** FA: Unknown, early '90s.

27   **The Big Pucker** FA: Tom Davis, David Rubine, 11/88. One bolt placed from stance, rest placed from aid. Bolts: ⅜" x 3¾" wedge anchors.

28   **The Wet Kiss** FA: David Rubine, Kelly Rich, 12/88. Bolts placed from aid. Bolts: ⅜" x 3¾" wedge anchors.

29   **Plague** FA: Jack Holmgren, Peter Ruben, 5/82. Bolts placed from stance. Bolts: ⅜" Star Dryvin.

30 **Trauma** FA: Jim Bridwell, Dave Bircheff, Bruce Smith, 3/65. FFA: Unknown. Bolts: two 2⅜" x 3¾" wedge anchors on top.

30a **Traumatize – Direct Finish** FA: Kelly Rich, David Rubine, Tim Reid, 1/91. Bolt placed from aid. Bolt: ⅜" x 3¾" wedge anchor.

31 **Zippety Doo-Dah** FA: David Rubine, Tom Davis, 11/89. Bolts placed from aid. Bolts: ⅜" x 3¾" wedge anchors and Rawl.

32 **The Gladiator** FA: Paul Gagner, Chris Bellizzi, 11/89. Bolts placed from stance and aid. Bolts: ⅜" split shaft.

33 **Dead Bird Crack** FA: Unknown.

34 **Bye-Bye Fly-By** FA: Scott Fitzgerald, Jeff Maudlin, 1984. Bolt: ⅜" Star Dryvin.

35 **Fly-By** FA: Dave Coates, Wayne Steinert, 2/65. FFA: Jim Bridwell, Mike Kilmer, Dave Bircheff, 65. Bolt: bad ¼".

36 **Swallow Crack** FA: Dave Bircheff, Phil Bircheff, 2/65 Bolts: Protection: ⅜" x 3" Rawl torque bolt, ⅜" split shaft. Anchors: ⅜" Rawl, ⅜" Star Dryvin.

37 **Jorgie's Crack** FA: Wayne Steinert, Bob Williams, Jack Gouday, 3/65. FA (to top): Tom Rohrer, 12/67. FFA: Barry Bates, Dave Hampton, 12/70. Bolts: ⅜" Star Dryvin. Anchor: two ⅜"wedge anchors.

37a **Jorgie's Crack Continuation** FA: Clint Cummins, Nancy Kerrebrook, 2/91. Bolts ⅜" Rawl.

38 **February Fools** FA: Barry Bates, Michael McDaniel, 2/74. Bolt: ¼".

39 **Pweeter** FA: David Rubine, Tim Reid, 11/90. One bolt placed from stance, rest placed from aid. Bolts: ⅜" Rawl torque bolts and wedge anchors.

40 **Ordeal** FA: Jim Bridwell, Dave Bircheff, Wayne Steinert, 3/65. Bolts: all ⅜" Rawl torque bolt.

41 **Buffalo Soldier** FL (bolts placed on rappel): Mike Carville, 7/86. Toproped before led. Bolts: ⅜" wedge anchors.

42 **Broken Arrow** FL (bolts placed on rappel): Mike Carville, 9/86. Toproped before led. Bolts: ⅜" wedge anchors.

42a **Broken Arrow Direct Variation** FL (rap): Mike Carville, 9/86.

43 **Here Comes the Judge** FA: Paul Gagner, Chris Bellizzi, 1989. Bolts placed from aid. Bolts: ⅜" split shaft.

44 **Trial** FA: Jim Bridwell, Mike Kilmer, 2/65. FFA: David Rubine, Tom Davis, Kelly Rich, 10/88. Bolts placed from aid. Bolts: ⅜" x 3¾" wedge anchors, one original ⅜" Star Dryvin.

45 **The Verdict** FA (tr): David Rubine, Tom Davis, Kelly Rich, 12/88. FL: Chris Bellizzi, Paul Gagner, 2/89. Bolts placed from aid. Bolts: ⅜" split shaft.

45a **Verdict Direct Variation** FL: Clint Cummins, 11/89. One bolt placed on lead from aid, one from rappel. Bolts: ⅜" Rawl torque bolts.

46 **Pistol Whipped** FA: Todd Telander, Mike Carville, Robert Cox, 4/87. Bolts placed from hooks and stance after toproping. Bolts: ⅜" wedge anchors.

47 **Cleft** FA: Jim Bridwell, Larry Kilmer, Mike Kilmer, 3/62. Bolts: ⅜"" Star Dryvin and split shaft, ⅜" Rawl torque bolts at belay

47a **Lithium** FA: Clint Cummins, Dennis Erik Strom, 3/1/92. Bolts: ⅜" Rawl torque bolts

48 **Stupendous Man** FA: David Rubine, Eric Topel, 7/90. One bolt placed from stance, rest placed from aid. Bolts: ⅜" Rawl torque bolts, wedge anchors.

49 **Entrance** FA: Jim Bridwell, et al., 2/65. Bolts: ⅜" Rawl torque bolt and ⅜" split shaft.

49a **Power Point** FA tr: Mark Swank, 1/1/91. FL: Unknown.

49b   **Mammary Junk**   FA tr: Joel Ager, Clint Cummins, 1/1/91.

50   **Mammary Pump**   FA: Paul Gagner, Chris Bellizzi, 1988. One bolt placed from stance, rest placed from aid. Bolts: ⅜" split shaft.

51   **Lost Horizons**   FA: John Barbella, Tom Templemen, 2/76. Bolts: ⅜" Star Dryvin.

52   **Cosmos**   FL (bolts placed on rappel): Mike Carville, 10/86. Bolts: ⅜" wedge anchors.

53   **Forty Days of Rain**   FA: Tom Davis, Kelly Rich, David Rubine, 10/88. Bolts placed from aid. Bolts: ⅜" x 3¾" wedge anchors and Rawl.

54   **Gutter**   FA: Tom Rohrer, Robert Todd, 2/68. FFA: Jim Beyer, Bob Sullivan, 10/78.

55   **Roof**   FA: Jim Bridwell, Craig Little, 10/65. FFA: Unknown. Bolts: ¼" at start of roof, ⅜" Rawl Torque at end of roof.

56   **Slot**   FA: Jim Bridwell, Mike Kilmer, Dave Bircheff, 10/65.

57   **Welcome to the Machine**   FA: Kelly Rich, Eric Topel, 1989.

57a   **Spaceman Spiff**   FA: Brad Young, Tom Barney, Sam Davidson, 12/17/93. Bolt Pro.: 6 ⅜" x 3" Rawl Torque, Anchor: many ⅜" Star Dryvin.

57b   **Dismemberment Gorge**   FA: Brad Young, 12/17/93.

58   **Happy Birthday George**   FA: Rupert Kammerlander, John Schaffert, 2/76, ?? Bolts placed from stance. Bolts: ¼".

59   **Agrarian**   FA: Jim Beyer, Janice Linhares, 12/77. Bolts placed from stance. Bolts: ¼"

60   **Exiles**   FA: John Barbella, James McConachie, 2/85. Bolts placed from stance. Bolts: ⅜".

61   **Heat Seeking Moisture Missile**   FA: John Barbella, James McConachie, Paul Gagner 2/84. Bolts placed from aid and stance. Bolts ¼" and ⅜" split shaft.

62   **Crash Buds**   FA: Jim Beyer, Tim Washick, 1977. FFA: Paul Gagner, 11/81. Bolt: ⅜" split shaft on first pitch.

63   **Buzzard Bait**   FA: James McConachie, John Barbella, 2/85. Bolts: one ¼" and one ⅜" split shaft.

63a   **Voyeur**   FA: James and Jon McConachie, 2/1/91.

64   **Scorpion**   FA: Jim Beyer, Tim Washick, 1977, ??

65   **An-archy**   FFA: Kelly Rich, David Rubine, Tom Davis, 2/86. The arch was initially led without the bolt. Bolts: ⅜" split shaft.

65a   **Zig-Zag Man**   FA: Kelly Rich, '92.

66   **Zig-zag Left**   FA: Jim Bridwell, Craig Little, 2/65. FFA: Barry Bates, Buff Njoa, 4/74.

67   **Zig-zag**   FA: Jim Bridwell, Craig Little, 2/65. FFA: Barry Bates, Buff Njoa, 4/74.

68   **Surf's Up**   FA: Lanny Johnson, ?? Bolt: ⅜" wedge anchor.

69   **Torque Twister**   FA: John Barbella, Chris Bellizzi, 2/82.

70   **Honeycomb**   FA: Jim Beyer.

71   **Limp at Last**   FA: David Rubine, Raoul Rickenberg, Ben Carlson, 4/89. Bolts placed from aid. Bolts: ⅜" x 3 ¾" wedge anchors.

72   **Mr. Hugh G. Rection**   FA: Unknown.

73   **Auto Cream aka Sunwheel**   FA: David Rubine, Pat Kent, 4/89. Bolts placed from aid. Bolts: ⅜" x 3¾" wedge anchors.

74   **The Gag**   FA: John Barbella, James McConachie, 8/85. Bolts: ¼".

75   **The Vigilante**   FA: David Rubine, Paul Gagner, 4/89. Bolts placed from aid. Bolts: ⅜" x 3¾" wedge anchors, except for first bolt – ⅜" split shaft.

76 **Fringe Dweller** FA: David Rubine, Tom Davis, 3/89. Two bolts placed from stance, two from aid. Bolts: ⅜" x 3¾" wedge anchors.

77 **The Druid** FA: David Rubine, Tom Davis, 3/89. Bolts placed from aid. Bolts: ⅜" x 3¾" wedge anchors, one Rawl at start.

78 **Men at Work** FA: Paul Gagner, Chris Bellizzi, 1989. Bolts placed from aid. Bolts: ⅜" split shaft.

78a **The Jerk** FA: Chris Belizzi, early '90s. Bolts placed from aid. Bolts: ⅜" split shaft.

78b **Wet Willie** FA: Eric Gable, early '90s. Bolts: ⅜" Rawl torque.

79 **Ranger Bolts** FA: Doug Cardinal, et al, 1973. FL (to double bolts): Tom Davis '88. Retrobolted on lead from hooks. Bolts: ⅜" wedge anchors. FA (direct start): Tom Davis, Jeff Gorris. Bolts placed from stance. Bolts: ⅜" wedge anchors. FFA (tr entire route): Jim Thornburg, 10/89. FL: John Yablonski, Scott Frye, Jim Thornburg, 11/89 Retrobolted on rappel. Bolts: ⅜".

80 **Ape Index** FA: Paul Gagner, Dave Caunt, 1989. First bolt from stance, rest from aid. Bolts: ⅜" split shaft.

81 **Lower North Face** FA: Unknown. FFA: Unknown retrobolted with ⅜" wedge anchors and Rawl, also ¼" and ⅜" split shaft and Star Dryvin from earlier ascents. Rawl bolt in boulder at base as anchor.

82 **Rocket in my Pocket** FA: Tom Davis, Mike Harrington. Bolts placed from stance, one bolt placed from aid. Bolts: ⅜" wedge anchors.

83 **Future Shock** FA: Tom Davis, David Rubine, 9/88. First two bolts placed in stance, rest placed from aid. Bolts: ⅜" x 3¾" wedge anchors.

84 **Cataract Corner** FA (tr): Mike Carville, 7/86. FL: Tom Davis (bolts placed on rap by Mike Carville) Bolts: ⅜" wedge anchors.

85 **Foreplay** FA: Tom Davis, Kelly Rich, David Rubine, Ruselle Rubine, 12/88. Bolts: 2 ⅜" Rawl torque bolt, rest are ⅜" wedge anchors. Bolts placed from aid.

86 **Several Small Species** FA (tr): Karl McConachie, circa 1979.

87 **Post Orgasmic Depression (P.O.D.)** FL: Chris Bellizzi, 1981 (bolts placed on rap and lead by several people) Bolts: ⅜" Rawl torque bolt, ⅜" split shaft. Top anchor has ⅜" wedge anchors and Star Dryvin. Top block rappel station has two ⅜" Star Dryvin and one wedge anchor.

88 **Indirect Traverse** FA: Blake Hinman, Doug Cardinal, 5/74. Bolts: ⅜" Rawl, split shaft, Star Dryvin.

89 **Hawaiian Noises** FL (bolts placed on rappel): Mike Carville, Joel Richnak, 6/86. Bolts: ⅜" wedge anchors.

90 **Subterranean Tango** FA: Tom Davis, Mike Harrington, Sylvain Malchelosse, 2/88. Placed in stance. Bolts: ⅜" wedge anchors.

91 **Direct Route (Monolith)** FA: John Whitmer, Dave Hammack, 12/53. Route was initially led with one bolt and pitons. Retrobolted with ⅜" wedge anchors or split shaft.

91a **Way Below the Direct** FA: Jeff Schoen, 1/1/93.

91b **Baby Blues (aka—Post Partum Depression)** FA tr: Peter Lataille, 1/1/91.

92 **Richnak's Revenge** FL (bolts placed on rappel): Joel Richnak, Mike Carville, 6/86. Bolts: ⅜" wedge anchors.

92a **Lodestone var.** FA (tr): Clint Cummins 12/89.

93 **Monolith – Regular Route** FA: John Whitmer, Craig Holden. Anchors: ⅜" Star Dryvin. Pro: ⅜" Rawl torque bolt.

93a **Hard Variation** FA: Unknown. Bolts: ⅜" Rawl.

93b **God is Gravity** FA tr: Unknown.

94   **Monolith—Northeast Corner var.** FA: Mark Powell, Sully Cooper, '56.

94a   **Piton Traverse** FA: Al Baxter, John Hood, Bud Gates, 2/47.

95   **Feed the Beast** FA (tr): Unknown. FL: David Rubine, 8/89. Bolts placed from aid. Bolts: ⅜" x 3¾" wedge anchors, ⅜" Rawl Torque.

96   **Canteloupe Death** FL (bolts placed on rappel): Mark Chapman, 1989. Bolts: ⅜" Red Head sleeve anchor.

97   **Hot Lava Lucy** FL (bolts placed on rappel): John Yablonski, 1989. Bolts: ⅜" Rawl.

97a   **Lard Butt** FL: (bolts placed on rappel): Jim Thornburg, 11/1/93.

98   **Bridwell Bolts** FA: Jim Bridwell, Larry Kilmer, Craig Little, 1/63. Bolts: many ¼".

99   **Black Dagger** FA: Kelly Rich, David Rubine, 4/89. One bolt placed from stance, rest placed from aid. Bolts: ⅜" x 3¾" wedge anchors.

99a   **The Pearl Sheath** FA: Kelly Rich, David Rubine, 1/1/95. Bolts: ⅜" x 3½" Rawl Torque. Bolts placed from stance and aid.

100   **Castles Made of Sand** FA: Kelly Rich, Tom Davis, 1/90. One bolt placed from aid, one placed from stance. Bolt: ⅜" Rawl or wedge anchors.

102   **Sound Chaser** FA: John Barbella, Paul Gagner, 1/83 Bolts: ⅜" Rawl.

103   **Relayer** FA: David Rubine, Jeff Gorris, 1/90. Bolts placed from aid. Bolts: ⅜" x 3¾" wedge anchors, ⅜" Rawl Torque.

104   **Organgrinder** FA: Eric Topel, David Rubine, 3/90. Bolts placed from aid. Bolts: ⅜" x 3¾" wedge anchors.

105   **Me and My Monkey** FA: Eric Topel, David Rubine, 3/90. Last bolt placed from stance, rest placed from aid. Bolts: ⅜" x 3¾" wedge anchors.

106   **Baboon Crack** FA: David Rubine, Sam Davidson 5/95.

107   **When in Doubt Run it Out** FA: John Barbella, Paul Gagner, 1/83.

108   **Japanese Water Torture** FA: John Barbella, Paul Gagner, 1/82. Bolts placed from stance. Bolts: ⅜" split shaft.

109   **Nodal Line** FA: Bob Katsma, Dave Parks, 12/76. Bolts: ⅜" Star Dryvin, ⅜" Rawl torque bolt.

110   **Hard as a Rock** FA: Kelly Rich, 11/90. First bolt placed from stance, rest placed from aid. Bolts: ⅜" Rawl and wedge anchors.

111   **Cross Your Heart** FA: Kelly Rich, David Rubine, Tom Davis, 1/89. First Bolt placed from stance, rest placed from aid. Bolts: ⅜" Rawl and wedge anchors.

112   **Coyote Ugly** FA: David Rubine, Eric Topel, 3/89. Two bolts placed from stance, rest placed from aid. Bolts: ⅜" x 3¾" wedge anchors. One ⅜" Rawl torque and four ⅜" x 3¾" wedge anchors on top.

112a   **Coyote Ugly** direct finish FA (tr): David Rubine 4/90.

113   **Sidesaddle** FA: Unknown.

114   **Backside Route** FA: Unknown. Bolt: ¼".

115   **Toprope Wall** FA: Tom Davis 1988. Bolts: ⅜" wedge anchors, ⅜" Rawl torque.

116   **Ali Baba** FA: Mike Harrington, Tom Davis, 2/88. Bolts placed from hooks and stance. Bolts: ⅜" wedge anchors.

117   **Love Handles** FA: Kelly Rich, David Rubine, Tom Davis, Chris Bellizzi, 1989. Third bolt placed from stance, rest placed from aid. Bolts: ⅜" wedge anchors, one ⅜" split shaft.

118   **First Sister—Left Route** FA: Unknown. Bolts: ⅜" Rawl torque bolts.

119   **First Sister—Center Route** FA: Unknown. Bolts: ⅜" Rawl torque bolts.

120 **First Sister—Back side** FA: Unknown, ?? Bolt; ⅜" Star Dryvin.

121 **Second Sister** FA: Unknown.

122 **Third Sister** FA: Unknown. Bolts: ¼ ".

123 **Third Sister—Little Sister Spire** FA: Unknown. Bolts: ¼".

124 **Fourth Sister—West Face** FA: Unknown.

125 **Fourth Sister—North Shoulder** FA: Unknown. Bolt: hangerless ⅜" split shaft.

126 **Fourth Sister—Silhouette Arête** FA: Jim Beyer, Courtney Simpkins, 12/76.

126a **Ghost of Tiburcios** FA: Unknown. Bolts pro. and anchor: ⅜" Rawl Torque.

126b **Going The Wong Way** FA: Steve and Beverly Wong, Phil Marr, 1/1/94. Bolts: ⅜" Rawl torque.

127 **Fifth Sister** FA: Unknown.

128 **Hatchet** FA (kite, strings, and prusik): Jim Wilson, 1946. FA (plain prusik): Anton Nelson, Robin Hansen, Dick Houston, 1946. FA (bolts to Nail Puller notch): Don Evers, Bill Dunmire, Floyd Burnette. FA (bolts to summit): Jim Moore. FFA: Unknown, by 1966.

129 **Gerties Pinnacle – Regular Route** FA: Unknown.

130 **Ramble and Gamble** FA: Jim Beyer, Courtney Simpkins, 11/76, ??

131 **Maniac's Delight—Regular Route** FA: Jim Harper, Steve Roper, 2/63.

132 **Maniac's Delight—West Side** FA: Unknown, ??

133 **Knee—Regular Route** FA: Earl Furman, Mark Roest, Margaret Young, 4/69, ??

134 **Blowing Chunks** FA: John Barbella, Paul Gagner, 5/82. Bolts: some ¼" and ⅜" split shaft.

135 **Nit-Wit Knob** FA: Earl Furman, Roger Breedlove, Gordon Lien, 10/69, ??

136 **Little Mustagh** FA: Bob Swift, Terry Tarver, Fred Schaub, 3/57. Bolts: many ¼".

137 **Crud and Mud** FA: Unknown, ??

138 **South Side Shuffle** FA: Anton Nelson, Robin Hansen, Dick Houston, 1946.

139 **East Chimney** FA: Unknown.

140 **Big Sky** FA (solo): Jim Beyer, 3/78.

141 **Atlas Shrugs** FA: Jim Beyer, Tim Washick, 1977.

142 **MaGootchy Bird Chimney** FA: Al Baxter, Bill Kershaw, 1947. Bolt: ¼"

143 **Tuff** FA: Jim Beyer, Bob Sullivan, 10/78. Bolts: ⅜" Star Dryvin.

144 **Fear and Perspiration** FA: Jim Beyer. Bolts: ⅜" Star Dryvin.

145 **Dirty Bird Crack** FA: Jim Smith, John Whitmer, 1959. Bolts: Star Dryvin.

146 **Pinch Gripped** FA: Jim Beyer, Courtney Simpkins, 10/76, ??

147 **Ski Jump** FA: Rupert Kammerlander, Bev Belanger, 3/75. Bolts: ¼".

148 **Lonesome Dove** FA: Unknown. Bolts: ⅜" wedge anchors or split shaft.

149 **Getchy-Getchy Bird** FA: Earl Furman, et al., 2/70, ??

150 **Snail** FA: Unknown.

151 **Salathé** FA: John Salathé, Robin Hansen, Dick Houston, 2/47. Bolts: ⅜" Star Dryvin.

151a **Burnette Bolt var.** FA: Floyd Burnette, Al Steck, 1949. Bolts: ⅜" Star Dryvin.

151b **Wilts Bolt var.** FA: Chuck Wilts, Ellen Wilts, 1956, ??

152 **Lifeline** FA: Dave Parks, Stu Polack, 2/86. Bolt: ⅜" Star Dryvin.

153 **Carpel Tunnel Syndrome** FA: James McConachie, Clint Cummins, early '90s. One bolt placed from stance, rest placed from aid. Bolts: ⅜" split shaft and Rawl.

154   **Back of Hand**   FA: John Whitmer, Bill Kyle, 4/58.

155   **Bolt Ladder**   FA: Unknown, ??

156   **Regular Route (Thumb)**   FA: Dick Houston, Robin Hansen, Anton Nelson 1946. Bolts: ¼".

157   **Fifty Meter Must**   FA: Rupert Kammerlander, Bev Belanger, 11/75. Bolts: ¼".

158   **Bicuspid**   FA: Jim Smith, Bob Smith, Bruce Edwards, 12/62, ??

159   **Incisor**   FA (prusik): Jim Smith, Bob Smith, Bruce Edwards, 12/62. FFA: Earl, Eric and Tim Furman, Bernie Aaen, 12/67, ??

160   **First Tooth**   FA (prusik): Jim Smith, Bob Smith, Bruce Edwards, 1963. FFA: Earl, Eric and Tim Furman, Bernie Aaen, 12/67, ??

161   **Second Tooth**   FA (prusik): Jim Smith, Bob Smith, Bruce Edwards, 63. FFA: Earl, Eric and Tim Furman, Bernie Aaen, 12/67, ??

162   **Third Tooth**   FA: Earl, Eric and Tim Furman, Bernie Aaen, 12/67, ??

163   **Spasm Block**   FA: Jim Harper, Steve Roper, 2/63. Bolts: 1¼".

164   **Chimney Sweep**   FA: James McConachie, Jon McConachie, mid-1980s.

165   **Mollusk**   FA: Jim Smith, Dave French, Bruce Edwards, 11/62 Bolt: Star Dryvin.

166   **Little Flatiron**   FA: Jim Smith, Bruce Edwards, 11/62. Bolts: ¼".

167   **Toadstool**   FA: Jim and Bob Smith, Howard Lewis, Bruce Edwards, 12/62.

168   **Triple Decker**   FA: Jim and Bob Smith, Howard Lewis, Bruce Edwards, 12/62.

169   **Lion's Head**   FA: Jim Smith, Bruce Edwards, Dave French, 11/62, ??

170   **Outcast—West Face**   FA: Jim Smith, Bruce Edwards, Dave French, 11/62.

171   **Outcast—West Face Right**   FA: Unknown.

172   **Outcast—South Face**   FA: Jim Harper, Steve Roper, 2/63.

173   **Outcast—East Face**   FA: Dick Irvin, Richard Hechtel, 1/63.

174   **Outcast—Northeast Rib**   FA: Unknown. Bolts: ¼".

174a   **Back Alley Driver**   FA (tr): Dennis Erik Strom, Steve Wilcox, David Wood, 1/1/91.

175   **Knuckle Ridge**   FA: Jim Smith, Bruce Edwards, Dave French, 11/62, ??

175a   **The Darkness Within**   FA: David Wood, Dennis Erik Strom, 11/1/94.

175b   **The Edge of Sundown**   FA: Dennis Erik Strom, David Wood, 12/1/91.

175c   **Catatonic Stupor**   FA: Bradley Young, Vickie Young, Martin Bez, 1/1/91.

175d   **The Agony of Defeat**   FA: Dennis Erik Strom, David Wood, Steve Wilcox, 1/1/94.

176   **Gargoyle**   FA: Jim and Bob Smith, Howard Lewis, Bruce Edwards, 12/62, ??

176a   **The Gargoyle—Que Lastima**   FA: Sam Davidson, Jack Holmgren, Bob Walton, '93. Bolts: ⅜" Rawl Torque. Bolts placed from stance.

176b   **The Gargoyle—La Gruniga**   FA: Bob Walton, Jack Holmgren, early '90s. Bolts placed from stance.

176c   **Viva Zapatos**   FA: Jack Holmgren, Sherry Vaughn, early '90s. Bolts placed from stance.

176d   **La Margen de la Vida**   FA: Jack Holmgren, Sherry Vaughn, early '90s. Bolts placed from stance.

177   **Marauder**   FA: Paul Gagner, John Barbella, 1987. Bolts: ⅜" split shaft.

178   **Wrinkle Remover**   FA: Steve Smith, Paul Gagner, Bill Crouse, 1988. Bolts: ⅜" split shaft.

179   **Asleep at the Wheel**   FA: Paul Gagner, Bill Crouse, 1988. Bolts: ⅜" split shaft.

180 **Marmot With a Hand Grenade** FA: Paul Gagner, Gary Thunen, 12/86. Bolts: ⅜" split shaft.

181 **The Heretic** FA: John Barbella, James McConachie, 3/87. Bolts placed from stance and aid. Bolts: ¼" and ⅜" split shaft.

182 **Little Marmot** FA: Dick Irvin, Jerry Leonard, Randy Lawrence, date unknown.

183 **Big Marmot** FA: Allan Kreiss, Randy Lawrence, Paul Porter, 8/63. FFA: Unknown. Bolts: ¼".

184 **Furry Marmot Substitute** FA: Paul Gagner, Gary Thunen, 12/86. Bolts: ⅜" split shaft.

185 **Making Puppies** FA: Paul Gagner, Gary Thunen, 3/87. Bolts: ⅜" split shaft.

186 **On a Pale Horse** FA: John Barbella, James McConachie, 9/86. Bolts placed from stance. Bolts: ⅜" split shaft.

187 **Frontiers of Chaos** FA: Paul Gagner, John Barbella, 4/87. Bolts: ⅜" split shaft.

188 **Murky Bong Water** FA: Paul Gagner, John Barbella, 11/86. Bolts: ⅜" split shaft.

189 **Only a Lad** FA: Paul Gagner, John Barbella, 11/86. Bolts: ⅜" split shaft.

190 **The Tom-Tom Club** FA: Paul Gagner, Gary Thunen, 12/86. Bolts: split shaft.

191 **Northwest Face—North Yak** FA: Craig Holden, Dave Sowles, John Whitmer, 3/56. Bolts: ¼". FFA: Unknown

191a **North Yak Tyrolean** FA: Dave Hammack, George Larimore, Manford Samuelson, Alice Ann Dayton, 6/51, ??

192 **North Face—North Yak** FA: Unknown. Bolts: ¼".

193 **South Yak** FA: Dave Hammack, George Larimore, 3/51, ??

194 **South Face—South Yak** FA: Unknown. Bolts: ¼".

195 **Beast of Burden** FA: Dave Parks, Stu Polack, 12/82. Bolts: ¼", top anchors are ⅜" Star Dryvin.

196 **Bullrun** FA: Dave Parks, Stu Polack, 1986. Bolts: ⅜" Star Dryvin.

197 **Shoot the Tube** FA: James McConachie, Jon McConachie, 2/84. Bolts placed from stance. Bolts: Two are ¼", two are ⅜", probably split shaft.

198 **Orion** FA: Rupert Kammerlander, Bruce Cooke, 2/78. Bolts: ¼".

199 **White Punks on Rope** FA(so far): James McConachie, Jon McConachie, mid-1980s.

200 **Split Infinity** FA: John Barbella, James McConachie and others, 5/86. Bolts: ⅜" and ¼", probably split shaft.

201 **Slip Stream** FA: Jim Beyer, Courtney Simpkins, 12/77. FFA: James McConachie, Jon McConachie, 84. New bolts added from stance.

202 **Tato Pani** FA: James McConachie, Bill McConachie, 11/86.

203 **Dance on a Volcano** FA: James McConachie, Jon McConachie, 10/87.

204 **Naked Lunge** FA: Joe Bryant, Malintha Winwood, Keith Vandevere, Jack Holmgren, 2/84. Bolts: first bolt is ¼", rest ⅜" Star Dryvin.

205 **Liebacker's Lullaby** FA: Rupert Kammerlander, Craig Mackay, 1/73.

206 **Crack Climber's Concerto** FA: Joe Bryant, Malintha Winwood, Keith Vandevere, Jack Holmgren, 2/84.

207 **Terminal Buttress** FA: Jack Holmgren, Joe Bryant, Malintha Winwood, Keith Vandevere, 1984.

207a **Terminal Buttress—McConachie/Barbella Var.** FA: James McConachie, John Barbella, 2/85, ??

208 **Venus Fly Trap** FA: Paul Gagner, Dave Caunt, 12/87. Bolts: ⅜" split shaft.

209 **Reach for the Sky** FA: Bill McConachie, James McConachie, 12/86. Anchors: 2 ⅜" wedge anchors.

210 **The High Chair** FA: Unknown, ?? Bolt: ⅜" Star Dryvin.

211 **Kasparek's Delight** FA: Anton Nelson, Robin Hansen, Dick Houston, 1946. FFA: Unknown. Bolts: one ¼" and one ⅜" Star Dryvin.

212 **Pinky Pinnacle** FFA: Unknown. Bolts: ⅜" Star Dryvin for protection, one ¼" on top.

213 **Toilet Seat** FA: Will Piper, Jim Smith, John Armitage, 3/65, ??

214 **Toilet Seat—The Drain Chimney** FA: Unknown, ??

215 **Hidden Pinnacle** FA: Bob Smith, Ed Sutton, 12/61. Bolts: Two ⅜" Star Dryvin.

216 **Teter-Tower** FA: Jim and Bob Smith, Ed Sutton, Ed Gammon, Al Timmons, Doug Wendt, 3/62.

217 **Nip and Tuck** FA: The Smiths, Sutton, Gammon, Timmons, Wendt, 3/62. Bolt: ¼".

218 **Wart** FA: The Smiths, Sutton, Gammon, Timmons, Wendt, 3/62.

219 **Wad—Left** FA: The Smiths, Sutton, Gammon, Timmons, Wendt, 3/62. Bolt: ⅜".

220 **Wad—Right** FA: The Smiths, Sutton, Gammon, Timmons, Wendt, 3/62.

221 **The Carousel** FA: Unknown. Bolts: Two ¼", two ⅜" wedge anchors.

222 **The Mushroom Cloud** FA: Unknown.

223 **The Anvil** FA: Unknown. Bolts: one ⅜" Star Dryvin and hangerless split shaft for anchors.

224 **Pipsqueak Pinnacle—Regular Route** FA: Bill Amborn, Joe McKeown, Dave McFadden, 11/60. Bolts: ¼" split shaft and ⅜" Star Dryvin on top.

225 **Pipsqueak Pinnacle—Rightfoot** FA: Bob Walton, Lincoln Hatch, 1/88 . Bolts: ⅜" Star Dryvin.

226 **The Snout** FA: Unknown. Bolts: one ¼" and ⅜" carriage-looking bolt on top.

227 **The Unmentionable** FA: Unknown. Bolts: ⅜" Star Dryvin. Two bolts on top.

228 **Bobbin** FA: Frank Tarver, Mary Kay Pottinger, Richard Irvin, 1954, ??

229 **Assault and Battery** FA: Jon McConachie, James McConachie, 3/89. Bolts placed from stance.

230 **Poodle With a Mohawk** FA: Jon McConachie, Bob McConachie, 1986. Bolts placed from stance. Bolts: ¼" and ⅜" split shaft.

231 **Pinch or Lynch** FA: Bill Griffen, Bob Katsma, Dave Parks, 4/76. Bolts: ¼".

232 **Generation Gap** FA: Tim Kemple, John Ramos, 1/1/83. Bolts: one ⅜" Star Dryvin for pro and one ⅜" Star Dryvin and ¼" split shaft on top.

233 **Thin Man** FA: Tim Kemple, John Ramos, 1/1/83. Bolts: ¼" and ⅜" split shaft.

234 **Salathé's Sliver** FA: John Salathé, Anton Nelson, '47. Bolts: Two ⅜" Star Dryvin on top.

235 **Nelson's Needle—Regular Route** FA: Unknown. Bolts: ⅜" Star Dryvin, two on top.

236 **Nelson's Needle—East Face** FA: John Servais, Dan Cutshall, R.F. Shimek, 11/72, ?? Bolts: ¼" protection bolt.

236a **Cemetary Gates** FA: Tim Kemple, Jon Ramos, 1/1/85.

237 **Nebulous Knob** FA: Dick Brown, Al Timmons, George Oetzel, 2/65. Bolts: ¼".

238 **Popcorn Pinnacle—Northeast Corner** FA: Dick Brown, Al Timmons, George Oetzel, 2/65, ??

239 **Popcorn Pinnacle Chimney** FA: Unknown.

240 **Raven** FA: Al Timmons, Dick Brown, George Oetzel, 2/65. Bolt: one ⅜" Star Dryvin on top.

241 **Buzzard** FA: Al Timmons, Dick Brown, George Oetzel, 2/65, ??

242 **Buzzard—Westside Layback** FA: Unknown.

243 **Vulture** FA: George Oetzel, G. Converse, R Flores, B. Covey, 3/65.

244 **Hip Hip Hooray** FA: Unknown.

245 **Hippo Stomp** FA: James McConachie, Kelly Wells, 6/87. Bolts: some ⅜", probably split shaft.

246 **Hippopotamus** FA: Unknown, ??

247 **Dutch Goose** FA: John Servais, Dan Cutshall, 3/73, ??

248 **Don Genaro's Waterfall** FA: John Servais, Dan Cutshall, 6/73.

249 **Crap Chute** FA: Brett Bernhardt, Tom Higgins, 4/86. Bolts placed from stance

249a **Drilling in My Dreams** FA: Tim Kemple, 5/1/89.

250 **High Stakes Breaks** FA: First pitch (old bolts): Tim Kemple, Scott Ennis, 1/85. Bolts placed from stance.

251 **Lobster Claw** FA: Unknown, ??

252 **Doodlin' Dody** FA: Jim Smith, John Armitage, 8/64, ??

253 **Peanuts** FA: Jeff Foott, Al Macdonald, Les Wilson, 11/60, ??

254 **Toes** FA: Dave French, Bill French, Jim Smith, 10/62.

255 **Dionysian Towers** FA: Al Steck, Joe Fitschen, Andy Lichtman, 12/65. Bolts: ⅜" Allen head.

256 **Jamcrack Rock** FA: Jim Smith, John Armitage, Al Timmons, 4/64, ??

257 **Rook—Regular Route** FA: Jim Smith, Bruce Edwards, Howard Lewis, 1962.

258 **Rook—North Face** FA: Steve Roper, Andrew Emery, 12/65. Bolts pro. ¼"; anchor, one ⅜" Star Dryvin.

259 **Torso** FA: John Whitmer, Jim Peabody, Monte Crowl, 11/54. FFA: Steve Roper, Nick Stevens, 1960.

260 **The Shepherd** FA: Unknown. FFA: David Rubine, 8/90. Bolts: mostly ¼" split shaft and ⅜" Star Dryvin. Retro-bolted with 3/8" Raw; Torque at crux, one ⅜" Rawl Torque for belay.

261 **The Lamb** FA: Unknown.

262 **Passion Play** FA: David Rubine, Martin Wensley, Sheri Levine, 4/80. Bolts placed from stance. Bolts: ⅜" split shaft.

263 **Mousetrap** FA (tr): David Rubine, 4/80.

264 **Elephant Crack** FA: Unknown.

265 **Elephant Rock —Regular Route** FA: Tom Rixon, Jack Arnold, Fred Kelly, 1/40.

266 **Citadel Stream Boulder—East Face** FA: Jonathan Richards, Douglas Martin, late 1980s.

267 **Citadel Stream Boulder—North Face** FA: Jonathan Richards, Douglas Martin, late 1980s.

268 **Citadel Stream Boulder—North Face, Right** FA: Jonathan Richards, Douglas Martin, late '80s.

269 **Peon's Delight** FL: Unknown. FA (tr): Jonathan Richards, Douglas Martin, late 1980s.

270 **Mission Impossible** FL (bolts placed on rappel): Jonathan Richards, Douglas Martin, late 1980s.

271 **Costanoan** FL (bolts placed on rappel): FA: Jonathan Richards, Douglas Martin, late 1980s. Bolts: ¼".

272 **Anasazi** FL (bolts placed on rappel): Jonathan Richards, Douglas Martin, late '80s, ??

273 **Berserker Route** FA: Larry Johnson, Todd Vogel, 2/88. FFA: Jack Holmgren, Sherry Vaughn, 3/88. Bolts: ⅜" Star Dryvin.

274 **Power Tools** FL (bolts placed on rappel): Jonathan Richards, Douglas Martin, 7/88.

275 **Power Corrupts** FL: David Rubine, 8/90. Last four bolts were initially placed on rappel by Richards and Martin. First two bolts were later placed from hooks and the route finally led. Bolts: ⅜" Rawl, split shaft and/or wedge anchors.

276 **Hummingbird Spire—East Face** FA: Tom Rohrer, Bob Smith, 8/56. Bolts: ¼" Star Dryvin.

277 **Hummingbird Spire—Buckwheats Bender** FA: Steven Bosque, Larry Johnson, 3/86. Bolts: ¼".

278 **Bouldering Rock** FA: Unknown. Bolt: ⅜" Star Dryvin.

279 **The Rookie** FA: Unknown. Bolts: ⅜" Star Dryvin.

280 **Jeopardy** FA (tr): Unknown. FL: Tom Davis, David Rubine, 3/89. Bolts placed from hooks. Bolts: ⅜" x 3¾" wedge anchors.

281 **Truth or Consequences** FA (tr): unknown. FL: Tom Davis, David Rubine, 2/89. Bolts placed from hooks. Bolts: ⅜" x 3¾" wedge anchors.

282 **Vanna** FA (tr): Unknown.

282a **Came In Second** FA: Unknown. Bolts: ⅜" Rawl.

282b **Glorious** FA tr: Teresa Deruntz, Michael Leonard, 1/1/92.

283 **Feeding Frenzy** FA: Paul Gagner, James McConachie, 8/88, ??

284 **Groto Chimney** FA: Unknown, ??

284 **Flimsy Flume** FA: Andrew Emery, Steve Roper, 12/65.

286 **Flames Face** FA: Robin Riner, Chuck Coon, 2/85. Bolts: some ¼".

287 **Drizzly Drain** FA: Ward Allison, Norm Melride, Jim Shipley, 10/66.

288 **Drizzly Drain—Direct Finish** FA: Unknown.

288a **Bits 'n Pieces** FA: Chris Belizzi, Paul Gagner, 1/1/88. Bolts: ⅜" split shaft.

289 **Tilting Terrace** FA: Dave Haller, Chuck Richards, 5/73. Bolts: bad 1/4". Retro-bolted: ⅜".

289a **Adam's Apple** FA: Geoff Norris, Adam Herrin, 1/1/92. One bolt placed from aid, rest from stance. Bolts Pro: ⅜". Anchor: Two ⅜".

289b **Rumbling Rampart** FA: Doug Wolff, Jon Cochran, Esplins, 1/1/93. Bolts: Two ⅜" x 2", 2⁵⁄₁₆" x 2½", Anchor: 2⁵⁄₁₆". Bolts placed from stance.

290 **Once Around the Backside** FA: Seth Boatright, Chuck Richards, 4/72. FFA: Unknown. Bolts: ¼".

291 **Crowley Towers—Tower 1** FA: Dave and Fran Stevenson, Dick Brown, Allen Henshaw, Carl Dreisback, 1961, ??

292 **Crowley Towers—Tower 2** FA: The Stevensons, Brown, Henshaw, Dreisback, 1961, ??

293 **Crowley Towers—Tower 3** FA: The Stevensons, Brown, Henshaw, Dreisback, 1961, ??

294 **Crowley Towers—Tower 4** FA: The Stevensons, Brown, Henshaw, Dreisback, 1961, ??

295 **Crowley Towers—Tower 5** FA: The Stevensons, Brown, Henshaw, Dreisback, 1961, ??

295a **If We Bolt It They Will Come** FA: Clint Cummins, Dennis Erik Strom, 11/1/93.

296 **Bongloadash** FA: James McConachie, Jon McConachie, 10/85. Bolts: ⅜" split shaft.

297   **Premeditated**   FA: Jim Bridwell, Craig Little, 2/65, ??

298   **Where the Birds Hang**   FA: abandoned , Jack Holmgren, Joe Bryant, ??

299   **Peregrine**   FA: Dave Parks, Stu Polack, 86. Bolts: many ¼" in bolt ladders, ⅜" Star Dryvin, one ⅜" wedge anchor plus Star Dryvin at anchors. FFA: Stu Polack, Marty Garrison, 12/88

300   **Conduit to the Cosmos**   FA: John Barbella, James McConachie, '83. Bolts: ⅜" split shaft.

301   **Pipeloads To Pluto**   FA: Paul Gagner, James McConachie, in progress. Bolts: ⅜" Rawl torque bolt.

302   **Lava Falls**   FA: Jack Holmgren, W.V. Graham Matthews, Keith Vandevere, 3/82. Bolts drilled from stance. Bolts: some ¼" at start, ⅜" Star Dryvin.

303   **No Sense of Measure**   FA: James McConachie, Jon McConachie, 10/89. Bolts: ⅜" Rawl.

304   **The Powers That Be**   FA: Paul Gagner, James McConachie, 10/89. Bolts: ⅜" split shaft.

305   **Electric Blue**   FA: Paul Gagner, Chris Bellizzi, 1988. Bolts: ⅜" split shaft.

306   **Shake and Bake**   FA: Tom Higgins, Chris Vandiver, 5/76. Bolts placed from stance. Bolts: ⅜" split shaft.

307   **On the Threshold of a Scream**   FA: James McConachie, et al. In progress.

308   **Balconies Regular Route**   FA: Frank Sacherer, Howard Bradley, Steve Roper, 12/61. Bolts: many ¼" on bolt ladders. FFA: Tom Higgins, Chris Vandiver, 5/79

309   **Digger**   FA: Jim Beyer, Bob Sullivan, 10/78

310   **Hook and Drill**   FA: Jim Beyer, Janice Linhares, late '70s.

311   **Crack Climb**   FA: Unknown.

312   **Knifeblade direct**   FA: Ken Philips, Carl Martin, 2/73, ??

313   **Knifeblade**   FA: Unknown.

314   **Blade Runner**   FA: John Barbella, James McConachie, 11/84.

315   **Echoes**   FA: James McConachie, Jon McConachie, 5/86. Bolts placed from stance. Bolts: ⅜" split shaft.

316   **Prairie Home Companion**   FA First Pitch: Jon Cohran, Gabe Carvey, '84. FA rest of climb: Jack Holmgren, Keith Vandevere, David Zola, 5/84. Bolts placed from stance. Bolts: ¼".

317   **Nexus**   FA: Jack Holmgren, Malintha Winwood, Keith Vandevere, 9/84. Bolts placed from stance.

318   **Sexus**   FA: Jack Holmgren, Malintha Winwood, 9/84. Bolts placed from stance.

319   **Plexus**   FA: Jack Holmgren, Malintha Winwood, 9/84. Bolts placed from stance.

320   **Osiris—Regular Route**   FA: Andrew Emery, Steve Roper, 12/65, ??

321   **Escape From Soledad**   FA: John Barbella, James McConachie, 2/83. Bolts: ⅜" split shaft.

322   **Toog's Terror**   FA: Jim Smith, John Armitage, 4/64, ??

323   **Toog's Trailside**   FA: Al Swanson, et al., late 1970s. Bolts: ⅜" Rawl.

323a   **Toog's Trailside Direct**   FA: Unknown. Bolt: ⅜" Rawl.

324   **Smiling Simian—Easy Route**   FA: Andrew Emery, Steve Roper, 12/65

325   **Smiling Simian**   FA: Greg Schaffer, Ralph Foster, Jeff Schaffer, 12/16/67. Bolts: ¼".

326   **Little Big Dog**   FA: David Rubine, Tom Davis, 1/89. Bolts placed from aid. Bolts: ⅜" Rawl.

326a **Windmills** FA (tr): Clint Cummins, 11/92.

327 **No Smiles** FA: Bruce Cooke, Tom Higgins, 4/76. Bolts placed from stance. Bolts: ⅜" Star Dryvin.

327a **Bad Ape** FA (tr): Unknown.

328 **Even Coyotes Like It Doggie Style** FA: James McConachie, Paul Gagner, 2/87. Bolts: ⅜" Rawl.

328a **Stance Dance** FA: Jon Cochran, Caleb Rightmeyer, Tom Green, Geoff Norris, 1/1/94. Bolts placed from stance. Bolts: Two ⅜" x 2", 1 ⅜" x 3" (crux).

329 **Sombrero** FA: Unknown. Bolts: ¼".

330 **Wild Mexican** FA: Unknown.

331 **Walk the Plank** FA: Mark Spencer, Shirley Spencer, 1/86. Bolts: Six ⅜" x 2¼" Rawl.

331a **Overboard** FA: Mark Spencer, Shirley Spencer, 6/95. Bolts: Six ⅜" x 2¼" Rawl.

332 **Chockstone Dome** FA: Joe McKeown, Jim Harper, Steve Roper, 2/63. Bolts" Two ¼" split shaft.

333 **Kamikazzi Kommute** FA: (1st pitch) James McConachie, Jon McConachie, 12/85. Bolts: ⅜" Rawl. FA: (2nd pitch) James McConachie, Paul Gagner, 4/87. Bolts: ⅜" Rawl.

334 **Toog's Gallery** FA: Bill Craig, Randy Hurret, 4/77. Bolts: ⅜" split shaft and Star Dryvin.

334a **Toog's Gallery Direct Var.** FA: Unknown. Bolts: ⅜" split shaft and Star Dryvin and ⅜" Rawl Torque, Anchor: One ⅜" Rawl Torque.

335 **Toog's Alligator** FA: Steve Chidester, Chuck Richards, 12/72.

336 **Toog's Tarbaby** FA: Chris Hadland, Caleb Rightmyer, 12/90. Bolts: ⅜" Star Dryvin. Route starts right of the "Alligator Chimney" on **Toog's Alligator**.

337 **Powerslave** FL (bolts placed on rappel): Jonathan Richards, Douglas Martin, 10/88. Bolts: Either ⅜" wedge anchors or split shaft.

338 **Thundering Herd** FA: Steve Chidester, Chuck Richards, 12/72, ??

339 **Tugboat** FA: Unknown, ??

339a **Cuidado!** FA: Eric Brand, Jeff Dopp, John McCoy, '94. Bolts: ⅜" Rawl Torque. Bolts from hooks and stance.

340 **Tiburcio's Ambush** FA: Dave Haller, Chuck Richards, 10/73.

341 **Ambush Cutoff** FA: Gary Colliver, Glen Denny, 3/74.

342 **Flies On a Pile** FA: Clint Cummins, Hubert Shen, 2/90. Bolts: ⅜" Rawl.

343 **Machete Direct** FA: Gary Colliver, Glen Denny, 4/74. FA: (all pitches together) Dave Haller, Dave Crough, Christian Straight, 5/74. FFA: Barry Bates, Glen Garland, 1978. FA: (Pitch One direct start) John Barbella, Jon McConachie, 11/82. Bolts: direct start has one bad ¼" and one ⅜" split shaft. First pitch retro bolted for free lead at bolt ladder: Three ⅜" Rawls. Rest of route is mostly ⅜" Star Dryvin.

344 **My Mistake var.** FA: Michael McDaniel, John Mirk, 2/82.

345 **West Face** FA: Dave French, Jim Smith, Bruce Edwards, Lee Donaghey, 2/63.

346 **Tower Bypass var.** FA: Frank Cole, Lee Donaghey, 9/64. Bolts pro.: Two ⅜" Star Dryvin. Anchor: Three ⅜" split shaft.

347 **Swanson's Crack** FA: Al Swanson.

348 **The Arch** FA: Unknown.

349 **Alias Bandits Bench** FA: Steve Chidester, Seth Boatright, Chuck Richards, 5/72. Bolts: ¼".

350 **Bandits in Bondage** FA: James McConachie, Karl McConachie, 10/87. Bolts placed from stance and aid. Bolts: ⅜" split shaft for protection, ⅜" Rawl for belay.

351 **Upper Bandits Bench** FA: Unknown. Bolts: some ¼".

352 **Bill's Bad Bolts** FA: Bob Walton, Lincoln Hatch, 6/87. Bolts pro.: Mostly ¼" Star Dryvin interspersed with ⅜" Rawl Torque and Star Dryvin. First belay: Two ⅜" Star Dryvin, one Rawl buttonhead, one ⅜" Rawl Torque. Second Belay: One ⅜" and one ¼" Star Dryvin. Top Belay: One ⅜" and one ¼" Star Dryvin.

352a **Bill's Bad Bolts direct finish** FA: Unknown.

352b **Young In Deed** FA: Steve Wong, Phil Marr, 4/1/91. Bolts: ⅜" x 3" Rawl Torque.

353 **Twinkle Toes Traverse** FA: Seth Boatright, Chuck Richards, 4/72.

354 **Destiny aka Dos Equis** FA: Unknown. Bolts: ⅜" split shaft, ⅜" Star Dryvin, one bolt at anchor is a ⅜" wedge anchor.

354a **Crackaphobia** FA: Clint Cummins, Jon McConachie, 4/1/91.

354b **Pigeon Crack Aid Route** FA: Unknown, ??

355 **Son of Dawn Wall** FA: Dave Crough, Christian Straight, 1978. FFA (first pitch): Al Swanson. Bolts: ¼" and ⅜" Star Dryvin.

356 **Desperado Chute-Out** FA: Christian Straight, Dave Haller, Chuck Richards, 2/73. FFA: Unknown.

357 **Desperado Chute-Out direct finish var.** FA: Gary Colliver, Glen Denny, 5/74.

357a **Serpiente de Cascabel** FA: Bob Walton, Lincoln Hatch, 11/1/90. FFA: Jack Holmgren, Sherry F. Vaughn, 11/1/90.

358 **Derringer** FA: George Giddings, Chuck Richards, 11/72. Bolts: ¼" and ⅜" Star Dryvin.

358a **Derringer - Direct Start (Bullseye Variation)** FA: Larry Johnson, Steve Bosque, 3/15/92. Bolts: ⅜" wedge.

359 **Old Original** FA: John Dyer, Robin Hansen, Tom Rixon, 2/40. Bolts: ¼" and ⅜" Star Dryvin and wedge anchors. On the first rappels the first anchor is two ⅜" Star Dryvin and one ⅜" wedge anchor, the others have ¼" bolts mixed with the ⅜" Star Dryvin.

360 **Middle Tower Continuation** FA: John Dyer, Robin Hansen, Tom Rixon, 2/40.

360a **Middle Tower Arête** FA: David Rubine, '83.

361 **Cleaver Buttress** FA: Jack Holmgren, Keith Vandevere, 1/82, ?? Bolts: ⅜" Star Dryvin. Direct var. FA: Jack Holmgren, 5/82, ??

362 **Casper** FA: Larry Johnson, Bob Ost, 9/1/86. Bolts: ⅜" split shaft or wedge anchors.

363 **Dog Do Afternoon** FA: Steven Bosque, Larry Johnson, 3/87. Bolts: ⅜" Red Head sleeve anchors.

364 **Numbskull's Needle** FA: Steven Bosque, Larry Johnson, Raoul Rodriguez, 1/87. Bolts: ⅜" Red Head sleeve anchors.

365 **ICBM** FA: Larry Arthur, Dan Hikel, 11/87. Bolts placed from stance, Bolts: ⅜" Star Dryvin.

365a **Y.F.T.** FA: Andrew Aliguiga, Dave and Jon Cochran, 1/1/94. Bolts placed from stance. Bolts: ⅜" x 2".

366 **Life's Still Scary** FA: Larry Arthur, Rick Erker, 1/88. Bolts placed from stance. Bolts ⅜" Star Dryvin.

367 **Ready For Lift Off** FA: Larry Arthur, Rick Erker, 1/88. Bolt: ⅜" Star Dryvin.

368 **Herchel Berchel** FA: Eric Collins, et al., 9/76. FFA: Paul Gagner, John Barbella, 1982, ??

369 **Resurrection Wall** FA: Rupert Kammerlander, Anton Karuza, 4/78. FFA: Tom Higgins, Frank Sarnquist, 5/78. Bolts: ¼" bolts in the ladders, ⅜" Star Dryvin.

370 **Reincarnation var.** FA: Jack Holmgren, Larry Martin, 5/85, ??

371 **The Great Spectacular** FA: Chris Bellizzi, Paul Gagner, et al., late 1980s. Bolts placed from aid. Bolts: ⅜" split shaft.

372 **What If** FA: Paul Gagner, Chris Bellizzi, 1987. Bolts placed from aid. Bolts: ⅜" split shaft.

373 **Crumbling Castle—Regular Route** FA: Mort Hempel, Steve Roper, 1961. Bolts: Two ⅜" Star Dryvin, one ¼".

374 **Crumbling Castle—Original Route** FA: Dave Hammack, George Larimore, Bob Smith, Alice Ann Dayton 5/52.

374a **Crumbling Castle—Direct Finish** FA: Unknown. Bolts: ⅜" Star Dryvin.

375 **Monument** FA: Bob Smith, Jim Smith, Howard Lewis, Don Ralston, 4/61. Bolt: ⅜" Star Dryvin.

376 **Tombstone** FA: John Whitmer, Clinton Kelly, 2/53. Bolts pro.: ⅜" Star Dryvin. Anchor: two ⅜" Star Dryvin.

377 **Tombstone—Doc Holiday Direct** FA: Bill Briggs, Karen McMurtry, 5/89. Bolt: ⅜" Rawl Torque.

378 **Cave Pinnacle** FA: Bob and Jim Smith, Howard Lewis, Don Ralston, 4/61, ??

379 **Brittle Palace** FA: Bob and Jim Smith, Howard Lewis, Don Ralston, 4/61, ??

380 **Yankee Pinnacle** FA (tyrolean): Jim Smith, Bruce Edwards, 4/60. FA (base): Chuck Ostin, Steve Roper, 1961. FFA: Jack Holmgren, Sherry Vaughn, 3/88. Bolts: mostly ¼", a couple ⅜" Star Dryvin on the bolt ladder, two ⅜" Star Dryvin on top.

381 **Jubilation Pinnacle** FA: Chuck Ostin, Steve Roper, 3/61, ??

382 **Chaos Crag** FA: Dave Hammack, Charles Crawford, 1949, ??

383 **Pyramid Pinnacle** FA: Dave Hammack, Charles Crawford, 1949.

384 **Trafalgar Tower** FA: Unknown, ??

385 **The Cone—Regular Route** FA: Jeff Foott, Steve Roper, 11/62.

386 **Wanderlust** FA: Jim Beyer, Courtney Simpkins, 11/77, ??

387 **Axe Pinnacle** FA: Jeff Foott, Steve Roper, 10/60. Bolts ¼" on the ladder.

388 **Jam It!** FA: Jon McConachie, James McConachie, Bill McConachie, 12/89, ??

389 **Dwarf Pinnacle** FA: Jeff Foott, Steve Roper, 10/60. Bolts ⅜" Star Dryvin on top.

390 **Possibility Pinnacle** FA: Unknown.

391 **Pop Pinnacle** FA: Unknown. Bolts: one ⅜" wedge anchor for protection, one ⅜" split shaft and ⅜" wedge anchor on top.

392 **Scout Peak—Regular Route** FA: Unknown. Bolts two ⅜" Star Dryvin on top.

393 **Scout Peak—Tracker** FA: Unknown. Bolt: ⅜" split shaft or wedge anchor.

394 **Scout Peak—South Face** FA: Unknown, ??

395 **Leonard-Horsfall** FA: Dick Leonard, Bill Horsfall, 1939. Bolts: ¼" bolt ladder. Anchor: one ⅜" Star Dryvin on top.

396 **Shaft** FA (prusik): Tom Rohrer, Bob Smith, 1956. FA (base): Unknown. FFA: Unknown. Bolts: ¼" bolt ladder; anchor: one ⅜" Star Dryvin on top.

397 **Beak Peak—Regular Route** FA: Unknown, ??

398 **Subtle Slopes** FA: Don Korcthner, Dave Parks, 4/82. Bolts: ⅜" Star Dryvin.

399 **Embraceable You** FA: Jack Holmgren, Malintha Winwood, 9/86, ??

400   **Lonely Sheepherder** FA: Dave Haller, Dave Crough, Chuck Richards, 11/73.

401   **Piece of Ewe** FA: Dave Crough, Dave Haller, 3/74.

402   **Return of Piece of Ewe** FA: Dave Haller, Chuck Richards, 1/74.

403   **Photographer's Delight—Regular Route** FA: Unknown. Bolt: ⅜" Star Dryvin.

404   **Photographer's Delight—Northeast Corner** FA: Jim Beyer, Courtney Simpkins, 12/76, ??

405   **Mechanic's Delight** FA (prusik): Unknown, before 1955. FA (base): Jeff Foott, Steve Roper, 10/60. FFA: Barry Bates, Dave Hampton, 12/70. Bolts: ¼" and ⅜" Star Dryvin on the ladder.

406   **Flatiron—Regular Route** FA: Manford Samuelson, Alice Ann Dayton, 10/51. Bolt: ¼", hangerless.

406a   **Burton's Below** FA: Steve Wong, Brad Young, Janet Burton, 3/21/93. Bolts: ⅜" x 3" Rawl.

407   **Lost Fortune** FA: Jim Lewis, Ed Tharp, 11/88. Bolts: ⅜" Star Dryvin.

408   **Flatiron—Regular Route—Variation 1** FA: Unknown. Bolts: a few ¼", mostly ⅜" Star Dryvin.

409   **Flatiron—Regular Route—Variation 2** FA: Unknown. Bolt: ⅜" Star Dryvin.

409a   **Mungy Bulgy** FA: Unknown.

410   **Flatiron—Regular Route—Variation 3** FA: Unknown. Bolt: ⅜" Star Dryvin.

411   **Silent Running** FA (tr): David Rubine, 1980. FL: Unknown. Bolts: ⅜" Star Dryvin.

412   **Long's Folly** FA: Dave Hammack, Dick Michael, 3/50. Bolts: mostly ⅜" Star Dryvin.

413   **South Finger** FA (tyrolean): Tom Rixon, Fritz Lippman, 1940. FA(base): Unknown. Bolts: ¼".

414   **South Finger—Earth Magnet** FA (tr): David Rubine, Jeffrey Thranow, 1980.

415   **North Finger—Regular Route** FA: Dave Brower, Hervey Voge, George Rockwood, 4/34.

416   **East Edge** FA: Unknown. Bolts: ¼".

417   **Slippery People** FA: Chris Bellizzi, Gary Thunen, 1986.

418   **Monga Bonna Memorial Route** FA: Chris Bellizzi, Paul Gagner, 3/86. Bolts: ¼" split shaft, ⅜" split shaft.

419   **Condor Crags—Original Route, South Summit** FA: Dave Brower, Hervey Voge, George Rockwood, 11/33.

420   **South Traverse** FA: Unknown. Bolts: ¼" on traverse, ⅜" Star Dryvin at belay at beginning of traverse.

421   **Condor Crags—Original Route, North Summit** FA: Dave Brower, Hervey Voge, George Rockwood, 11/33.

422   **St. Valentine's Day Massacre** FA: Mark Engstrom, Joe Rock, 2/14/76. Bolts pro.: Two ¼", three ⅜" Star Dryvin. Anchor: One ⅜" split shaft, one Star Dryvin.

423   **For M.E.** FA: Chris Bellizzi, Gary Thunen, 1986. Bolts: ⅜" Star Dryvin on first pitch, several ¼" on second pitch.

424   **C.C.N.S. Right Variation** FA: Gary Colliver, Glen Denny, 2/74. Bolts: ⅜" Star Dryvin.

425   **Condor Condom Condiment** FA: Keith Vandevere, Bob Walton, Jack Holmgren, 12/3/89. Bolts: ⅜" Star Dryvin, several ⁵⁄₁₆" split shaft. Bolts placed from stance.

426   **Condor Conduit** FA: Greg Schaffer, Jeff Schaffer, 9/68, ??

427   **The Great Chimney** FA: Glen Denny, Ellen Fry, 5/70, ??

428   **Pot Pinnacle** FA: Steve Roper, George Griffin, Andrew Emery, 1/66, ??

429 **Peyote Pinnacle** FA: Unknown.

430 **Sponge—Direct Northeast Face** FA: Dan Cutshall, John Servais, 12/72. Bolts: ⅜" Rawl torque.

431 **Sponge—Holes** FA: Unknown.

432 **Sponge—Regular Route** FA: Unknown. ⅜" Star Dryvin for protection, several ⅜" Star Dryvin and ¼" bolts on top.

433 **Burgundy Dome—Original Route** FA: Unknown.

434 **Burgundy Dome—Rappel Route** FA: Rupert Kammerlander, Bev Belanger, Jerry Tinling, 4/75. Bolts: ⅜" Rawl torque.

435 **Burgundy Dome—Vin Ordinaire** FA: Joe Bryant, Jack Holmgren, 3/86. Bolts: ¼" split shaft and ⅜" Star Dryvin.

436 **Pluvius Pinnacle** FA: Unknown.

436a **Piglet Pinnacle** FA: Unknown. Bolts pro.: ⅜" Star Dryvin. Anchor: Two ⅜" Star Dryvin.

436b **The Sow—East Shoulder** FA: Unknown.

436c **The Sow** FA: Unknown.

437 **Tuff Dome—Regular Route** FA: Dave Brower, Ralph Brower, Dick Leonard, 11/34. Bolts: ¼", top anchor has large eye bolt.

437a **Tuff Dome—Direct Start** FA: Unknown. Bolt: ¼".

438 **Tuff Dome—Traverse** FA: Gary Fox, 9/73.

438a **Tuff Dome—Prelude** FA: Jack Holmgren. Bolts placed in stance.

439 **Aliens Ate My Buick** FA: Paul Gagner, 1988. Bolts: ⅜" split shaft.

439b **Tuff Dome—Adagio** FA: Steve Wong et al., early '90s.

440 **H&L Dome—Regular Route** FA: Fritz Lippmann, Dick Houston, 1947. Bolts: ⅜" Star Dryvin.

440a **Catch Me** FA: Unknown.

441 **Feather Canyon** FA: Jim Langford, Ed, Ron and Ken Payton, 10/73, ??

442 **Bynum's Spire—Chocolate Face** FA: Unknown.

443 **Bynum's Spire—Rock Steady** FA: Unknown.

444 **Bynum's Spire—Regular Route** FA: Al Steck, Andy Emery, Joe Fitschen, Andy Lichtman, Steve Roper, 12/65. Bolt pro.: ⅜" split shaft. Anchor: Two ⅜" Star Dryvin.

444a **Begin It Now** FA: Unknown. Bolts Pro: ⅜" Star Dryvin. Anchor: Two ⅜" Star Dryvin.

445 **Spike's Peak** FA: Dick Brown and son. Date unknown.

445a **Little Javelina** FA: Grant Weeden, Paul McEwen, 4/1/92. Bolts: ⅜" x 3" Wedge Anchors. Bolts placed from stance and aid.

446 **Dragonfly Dome—Regular Route** FA: Steve Roper, Joe McKeown, 3/60. Bolts: ⅜" Rawl torque.

447 **Dragonfly Dome—School Daze** FA (tr): Unknown.

448 **Sidehorse—Regular Route** FA: Steve Roper, Andrew Emery, 12/65. Bolts: ⅜" Rawl torque.

449 **Egg Shell** FA: Jim Crooks, Tom Higgins, 11/75. Bolts pro.: two ⅜" Star Dryvin, one ⅜" Rawl torque. Anchors: ⅜" split shaft, ⅜" Rawl torque.

450 **Freedom Dome—Captain Crunch** FA: Unknown. Bolts: ⅜" Star Dryvin.

451 **Freedom Dome—Regular Route** FA: Chuck Ostin, Steve Roper, 3/61. FFA: Unknown. Bolts: one ⅜" Rawl split shaft, rest are ⅜" Rawl torque, including anchors.

452 **Freedom Dome—Preferred Freedom** FA: Jack Holmgren, Malintha Winwood, '85.

453 **Disintegration Pinnacle** FA: Bruce Cooke, Tom Higgins, 4/76. Bolt pro.: two ⅜" Star Dryvin. Anchor: two ⅜" Star Dryvin.

454 **Cinder** FA: Unknown.

455 **Smokestack—Original Route** FA: Kit Hanes, Frank Orme, 2/57, ??

456 **Smokestack—Swept Away** FA: Tim Kemple, Jeff Levin, 12/1/83. Bolts placed from stance.

457 **Smokestack—Clean Sweep** FA: Dave Parks, Stu Polack, 12/82. Bolts pro.: ¼" and ⅜" split shaft. Anchor: One ⅜" , one ¼".

458 **Cornflake** FA: George Oetzel, Dick Brown, Howell Helmke, Al Timmons, 12/64.

459 **Frothy Flake** FA: Kay Johnson, Tom Kimbrough, Steve Roper, 11/65.

460 **The Big Step** FA: Joe McKeown, Jeff Foott, Steve Roper, 12/62. Bolt pro.: ¼". Anchor: One ⅜" Star Dryvin.

461 **Papa Bear—Regular Route** FA: Earl Furman, Eric Furman, David McIntosh, 12/68, ??

462 **Papa Bear—April Fool's Route** FA: Bruce Cooke, Tom Higgins, 4/76. Bolts: ¼".

462a **Baby Bear** FA: Unknown.

462b **Mama Bear** FA: Unknown.

463 **The Lump** FA: Unknown. Bolts: ¼".

463a **Peace Of Heaven** FA: Unknown. Bolts pro.: Two ⅜" Star Dryvin. Anchor: One ⅜" Star Dryvin with lap link.

464 **Squareblock Rock Crack** FA: Unknown. Bolts: First pitch anchor: ¼" (very bad); Second pitch anchor: One ⅜" Star Dryvin, one ⅜" compression.

465 **Squareblock Rock—Buzzard's Breakfast** FA: Dave Haller, Chuck Richards,5/73, ??

465a **Scandal** FA: Sam Davidson, Jack Holmgren, 9/91. Bolts placed from stance.

466 **Teapot Dome—Regular Route** FA: Unknown.

467 **Teapot Dome Crack** FA: Christian Straight, Dave Crough, 5/74.

467a **Green Dolphin St.** FA: Steve Bosque, Larry Johnson, 9/25/94. Bolts: ⅜" wedge.

468 **Lower Teapot Dome** FA (tyrolean): Jim Smith, Bruce Edwards, Tony Hovey, Howard Lewis, 2/57. FA: Steve Roper, Mort Hempel, 3/61. FFA: Jack Holmgren, Joe Bryant, 3/86.

469 **Ball Pinnacle** FA: Dave Hammack, George Larimore, Bob Smith, Julius Siddon, Marga Urban, 11/51. Bolts: ¼" split shaft.

470 **Wedge** FA: Keith Anderson, Fred Schaub, 11/56. Bolts: ¼" ladder.

470a **Wedgie** FA (tr): Dennis Erik Strom, 11/1/93.

471 **Disintegration Point** FA: Jim Smith, Bruce Edwards, Tony Hovey, Howard Lewis, 1/57, ??

472 **Arch Pinnacle** FA: Unknown, ??

473 **The Groove** FA: Unknown. Bolts: ¼".

474 **Proclamation Pinnacle—South Summit** FA: Unknown.

475 **Proclamation Pinnacle—North Summit** FA: Unknown. Bolts pro.: ¼" and ⅜" split shaft. Anchor: One ⅜" Star Dryvin, one ¼" split shaft.

475a **Proclamation Pinnacle—North Summit Crack** FA: Christian Straight, Mark Martin, 10/73, ??

476 **Proclamation Pinnacle—Adrenalin Junkies** FA: Paul Gagner, Chris Bellizzi, 4/86. Bolts placed from aid. Bolts: ⅜" split shaft for protection, one ⅜" wedge anchor and ⅜" Star Dryvin for top anchor.

477 **Emancipation** FA: Jack Holmgren, et al., mid-1980s, ??

478 **The Egg—Regular Route** FA: Dave Hammack, George Larimore, 11/51. Bolts: ⅜" Star Dryvin.

479 **Sunny Side Up** FA: Larry Johnson, Steven Bosque, 11/86, ?? FFA: Jack Holmgren, Larry Martin, 4/87. Bolts: ⅜" wedge anchors.

480 **Hunky Dory** FA: Larry Johnson, Steven Bosque, 9/86. Bolts: ¼".

481 **Halloweenie** FA: Larry Johnson, Steven Bosque, 11/86. Bolts: ⅜" wedge anchors.

ROUTES BY RATING

Routes with plus or minus ratings below 5.9 were grouped with their respective ratings, i.e., 5.9+ is grouped with 5.9. Plus or minus ratings 5.10 and above were grouped as the following: plus ratings were grouped with "d," minus ratings were grouped with "a." Areas or formations that did not list specific routes, or that were listed with a range of ratings were omitted from this index.

R and X ratings were omitted from this listing. Page numbers are in parenthesis.

5.0 to 5.3

- ☐ Anvil, The 5.1 (98)
- ☐ Bynumn's Spire – Regular Route 5.2 ★★ (196)
- ☐ Catch Me 5.3 (195)
- ☐ Chockstone Dome – Regular Route 5.3 ★★ (142)
- ☐ Cone, The – Regular Route 5.3 ★ (172)
- ☐ Cornflake 5.3 (200)
- ☐ Dwarf Pinnacle 5.2 (174)
- ☐ Fourth Sister – North Shoulder 5.1 (69)
- ☐ Lamb, The 5.0 (118)
- ☐ Little Marmot 5.0 (83)
- ☐ Nebulous Knob 5.0 (109)
- ☐ Papa Bear – Regular Route 5.2 (200)
- ☐ Photographer's Delight – Regular Route 5.2 ★★ (180)
- ☐ Tiburcio's Ambush 5.2 (147)
- ☐ Tombstone – Regular Route 5.2 (168)
- ☐ Toog's Terror 5.2 (139)
- ☐ Jubilation Pinnacle 5.3, A3 (168)
- ☐ Old Original 5.3 ★★★ (156)
- ☐ Raven 5.0 (109)
- ☐ Scout Peak – Leonard-Horsfall Route 5.3 (175)
- ☐ Sponge, The – Regular Route, The 5.2 ★★ (190)

5.4

- ☐ Begin It Now (196)
- ☐ Bicuspid (76)
- ☐ Blade Runner (137)
- ☐ Costanoan (123)
- ☐ Dismemberment Gorge (44)
- ☐ Don Genaro's Waterfall ★ (112)
- ☐ First Sister – Center Route ★★★ (67)
- ☐ Hideout, The ★ (157)
- ☐ Lion's Head (79)
- ☐ Little Flatiron (79)
- ☐ Lobster Claw (114)
- ☐ Thumb, The – Regular Route ★ (76)
- ☐ Thundering Herd (145)
- ☐ Toes, The (114)
- ☐ Yak, South – South Face A1 (88)

5.5

- ☐ Chaos Crag (171)
- ☐ Crowley Towers – Tower 3 (129)
- ☐ Drizzly Drain (127)
- ☐ First Sister – Left Route ★★ (67)
- ☐ Flimsy Flume (126)
- ☐ Fourth Sister – West Face (69)
- ☐ H&L Dome – Regular Route ★★★ (195)
- ☐ Hidden Pinnacle A1 (95)
- ☐ Knee, The – Regular Route (72)
- ☐ Knifeblade, The (137)
- ☐ Lonesome Dove (74)
- ☐ MaGootchey Bird Chimney (73)
- ☐ Middle Tower Continuation ★ (157)
- ☐ Monument ★ (168)
- ☐ Mustache A3 (38)
- ☐ North Finger – Regular Route (184)
- ☐ Outcast, The – West Face ★ (80)
- ☐ Outcast, The – West Face Right (80)
- ☐ Pillbox Crack (38)
- ☐ Pinky Pinnacle (94)
- ☐ Pipsqueak Pinnacle – Regular Route ★ (98)
- ☐ Piton Traverse ★ (57)
- ☐ Pot Pinnacle (188)
- ☐ Premeditated A4 (131)
- ☐ Proclamation Pinnacle – South Summit (203)
- ☐ Rook, The – North Face (114)
- ☐ Scout Peak – Regular Route (174)
- ☐ South Finger – Regular Route ★ (184)
- ☐ Squareblock Rock Crack (201)
- ☐ Toilet Seat, The (94)
- ☐ Vulture ★ (109)
- ☐ Wad – Right (95)
- ☐ Wedge, The A2 (202)
- ☐ Y.F.T. (162)
- ☐ Mustache A3 (38)

5.6

- ☐ Arch Pinnacle   (202)
- ☐ Baby Bear   (201)
- ☐ Back of Hand ★   (76)
- ☐ Ball Pinnacle   (202)
- ☐ Big Marmot   (83)
- ☐ Big Step, The   (200)
- ☐ Buzzard – North Face   (109)
- ☐ Buzzard's Breakfast   (201)
- ☐ Cleft, The ★   (44)
- ☐ Dirty Bird Crack   (73)
- ☐ Disintegration Pinnacle   (198)
- ☐ Dragonfly Dome – Regular Route ★★★ (197)
- ☐ Elephant Rock – Regular Route ★★ (121)
- ☐ Fifth Sister   (70)
- ☐ Flip-a-Coin Chimney   (35)
- ☐ Getchy-Getchy Bird   (74)
- ☐ Ghost of Tiburcio's   (69)
- ☐ Heffalump   (35)
- ☐ Holes ★   (190)
- ☐ Jamcrack Rock A2   (114)
- ☐ Lonely Sheepherder   (179)
- ☐ Lump, The   (201)
- ☐ Monolith, The East Face – Direct Route ★★   (55)
- ☐ Nelson's Needle – East Face   (104)
- ☐ Nelson's Needle – Regular Route ★ (104)
- ☐ Nodal Line ★   (60)
- ☐ Outcast, The – South Face   (80)
- ☐ Pinch or Lynch   (102)
- ☐ Plexus   (137)
- ☐ Popcorn Pinnacle – Chimney   (109)
- ☐ Popcorn Pinnacle – Northeast Corner (109)
- ☐ Portent ★★★   (39)
- ☐ Proclamation Pinnacle – North Summit (204)
- ☐ Pyramid Pinnacle   (171)
- ☐ Rumbling Rampart   (127)
- ☐ Salathé ★★★   (75)
- ☐ Sow, The   (193)
- ☐ Spike's Peak   (197)
- ☐ Sponge, The – Direct Northeast Face ★★   (190)
- ☐ Swallow Crack ★★★   (42)
- ☐ Teapot Dome Crack   (202)
- ☐ Third Sister – Little Sister Spire   (69)
- ☐ Tower Bypass Variation   (147)
- ☐ Tracker   (174)
- ☐ Tuff Dome – Regular Route ★★★ (194)
- ☐ Tuff Dome Traverse   (194)
- ☐ Tugboat   (145)
- ☐ Twinkle Toes Traverse ★★   (149)
- ☐ Walk The Plank ★★   (142)
- ☐ Wanderlust   (172)
- ☐ Wilts' Bolt Variation   (75)
- ☐ Young In Deed   (149)

5.7

- ☐ Ambush Cutoff   (147)
- ☐ Axe Pinnacle – Regular Route A1 (174)
- ☐ Bill's Bad Bolts A1   (149)
- ☐ Bridwell Bolts A2   (57)
- ☐ Buckwheats Bender   (124)
- ☐ Burgundy Dome – Rappel Route   (193)
- ☐ Burnette Bolt Variation ★★   (75)
- ☐ Cinder ★   (198)
- ☐ Condor Conduit – Regular Route (188)
- ☐ Condor Crags North Summit – Original Route   (188)
- ☐ Condor Crags South Summit – Original Route   (187)
- ☐ Condor Crags South Summit – South Traverse ★★   (187)
- ☐ Crumbling Castle – Original Route (167)
- ☐ Crumbling Castle – Regular Route (167)
- ☐ Delusion Overhang A3   (29)
- ☐ Denny-Colliver Finish ★   (149)
- ☐ Denny-Colliver Route   (188)
- ☐ Derringer ★   (149)
- ☐ Dog Do Afternoon   (161)

5.7 cont.

- [ ] Doodlin' Dody   (114)
- [ ] Drilling In My Dreams   (113)
- [ ] Dutch Goose A2   (112)
- [ ] Elephant Crack ★   (121)
- [ ] Entrance ★   (44)
- [ ] Fifty Meter Must ★   (76)
- [ ] First Sister – Back Side   (67)
- [ ] Generation Gap ★   (104)
- [ ] Glorious   (124)
- [ ] Going The Wong Way   (69)
- [ ] Great Chimney, The A2   (188)
- [ ] Groove, The   (203)
- [ ] Halloweenie   (207)
- [ ] High Chair, The   (93)
- [ ] Hummingbird Spire – West Face ★ (124)
- [ ] Incisor   (76)
- [ ] Japanese Water Torture ★   (60)
- [ ] Kachink   (137)
- [ ] Mama Bear   (201)
- [ ] Maniac's Delight – Regular Route   (71)
- [ ] Marauder ★   (83)
- [ ] Monolith East Face, The – Northeast Corner ★   (57)
- [ ] Nit-Wit Knob   (72)
- [ ] North Finger – Northeast Face, East Edge   (186)
- [ ] Outcast, The – East Face   (80)
- [ ] Outcast, The – Northeast Rib ★   (80)
- [ ] Overhang Chimney   (36)
- [ ] Passion Play ★   (118)
- [ ] Pastie   (32)
- [ ] Piece of Ewe   (179)
- [ ] Pop Pinnacle   (174)
- [ ] Praire Home Companion   (137)
- [ ] Proclamation Pinnacle – North Summit Crack   (204)
- [ ] Ramble and Gamble   (70)
- [ ] Rat Race ★★   (31)
- [ ] Rock Steady ★★   (196)
- [ ] Rook, The – Regular Route   (114)
- [ ] Salathe's Sliver ★   (104)
- [ ] Sidesaddle ★   (62)
- [ ] Snail ★   (74)
- [ ] Snout, The   (99)
- [ ] St. Valentine's Day Massacre ★   (188)
- [ ] Toog's Alligator ★   (145)
- [ ] Toog's Gallery ★   (145)
- [ ] Tuff Dome – Direct Start   (194)
- [ ] Unmentionable, The ★★★   (99)
- [ ] Welcome to the Machine   (44)
- [ ] When In Doubt Run It Out   (60)
- [ ] Yak, South – West Face   (88)

5.8

- [ ] Agrarian   (46)
- [ ] Alias Bandit Bench   (149)
- [ ] Beak Peak – Subtle Slopes   (176)
- [ ] Big Sky   (73)
- [ ] Bill's Bad Bolts Direct Finish   (149)
- [ ] Bongloadash   (131)
- [ ] Burton's Below   (182)
- [ ] Casper   (161)
- [ ] Catatonic Stupor   (80)
- [ ] Condor Condom Condiment ★   (188)
- [ ] Contraband Crack A2   (28)
- [ ] Destiny ★★★   (149)
- [ ] Dionysian Towers   (114)
- [ ] Dos Equis ★★★   (149)
- [ ] Echoes   (137)
- [ ] Egg Shell ★   (198)
- [ ] Embraceable You   (179)
- [ ] Fourth Sister – Silhouette Arete   (69)
- [ ] H&L Dome – Feather Canyon   (196)
- [ ] Hunky Dory   (207)
- [ ] I.C.B.M.   (162)
- [ ] Indirect Traverse ★★   (55)
- [ ] Liebacker's Lullaby ★★   (93)
- [ ] Little Mustagh A2   (72)
- [ ] Long's Folly ★   (184)
- [ ] Lost Horizons ★   (44)
- [ ] Lower Teapot Dome   (202)
- [ ] Monolith, The East Face – Regular Route ★★★   (57)
- [ ] Mr. Hugh G. Rection ★   (53)

5.8 cont.

- [ ] Mushroom Cloud, The (98)
- [ ] My Mistake (147)
- [ ] Nailbox Crack ★ (38)
- [ ] Nip and Tuck (95)
- [ ] Nipple Jam ★ (32)
- [ ] Numbskull's Needle (161)
- [ ] Ordeal ★★★ (42)
- [ ] Organgrinder ★ (60)
- [ ] Orion ★ (93)
- [ ] Outcast, The – Back Alley Driver ★ (80)
- [ ] Overboard ★★ (142)
- [ ] Peace of Heaven (201)
- [ ] Photographer's Delight – Northeast Corner (180)
- [ ] Piglet Pinnacle ★ (193)
- [ ] Pipsqueak Pinnacle – Rightfoot ★ (99)
- [ ] Ready for Lift Off (162)
- [ ] Scorpion (48)
- [ ] Sexus (137)

- [ ] Ski Jump ★ (74)
- [ ] Smiling Simian ★ (140)
- [ ] Sombrero (141)
- [ ] Steve's Folly ★ (35)
- [ ] Teter-Tower (95)
- [ ] Thin Man (104)
- [ ] Thrill Hammer ★★ (32)
- [ ] Tilting Terrace ★★ (127)
- [ ] Toilet Seat, The – The Drain Chimney (94)
- [ ] Tom-Tom Club, The ★ (85)
- [ ] Tombstone – Doc Holliday Direct (168)
- [ ] Toog's Tarbaby (145)
- [ ] Triple Decker (79)
- [ ] Vin Ordinaire ★ (193)
- [ ] Viva Zapatos (81)
- [ ] Wart (95)

5.9

- [ ] Adam's Apple ★★ (127)
- [ ] Atlas Shrugs ★★ (73)
- [ ] Bienvenidos a Pinnacles ★ (62)
- [ ] Bits 'n Pieces ★ (127)
- [ ] Buzzard Bait ★ (48)
- [ ] Buzzard – Westside Lieback (109)
- [ ] Bye-bye Fly-by (42)
- [ ] Chocolate Face (196)
- [ ] Cigar, The (118)
- [ ] Citadel Stream Boulder – North Face right (123)
- [ ] Coyote Ugly ★ (62)
- [ ] Crack Climber's Concerto ★ (93)
- [ ] Crap Shoot (113)
- [ ] Crowley Towers – Tower 1 (129)
- [ ] Dead Bird Crack (42)
- [ ] Drizzly Drain – Direct Finish (127)
- [ ] Edge of Sundown, The (80)
- [ ] Egg, The – Regular Route ★ (206)
- [ ] Emancipation (204)
- [ ] February Fools (42)
- [ ] Flames Face (127)

- [ ] Flies on a Pile (147)
- [ ] Fly-by ★ (42)
- [ ] Fly-by (40)
- [ ] Freedom Dome – Regular Route ★★ (198)
- [ ] Furry Marmot Substitute (83)
- [ ] Happily Married Bachelor (31)
- [ ] Happy Birthday George (46)
- [ ] High Stakes Breaks (113)
- [ ] Hippopotamus A1 (110)
- [ ] Honeycomb (49)
- [ ] Hook and Drill (132)
- [ ] Jam It! (174)
- [ ] Kasparek's Delight ★ (94)
- [ ] La Margen de la Vida (81)
- [ ] Lava Falls ★★★ (132)
- [ ] Lava Falls (133)
- [ ] Life's Still Scary (162)
- [ ] Limp at Last ★ (53)
- [ ] Little Javelina (197)
- [ ] Lost Fortune (182)
- [ ] Marmot With a Hand Grenade (83)

5.9 cont.

- [ ] Me and My Monkey ★ (60)
- [ ] Middle Tower Arête ★ (157)
- [ ] Mungy Bulgy (182)
- [ ] Murky Bong Water ★ (85)
- [ ] Naked Lunge (93)
- [ ] Powerslave (145)
- [ ] Preferred Freedom ★ (198)
- [ ] Preferred Freedom (199)
- [ ] Return of Piece of Ewe (179)
- [ ] Scandal ★ (202)
- [ ] School Daze ★ (197)
- [ ] Slippery People (186)
- [ ] Slot, The ★ (44)
- [ ] Smokestack – Clean Sweep (198)
- [ ] Smokestack – Swept Away (198)
- [ ] Sound Chaser Indirect (60)

- [ ] Spaceman Spiff (44)
- [ ] Tato Pani (Hot Water) ★★ (93)
- [ ] Terminal Buttress ★ (93)
- [ ] Terminal Buttress – McConachie-Barbella Variation (93)
- [ ] Toadstool (79)
- [ ] Toog's Gallery Direct Variation ★ (145)
- [ ] Torso, The aka The Cigar (118)
- [ ] Trauma ★ (39)
- [ ] Voyeur ★ (48)
- [ ] Wad – Left (95)
- [ ] Wedgie (202)
- [ ] Wet Kiss, The ★★★ (39)
- [ ] Zig-Zag ★ (48)

5.10

- [ ] Anasazi (123)
- [ ] Cemetary Gates (109)
- [ ] Chimney Sweep ★ (79)
- [ ] Citadel Stream Boulder – East Face (123)
- [ ] Citadel Stream Boulder – North Face left (123)
- [ ] Delusion Overhang Right (29)
- [ ] Desperado Chuteout (149)
- [ ] Escape from Soledad ★ (138)

- [ ] Green Dolphin St. (202)
- [ ] Mollusk, The ★ (79)
- [ ] On the Threshold of a Scream (132)
- [ ] Once Around the Backside ★ (127)
- [ ] Stance Dance (141)
- [ ] Surf's Up A2 (48)
- [ ] Swanson's Crack (147)
- [ ] Where the Birds Hang (131)

5.10a

- [ ] Agony Of Defeat, The (80)
- [ ] Angstrom's Away (31)
- [ ] April Fool's Route (201)
- [ ] Baboon Crack ★ (60)
- [ ] Beast of Burden (88)
- [ ] Captain Crunch (198)
- [ ] Crash Buds ★ (46)
- [ ] Crumbling Castle – Direct Finish (168)
- [ ] Darkness Within, The (80)
- [ ] Digger (132)
- [ ] Even Coyotes Like it Doggie Style ★ (141)

- [ ] Exiles ★ (46)
- [ ] Fear and Perspiration (73)
- [ ] Flatiron Northeast Face – Regular Route, Variation 1 (182)
- [ ] Flatiron Northeast Face – Regular Route, Variation 2 ★ (182)
- [ ] Hatchet, The ★ (70)
- [ ] Hip Hip Hooray (110)
- [ ] Jorgie's Crack ★★ (42)
- [ ] Lifeline ★★ (75)
- [ ] Making Puppies (85)
- [ ] Monga Bonna Memorial Route ★ (186)

5.10a cont.

- [ ] Mousetrap   (121)
- [ ] No Holds Barred ★★   (36)
- [ ] No Smiles ★   (140)
- [ ] On a Pale Horse ★★   (85)
- [ ] Peon's Delight   (123)
- [ ] Pinch Gripped   (74)
- [ ] Plague ★   (39)
- [ ] Poodle with a Mohawk ★   (102)
- [ ] Racing Stripes ★   (39)
- [ ] Reach for the Sky ★   (93)
- [ ] Regular Route – Variation 3 ★   (182)
- [ ] Reincarnation Variation   (164)
- [ ] Roof, The   (44)
- [ ] Shaft, The ★   (176)
- [ ] Shake and Bake ★★★   (132)
- [ ] Shoot the Tube ★   (93)
- [ ] Sidehorse ★   (198)
- [ ] Silent Running ★   (182)
- [ ] Sound Chaser ★★   (60)
- [ ] Stupendous Man ★★   (44)
- [ ] Third Sister ★   (69)
- [ ] This Spud's For You   (36)
- [ ] Toog's Trailside ★   (139)
- [ ] Torque Twister   (49)
- [ ] Upper Bandit Bench ★   (149)
- [ ] Wet Willie ★★   (53)
- [ ] Wild Berry Crack   (32)
- [ ] Yak, North – Northwest Face ★★★ (88)
- [ ] Zig-Zag Man   (48)

5.10b

- [ ] Ali Baba ★★   (64)
- [ ] Balconies – Regular Route   (132)
- [ ] Blowing Chunks   (72)
- [ ] Bullrun   (88)
- [ ] Came in Second   (124)
- [ ] Castles Made of Sand ★   (60)
- [ ] Cross Your Heart   (62)
- [ ] Dance on a Volcano ★   (93)
- [ ] Frontiers of Chaos ★   (85)
- [ ] Gutter, The   (44)
- [ ] Nothin' Beats A Spud   (36)
- [ ] Only a Lad ★   (85)
- [ ] Sport Climber's Terror   (35)

5.10c

- [ ] Adrenaline Junkies ★   (204)
- [ ] Aliens Ate My Buick ★   (194)
- [ ] An-archy ★   (48)
- [ ] Asleep at the Wheel ★   (83)
- [ ] Assault and Battery   (102)
- [ ] Berserker Route   (123)
- [ ] Cantaloupe Death ★   (57)
- [ ] Carpal Tunnel Syndrome ★★   (75)
- [ ] Coyote Ugly – Direct Finish   (62)
- [ ] Crackaphobia   (149)
- [ ] Gag, The ★★   (53)
- [ ] Hard Variation   (57)
- [ ] Herchel-Berchel   (164)
- [ ] Heretic, The ★★★   (83)
- [ ] Hippo Stomp ★   (110)
- [ ] Jorgie's Crack Continuation ★   (42)
- [ ] Mission Impossible   (123)
- [ ] No Holds Barred – Direct Finish ★★ (36)
- [ ] Pearl Sheath, The ★★   (57)
- [ ] Prelude   (194)
- [ ] Que Lastima ★★   (81)
- [ ] Relayer ★★★   (60)
- [ ] Serpiente de Cascabel   (149)
- [ ] Slip Stream ★   (93)
- [ ] Split Infinity ★★   (93)
- [ ] Toog's Trailside Direct   (139)
- [ ] Traumatize – Direct Finish ★   (42)
- [ ] Tuff   (73)

5.10d

- [ ] Bad Ape ★ (141)
- [ ] Big Pucker, The ★★ (39)
- [ ] Broken Arrow ★ (44)
- [ ] Conduit to the Cosmos ★★ (132)
- [ ] Cuidado! ★★ (147)
- [ ] For M.E. (188)
- [ ] God Is Gravity ★ (57)
- [ ] Hawaiian Noises ★★ (55)
- [ ] Heat Seeking Moisture Missile ★★★ (46)
- [ ] La Gruniga (81)
- [ ] Love Handles, The ★ (67)
- [ ] Mammary Junk (44)
- [ ] Pistol Whipped ★ (44)
- [ ] Rocket in my Pocket ★★★ (55)
- [ ] Rookie, The (124)
- [ ] Sunny Side Up (206)
- [ ] Vanna (124)
- [ ] Venus Fly Trap (93)
- [ ] Wrinkle Remover ★★ (83)
- [ ] Yak, North – North Face (88)
- [ ] Yankee Pinnacle (168)

5.11

- [ ] Bat Cave ★ (28)
- [·] Chunky Monkey (35)
- [ ] Labor of Love (39)
- [ ] Lodestone Variation (57)
- [ ] Nexus ★★ (137)
- [ ] Shepherd, The (118)

5.11a

- [ ] Adagio ★ (194)
- [ ] Anchor Scream ★★ (29)
- [ ] Auto Cream ★★ (53)
- [ ] Bandits in Bondage ★★ (149)
- [ ] Between a Rock and a Hard Place ★ (39)
- [ ] Buffalo Soldier ★★★ (44)
- [ ] Coffin Nail (38)
- [ ] Electric Blue (132)
- [ ] Feeding Frenzy (126)
- [ ] Here Comes the Judge ★ (44)
- [ ] If You Bolt It They Will Come ★ (129)
- [ ] Jerk, The ★ (53)
- [ ] Kamikaze Kommute ★ (145)
- [ ] Little Big Dog ★ (140)
- [ ] Melvin ★★ (39)
- [ ] Post Orgasmic Depression (P.O.D.) ★★★ (55)
- [ ] Power Tools (123)
- [ ] Pweeter ★★ (42)
- [ ] Resurrection Wall – The Regular Route ★★ (164)
- [ ] Richnak's Revenge ★★ (57)
- [ ] Subterranean Tango ★★ (55)
- [ ] Sunwheel ★★ (53)
- [ ] Zig-Zag Left ★★ (48)

5.11b

- [ ] Bat Cave – Direct Finish (28)
- [ ] Broken Arrow – Direct Variation (44)
- [ ] Cosmos ★★ (44)
- [ ] Fat Lips ★★ (39)
- [ ] Foreplay ★★★ (55)
- [ ] Fringe Dweller ★★ (53)
- [ ] Gladiator, The ★ (42)
- [ ] Lithium (44)
- [ ] Lower North Face ★ (55)
- [ ] Mammary Pump ★★ (44)
- [ ] Mechanic's Delight ★ (180)
- [ ] Men at Work ★ (53)
- [ ] Powers That Be, The (132)
- [ ] Several Small Species ★ (55)
- [ ] Son of Dawn Wall A1 ★ (149)
- [ ] Time Stands Still ★ (36)
- [ ] Verdict, The ★★ (44)

5.11c

- ☐ Baby Blues ★ (57)
- ☐ Feed the Beast ★★★ (57)
- ☐ No Sense of Measure ★ (132)
- ☐ Pipeloads to Pluto (132)
- ☐ Post-Partum Depression ★ (57)
- ☐ Verdict, The – Direct Start ★★ (44)
- ☐ Windmills (140)

5.11d

- ☐ Black Dagger, The ★★★ (57)
- ☐ Daddy Long Legs ★★ (35)
- ☐ Price, The ★★ (29)
- ☐ This Bolt's For You ★★ (29)
- ☐ What If A0 (167)
- ☐ White Punks on Rope (93)

5.12

- ☐ Ape Index ★★ (55)
- ☐ Peregrine (132)
- ☐ Way Below The Direct (57)

5.12a

- ☐ Cantaloupe Death – Direct Start (57)
- ☐ December Shadows ★ (35)
- ☐ Earth Magnet ★ (184)
- ☐ Machete Direct ★★★ (147)
- ☐ Power Point (44)

5.12b

- ☐ Cataract Corner ★★★ (55)
- ☐ Druid, The ★★ (53)
- ☐ Future Shock ★★★ (55)
- ☐ Hard as a Rock ★★ (60)
- ☐ Jeopardy ★★ (124)
- ☐ Power Corrupts (123)
- ☐ Tarantula ★★★ (36)
- ☐ Truth or Consequences ★★ (124)

5.12c

- ☐ Forty Days of Rain ★★★ (44)
- ☐ Trial ★★ (44)
- ☐ Vigilante, The ★★ (53)

5.12d

- ☐ Great Spectacular, The A0 (167)
- ☐ Machete Ridge – West Face (147)
- ☐ Zippety-Doo-Dah ★ (42)

5.13a to 5.13c

- ☐ Hot Lava Lucy 5.13a ★★ (57)
- ☐ Lard Butt 5.13c (56-57)
- ☐ Ranger Bolts 5.13a ★★ (55)

ROUTES BY NAME